# Challenging Chomsky

To Walter Winckler, Word Wizard

# Challenging Chomsky

## The Generative Garden Game

Rudolf P. Botha

Basil Blackwell

Copyright©Rudolf P. Botha 1989

First published 1989

Basil Blackwell Ltd
108 Cowley Road, Oxford, OX4 1JF, UK

Basil Blackwell Inc.
432 Park Avenue South, Suite 1503.
New York, NY 10016, USA

*British Library Cataloguing in Publication Data*
Botha, Rudolf P.
   Challenging Chomsky: the generative garden game.
   1. Linguistics. Theories of Chomsky, Noam, 1928–
   I. Title
   410′ .92′ 4

   ISBN 0-631-16621-1

*Library of Congress Cataloging in Publication Data*
Botha, Rudolf P.
   Challenging Chomsky: the generative garden game/
   Rudolf P. Botha.
   p. cm.
   Bibliography: p.
   Includes index.
   ISBN 0-631-16621-1
   1. Chomsky, Noam.   2. Linguistics.   3. Generative grammar.
   I. Title.
   P85.C47B6 1989
   415–dc19

Phototypeset in 11 on 13 pt Sabon
by Dobbie Typesetting Limited, Plymouth, Devon
Printed in Great Britain by
T. J. Press Ltd, Padstow, Cornwall

This setting of human beings to kill one another in public, for entertainment, is by far the nastiest blood-sport ever invented.

Michael Grant, *Gladiators*, p. 8

'I was hoping that you, at least, would understand the appeal of the thing [i.e., the pitting of man against man in a maze]', he said at length. 'However . . . ' He paused again. 'To be honest,' he went on slowly, 'I'm not sure I wholly understand – myself – the deep attraction of the Game . . . I suppose the Game gives us the feeling of getting close to the roots of our profession . . . getting down to the fundamentals. . . . '

Jon Manchip White, *The Garden Game*, p. 102

The perceived need to outdo Chomsky has led him to be the most attacked linguist in history.

Newmeyer, 'Has there been a "Chomskyan revolution" in linguistics?'

Chomsky has rarely been defeated in argument on his own ground . . .

Gardner, *The Mind's New Science*, p. 214

The first essay [in *Rules and Representations*] and indeed much of the book provides us with critical examples illustrating the subtly controlled aggressive component of Chomsky's rhetoric and style . . .

Brame, 'Universal word induction vs Move $\alpha$'

Bloodsports, it is generally believed, are on the wane. But not so The Generative Garden Game.

Anonymous

# Contents

CONTENTS

CONTENTS

# CONTENTS

# Acknowledgements

Without the generous assistance of various colleagues and friends I would not have been able to complete this study, an early version of which was informally distributed as *The Generative Garden Game* (Stellenbosch Papers in Linguistics 16). My thanks go in particular to the following:

To Walter Winckler and Cecile le Roux, who read the entire manuscript more than once, inventively suggesting numerous improvements in the content and presentation of both the more serious sections and the playful parts.

To Professors Jean Aitchison, Keith Allan, Dwight Bolinger, Bob Dixon, Roger Lass, Peter Matthews, Gary Prideaux, Henk Schultink, Pieter Seuren, Bob Stockwell and Arnold Zwicky for comments that gave me a clearer idea of what I am trying to do here and, more important, should have been trying to do.

To Christine Anthonissen, Riekie Harm, Hildegard van Zweel and Elaine Leek (on the publishing side), who rendered valuable editorial assistance in weeding out technical flaws.

To Mrs L. Gildenhuys, who skilfully typed and retyped the manuscript, not once losing her patience in the protracted process.

And I would like to thank all these good people for not trying too hard to persuade me to leave my tale untold.

R.P.B.

The author and publishers are grateful to Noam Chomsky who generously granted permission to quote from his published works; also for permission to quote from N. Chomsky, *The Generative Enterprise. A Discussion with R. Huybregts and H. van Riemsdijk* (Foris Publications, 1982).

# Forewarning

*So you have heard about The Garden, Dear Reader. And you wish to challenge The Master at his Game. Boldly you aim to stalk him in his sprawling maze of forking and intersecting conceptual lanes. I say 'boldly' because, as you ought to know, the odds are against you. For years The Master has been playing The Game with superb – some would say, deadly – skill. Many of intellectual class have come to do battle with The Master about his ideas on language and mind. With woeful consequences, alas! Some entered The Garden, never to reappear. (May their minds rest in peace!) Others left The Garden in undignified hurry – hurt and, for the rest of their scholarly days, humiliated. Only a few were able to draw blood, to force The Master to acknowledge a flaw here, to concede a defect there in the foundations of his model of language and mind.*

*But, believing yourself to be intellectually fleet of foot and strong of limb, you are not one to be deterred by the more sinister details of Garden lore. So, before setting out to engage The Master, let me take you on a guided tour of the maze of lanes and paths so cleverly laid out in dense New England intellectual growth. Come with me and get the feel of the conceptual forks and intersections, the logical pitfalls and perils, the methodological dead ends and drops (plunging down into the Charles). Forearmed with this experience, you will know better where to fight and where to flee, when to lunge and when to parry in real action. Perhaps, even, you will learn how to avoid perishing at the hands of The Master in his alluring but lethal linguistic labyrinth.*

*Be warned: there will be distractions in The Garden, other Players with their own pursuits. Of some you will catch a fleeting glimpse; others you will hear in the distance only – roaring with rage, shrieking with fright or moaning in agony. (I do not mean to scare* you, but take care not to trip over the odd bleached bone sticking out of shallow structure.)

There will be Fiery Fighters and Guileful Gladiators who, in their prime, have come to prove their powers, to match The Master. Then there will be various members of the Gored Old Guard – those constitutionally incurable cases of brawling brains – back to revenge the terrible traumas suffered in past encounters with The Master. And you will become aware of the presence of a number of Fickle Friends – erstwhile admirers who, for reasons of their own, have turned against The Master and now stalk him with dour determination.

Also there will be a few Fanatic Followers who – having found The Game too tame, The Master too mellow – clamour for the radical reconstruction of The Garden. Oh, and do be careful not to startle the Nosy Novices sent by tutors to The Garden, not to provoke The Master, but to look, to listen and, above all, to learn how to survive a future fight.

And you might bump into any of a number of Stray Souls who, forever losing their intellectual way, have stumbled into The Garden by chance. A motley bunch – including Phantom Philosophers, Senile Psychologists, Asinine Anthropologists, AI-idiots, Computer Cranks and Wizened Whizz-kids of linguistic lineage – they would not know The Master from a maple. If they are permitted to loiter in the lanes, it is out of sheer charity. For reasons I need not mention, we won't concern ourselves with the capers of these clownish creatures. Before I forget, don't allow yourself to be distracted by the Flock of Frenzied Fans, metrically stamping their feet while cheering on their champ with the chant of 'Chomsky, Chomsky!'

Ultimately, of course, there is The Master: for ever patrolling the paths, modifying the maze – always ready to retaliate.

Why I call him 'The Master'? Certainly not out of subservience, servility or some other similarly silly sentiment. Nor for the want of a proper name. 'Great Generator', 'Garden Guru', 'Generative Genius' (or 'Genie', some would insist), 'Machiavellian Mentalist', 'Revengeful Rationalist' are but a few of the many names (by which) he has been called. 'The Master', however, says it all: it is he who has turned The Garden into a model maze, who has masterminded all major moves and manoeuvres, who has made The Garden the ground of the most magnificent matches in mentalist memory. But if the name touches a raw nerve or opens an old wound, please feel *free to read for 'The Master' a name of your own choice. Why not, for example, call him 'The Past Master (of The Maze)'?*

*Learning from the blunders, often crippling in their consequences, that have been committed by other Garden combatants is a must. To aid you in this, I will put up, as we move through the labyrinth, some signs marking places where in the past Plodding Players made misguided moves, selected suicidal stratagems, wielded weird weapons, or tumbled into treacherous traps. The inscriptions on these signs – e.g. 'The Milner Maneuver', 'Lemming Lane', 'The Bicycle Bifurcation', 'The Luria Lunge', 'Dennett's Decoy' and so on – I have taken, without permission, from The Master's memoirs, to be published at a distant date as* The Life and Times of a Gladiatorial Grammarian.

*But such mnemonic means won't see you through. Mobility of mind and agility in action – that's what The Game is all about. To give you a feel of this action, I will be making use of copious quotes from The Master's own writings and those of his adversaries. In this way, I will let you sense what it is like to be now in the shoes of the attacker, now in the shoes of the defender.*

*When playing for real, there is one thing never to forget: The Master is a mercurial mover. Don't rush a position where you saw a shadow some time ago. Chances are that you would be sailing into empty space, only to be attacked from an unexpected angle. And I won't recommend shooting from the hip: leave this to the Wild Men from the (Mid-) West. The Garden, after all, is in East Coast Country.*

*'So what are the rules of The Game?', I hear you ask. What, indeed, are the rules? For survival there is just this one: 'Anything goes'. Ah, and do remember: you will be no more than a player; you will not be a referee too. So it won't be for you to decide whether or not you have landed a crippling blow that set The Master reeling. Nor will it be your prerogative to say that a savage swipe by The Master left you with only a surface scratch. The Spectators, callously calculating, will be both judge and jury. This is the Raw Reality of The Game. If you would prefer not to face it, there is still time to retreat to the challenge of Chinese Checkers.* *

---

*If you happen to be a Serious Scholar – did I hear someone say 'Spoil Sport'? – who insists on a watered-down version of this Forewarning, Chinese Checkers is your fate. Or, what about a quiet game of conceptual croquet with your curate?*

# 1

## The Lie of the Land

*Getting to The Garden is not as easy as it may seem, Pupil Player. Along the way, you will come, rather unexpectedly, to some perilously concealed conceptual forks. Make a wrong choice at any of these, and you are bound to end up, like many before you, in some remote playground where, in your own opinion, you may well be having lots of fun. But you won't be really playing The Game.*

*Incidentally, don't let the playful pitch of the parts in italics put you on the wrong track: going after The Guru in The Garden is, most definitely, not child's play of the kindergarten kind. Are you ready then, Impatient Pupil, for some Preparatory Play?*

'Just where does Chomsky's linguistics fit into the bigger domain of the scientific study of human language?' This is one of the first worries of the newcomer or outsider. The present section provides a clear answer to this question by locating Chomsky's linguistics with reference to four other, related but distinct, linguistic concerns: generative grammar, Chomskyan linguistics, radical Chomsky-like linguistics and transformational grammar. The necessary boundaries will be drawn with the aid of five fundamental conceptual distinctions.

**1.1**  The first and most general distinction that has to be drawn in locating Chomsky's linguistics is that of **generative grammar vs non-generative grammar**. Chomsky's linguistics represents a form of generative grammar. Any approach to the study of human language is a form of generative grammar if it adopts the following requirement: a grammar, as a description of a particular human language, has to be perfectly explicit. Thus Chomsky (1965: 4) characterizes a generative grammar as follows:

> If the grammar is, furthermore, perfectly explicit – in other words, if it does not rely on the intelligence of the understanding reader but rather provides an explicit analysis of his contribution – we may (somewhat redundantly) call it a *generative grammar*.[1]

For a grammar to meet the requirement of explicitness, Chomsky initially proposed, it should take on the form of a system of formalized rules and other related devices which mechanically enumerate all and only the grammatical sentences of the language, assigning to each of these sentences an appropriate structural description.[2] Approaches to the study of language which do not subscribe to the requirement of explicitness are by definition nongenerative.

The explicitness of a generative grammar is meant to enhance its precision: the more explicit a grammar or description of a language, the easier it will be to check it for false claims, internal inconsistencies, gaps or lacunae, unjustified hidden assumptions, etc. Recently, Chomsky (1981b: 336) has reaffirmed his belief in formalization as a diagnostic and heuristic tool: 'formalization will not merely be a pointless technical exercise but may bring to light errors or gaps and hidden assumptions, and may yield new theoretical insights and suggest new empirical problems for investigation.'

Generative grammar, thus, differs from nongenerative grammar not in regard to WHAT is claimed about natural language(s), but rather in regard to HOW the claims are expressed. That is, the difference between a generative and nongenerative grammar is not one of linguistic content; the difference is one of metascientific format. This means that it is possible for two approaches to the study of language to differ greatly in regard to what they claim about language (structure etc.), but for both to be generative in virtue of the fact that they both adopt the criterion of explicitness for individual grammars.[3]

2

*In their frantic fervour to fling themselves at The Master, Prospective Players have from time immemorial floundered at the 'generative vs nongenerative' fork. In the beginning, when The Garden was still no more than a primaeval forest, a fundamental folly was to conflate, carelessly, 'generate' with 'produce' and to take a grammar to be a model of the speaker.[4] This mindless mistake, The Generative Gaffe, is being monotonously made to this very day. For a recent repetition, Dear Pupil, you may take a look at Schank's (1980: 36) criticisms of The Master's account of how wh-questions are formed, considering while you're at it also The Master's (1980b: 53) repartee. Meanwhile, however, the second conceptual fork on the way to The Garden is waiting to be negotiated.*

**1.2**   The second conceptual distinction that is fundamental to properly locating Chomsky's linguistics is **Chomskyan generative grammar vs non-Chomskyan generative grammar**. That is, within generative grammar a distinction has to be drawn between, on the one hand, the Chomskyan approach and, on the other hand, various non-Chomskyan approaches. This distinction reflects the fact that there may be, and are, differing conceptions of the primary aim, the guiding questions, and the fundamental problem in the study of language. The primary aim of the Chomskyan approach is mentalistic: to increase our understanding of the nature and properties of the human mind. Chomsky (1972: 103) puts the point as follows:

> There are any number of questions that might lead one to undertake a study of language. Personally, I am primarily intrigued by the possibility of learning something, from the study of language, that will bring to light inherent properties of the human mind.

In their pursuit of this primary aim, Chomsky (1986: 31) and others are guided by questions about knowledge of language: its nature, origin and use. Among such questions the following are considered 'basic' by Chomsky (1986: 3):

(1)   (a)  What constitutes knowledge of language?
      (b)  How is knowledge of language acquired?
      (c)  How is knowledge of language put to use?

As to question (1) (a), Chomsky (1980a: 166) considers a speaker's knowledge of his native language to be a complex, abstract system of rules.[5] For many of the properties of this system there is, in Chomsky's opinion, no evidence in the speaker's childhood experience of the language. This gives rise to question (1) (b), which Chomsky (1981a: 32) also frames as follows: 'How does such knowledge [of language] develop [in the individual]?' This question is assigned by Chomsky (1986: 7) the status of 'the fundamental problem' of his approach to generative grammar. To solve this problem, an explanation has to be given of how children can come to know their native language on the basis of what Chomsky considers to be severely limited experience of or evidence about the language.[6]

Chomsky's 'abstract system' view of the nature of knowledge of language is also reflected by his general approach to question (1) (c): he (1986: 4, 222) considers language use – e.g. in the expression of thought or the understanding of specimens of language – to be a case of rule-following or rule-governed behaviour. His approach to the questions of (1) leads him to postulate that human beings have a special innate mental faculty that makes language acquisition and language use possible. He refers to this as the 'language faculty'.

In non-Chomskyan approaches to generative grammar, by contrast, the primary aim for the study of language is not that of gaining insight into the properties of the human mind. In particular, such approaches do not consider question (1) (b) about language acquisition to be the fundamental problem to be solved by linguistic inquiry. That is, these approaches are nonmentalistic, pursuing non-psychological concerns about human language. Jerrold Katz (1981) has argued, for example, that a linguistic theory has to provide a description of a nonmental, abstract or Platonistic object 'language', a point that will be pursued in section 2.5.14 below. Still other linguists, e.g. Gerald Sanders (1980) and Michael Kac (1980), have taken human language to be a cultural object; in so doing, they have also assigned a nonmentalistic status/interpretation to linguistic theories.[7]

The point, then, is that an approach to the study of language may be at once generative and non-Chomskyan: generative in adopting the requirement that grammars, as descriptions of languages, have to be perfectly explicit, and non-Chomskyan in not having the aim of increasing our understanding of the human mind by pursuing questions such as (1) (a)–(c).[8]

*There has never been a time, Apprentice Player, when some Generative Gladiators did not attempt to change the character of The Game, contending creatively that The Garden was in fact a nonmentalistic maze. For example, Milner (1978) argued that one could do generative syntax in the Chomskyan style without assigning mentalistic import to the resulting theories. The Master (1982: 31) countered with a subtle side-swipe:*

> *I think a linguist can do perfectly good work in generative grammar without ever caring about questions of physical realism or what his work has to do with the structure of the mind. I do not think there is any question that that is possible. It just seems to me to indicate a certain lack of curiosity as to why things are the way they are.*

*Only if a lack of curiosity had ceased to rate as a scholarly vice, would these remarks have allowed Milner to get away unscathed. As for The Master, there is no doubt that he has kept The Garden a mentalistic maze, unmoved by what in his memoirs is called The Milner Maneuver.[9] Note, Dear Pupil, that, for his counterstroke, The Master preferred a rapier to a club. Clearly, being pierced with a rapier causes more permanent pain, particularly to a player's pride, than being clobbered with a club. So, here is a first Principle of Play that you might wish to commit to memory as The Rule of the Rapier:*

> *The more refined the rapier,*
> *the more painful the puncture it makes.*

**1.3** But locating Chomsky's linguistics also requires a third conceptual distinction to be clearly understood, namely **Chomskyan linguistics vs Chomsky's linguistics**. Within Chomskyan generative grammar, that is, a distinction has to be drawn between, on the one hand, Chomsky's own conception of the structure of human language – or linguistic structure, for short – and, on the other hand, a variety of deviating conceptions of other Chomskyan linguists. This distinction may be illustrated with reference to the status assigned by Chomsky to transformations as rules of syntax. Chomsky has always believed that transformations are fundamental to linguistic structure, though over the years his views on the nature of these rules have changed considerably. Various stages in the developmental history of Chomskyan linguistics have seen linguists, however, who accepted the questions (1) (a)–(c) as representing basic problems of linguistic inquiry, but who nevertheless did not share Chomsky's view that transformations were fundamental to linguistic structure. In pursuing these questions such scholars – e.g. Koster (1978a, 1978b) and Freidin (1978), to mention just two – were practising Chomskyan linguistics or Chomskyan generative grammar. In differing from Chomsky on the status of transformations, however, they did not subscribe to Chomsky's linguistics in a narrow sense.[10]

Chomsky's linguistics, then, represents the set of assumptions about linguistic structure held by himself at any particular moment. From a developmental perspective, Chomsky can be said to have been continuously revising these assumptions, thus making his linguistics a relatively volatile body of ideas. Chomskyan linguistics, by contrast, has undergone far fewer changes over the years – a fact that will emerge more clearly as we proceed.

*The lesson, Pondering Pupil? You cannot play The Garden Game, unless your adversary is The Master himself. Duelling with an adventurous understudy, however committed, might serve to warm you up; it would never count as a real contest. So, along the way, do not risk spilling your blood in a Number-Two Tussle.*

*Would those, by any chance, be 'snatches of song' floating in from afar? Indeed, Perceptive Pupil, those are stirring strains of martial music made by a special species of spectators as they march towards The Maze. It is a group of Generative Gypsies who, having serenaded The Master all over the Old World, are now trekking towards the terraces above the Charles. They have crossed the seas by clipper (the kind that cruises above cloud nine) and are on their way to wish The Master well, to sing for his survival the Battle Hymn of The Garden.*

*What they're singing right now? But of course, rephrased in boisterous double bars for raucous rendering, it is their signature tune with the rousing refrain:*

*'Glow Boys, Blow for Californioh . . . '*

*No, Dear Pupil, it wouldn't do for us to join the ranks of this tramping troupe of Transformational Troubadours. Theirs is an enterprise of cheering and chanting, ours a business of challenging and charging. Don't get me wrong, though: as practitioners of the performing arts, they most certainly are Charming Chaps and Winsome Wenches. But as for practising the martial arts in The Maze against The Master – that's a metier they are precluded from both by mood and mental mould.*

*What 'transformational' is supposed to signify? We'll come to that in a minute, Impatient Pupil.*

1.4   And so we come to the fourth fundamental conceptual distinction that has to be mastered in order properly to locate Chomsky's linguistics: **Chomsky's linguistics vs radical Chomsky-like linguistics.** Over the years, quite a number of variants of radical Chomsky-like linguistics have been vigorously championed by erstwhile followers of Chomsky's. What sets a variant of radical Chomsky-like linguists apart is the fact of adopting as a basic assumption some very strong version of a view held by Chomsky himself in a more nuanced form. Or, such a variant of Chomsky-like linguistics may retain as a basic assumption a view once held by Chomsky but now no longer endorsed by him.

In assuming that the deep structure of a sentence is identical to its semantic representation, generative semantics initially constituted a classic variant of radical Chomsky-like linguistics.[11] And Katz's assumption that the semantic interpretation of a sentence need not refer to any level of syntactic structure other than deep structure represents a related variant of radical Chomsky-like linguistics.[12]

It goes without saying that not all variants of Chomsky-like linguistics are equally radical. Some, moreover, are conceptually better founded and empirically more adequate than others. From a socio-historical perspective it is striking to see how many students

7

and once ardent followers of Chomsky's have ended up practising some variant of radical Chomsky-like linguistics.[13]

*In many cases, Dear Pupil, the radical nature of variants of Chomsky-like linguistics is reflected by a particular attitude of their proponents: they tend to see their variant of Chomsky-like linguistics as the only 'true' or 'pure' representation of The Master's views, often using the term 'generative grammar' in a monopolistic fashion to denote this, and no other, variant. 'I am not the one to fault', they often claim, 'it is The Master himself who has deviated from the straight and narrow road to linguistic salvation.' It would be most unwise, en route to The Garden, to let yourself be taken on a Deceptive Detour by some Old Boy who offers to show you – 'It will only take a moment' – where The Master 'has made a mess'. Chances are that you won't ever reach The Garden but will end up crazily confused in a corner of your distractor's own paltry piece of private property.*

1.5 The fifth conceptual distinction that has to be understood in order properly to locate Chomsky's linguistics is **generative grammar vs transformational grammar**. A linguist practises generative grammar if he subscribes to a particular metascientific condition for grammars, namely the condition of total explicitness. A linguist practises transformational grammar if he holds a particular substantive view of linguistic structure, namely that transformational rules are fundamental to natural languages. 'Generative vs nongenerative' constitutes a metascientific distinction; 'transformational vs nontransformational', by contrast, represents a substantive linguistic distinction. Thus, a generative grammar may or may not use transformational rules. And, analogously, a transformational grammar may be either generative or nongenerative. So in principle it is perfectly possible for a linguist to practise any of the following four: transformational–generative grammar, nontransformational–generative grammar, transformational–nongenerative grammar or nontransformational–nongenerative grammar. Chomsky's linguistics has always been both transformational and generative.

8

*In the history of The Garden, Dear Pupil, many an aspirant player confused 'generative' with 'transformational', thereby tumbling into The Transformational Trap. What you may take to be a simple slip-up was considered by some a serious sin. In the primordial past, for example, there was a Keeper of the Gates, a man called Dougherty, who showed no mercy to those who fell into the Transformational Trap. Rather than helping them out and letting them in, he passionately preached to them the part of Garden Gospel that is still remembered as Dougherty's Damnation.*[14]

In summary: in locating Chomsky's linguistics within the larger field of linguistics, we have found that his linguistics is

| | | |
|---|---|---|
| 1 | generative: | it adopts the requirement that grammars have to be perfectly explicit; |
| 2 | Chomskyan: | it is guided by questions about the nature, origin and use of knowledge of language, fundamental amongst which is the problem of language acquisition (1) (b); |
| 3 | transformational: | it accords syntactic transformations the status of fundamental units of linguistic structure. |

Although Chomsky-like linguistics and transformational grammar are not included in it, the diagram on page 10 does provide some visual pointers as to where Chomsky's linguistics fits into the larger field of linguistics. Many generative grammarians and Chomskyan linguists do not take the trouble to ensure that their terminology reflects systematically the conceptual distinctions represented in (2) on p. 10. Thus, the term 'generative grammar' is often used to denote Chomskyan (generative) grammar, even by Chomsky himself. Consider in this connection the way in which he (1986: 4–5) has recently used the distinction *theory vs topic* to clarify the metascientific nature of his approach to the study of language:

Generative grammar is sometimes referred to as a theory, advocated by this or that person. In fact, it is not a theory any more than chemistry is a theory. Generative grammar is a topic, which one may or may not choose to study. Of course, one

9

can adopt a point of view from which chemistry disappears as a discipline (perhaps it is all done by angels with mirrors). In this sense, a decision to study chemistry does stake out a position on matters of fact. Similarly, one may argue that the topic of generative grammar does not exist, although it is hard to see how to make this position minimally plausible.

From the context, it is clear that the phrases 'generative grammar' and 'the topic of generative grammar' in these remarks are intended by Chomsky to refer to (the nature, origin and use of) knowledge of language – which of course, strictly speaking, is 'the topic' of Chomskyan linguistics. In sum: newcomers to the field should take particular care not to be thrown off the track by shorthand statements by old hands of the nature, aims, concerns etc. of 'generative grammar', 'Chomskyan linguistics', 'transformational grammar' etc.

(2)

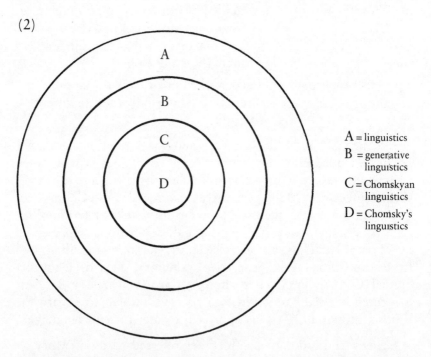

A = linguistics
B = generative linguistics
C = Chomskyan linguistics
D = Chomsky's linguistics

*So, thanks to expert guidance I dare say, you have been prevented from making The Generative Gaffe, from being led astray by a Milner Maneuver, from becoming embroiled in a Number-Two*

*Tussle, from being taken on a Deceptive Detour, and from tumbling into The Transformational Trap. Happily, you find yourself at the gates of The Garden. Are you ready then, Impatient Pupil, for some Propaedeutic Play?*

# 2

## The Maze of Mentalism

*Let us then start moving, Dear Pupil, into the heart of The Garden: The Maze of Mentalism, where matters of mind have been firing the fighting, fuelling the feuding. As we push on purposefully, but with patience, I will reveal to you many of the mysteries and marvels of The Maze, marking out areas of maximum menace. And I will introduce you to Possessed Players, past and present, along with the moves and manoeuvres, ploys and passions, flops and follies for which they have gone down in The Annals of The Game. Also, you will be told tales of terror and tumult about nasty things that have been done in the name of The Game. And there will be more than the occasional warning about strategies leading to self-destruction and about recipes for ruin. Most important of all, I will give you ample opportunity to observe the might of The Master, the power of his play, his ruthlessness in retaliation. You will be allowed, as it were, to taste the meat of mentalism.*

What in essence, then, is the substance of Chomsky's answers to the questions (1) (a)–(c) in section 1.2 above? That is, what is the core of his answers to the questions about the nature, origin and use of language? These are the questions with which the present section will be concerned. It will address these questions by laying out seven constellations of conceptual distinctions. These are the respective sets of distinctions that Chomsky has used to clarify the nature of the following topics: the 'fundamental' problem of language acquisition, the nature of the linguistic experience involved in language acquisition, the nature of the genetic basis of knowledge of language, the nature of the process(es) by means of which such knowledge is acquired, the nature of the acquired knowledge itself, the nature of the rules and the rule-following involved in the use of language, and the nature of mind in general.

**2.1**   In section 1.2 we saw that Chomsky considers question (1) (b), i.e., 'How is knowledge of language acquired?', to represent the fundamental problem of his linguistics. Obviously, his linguistics would make little sense to anyone who failed to take a closer look at the nature of this **problem of language acquisition**. So let us examine a constellation of Chomskyan distinctions whose function it is to elucidate and legitimate this problem.

*2.1.1*   A first conceptual distinction that bears on the nature of this problem is *the logical problem of language acquisition vs the psychological problem of language acquisition*. To Chomsky, what he calls 'the logical problem of language acquisition' is represented by his question (1) (b): How is it possible for children, on the basis of insufficient evidence about or severely limited experience of their language, to acquire the complex and rich system that represents their knowledge of the language? On Chomsky's view this system, as we noted in section 1.2, has many properties for which the speaker's linguistic experience contains no evidence. As a stimulus for language acquisition, this evidence is therefore considered by Chomskyans to be too 'impoverished'. For this reason, the logical problem of language acquisition has also been referred to by Chomsky (1986: xxv) and others as 'the problem of poverty or deficiency of the stimulus'.[1] In what sense the stimulus is claimed to be 'impoverished' we shall consider in section 2.2.1 below.

The psychological problem of language acquisition, by contrast, is the problem of 'real-time acquisition': How does a child acquire its language in stages over a period of time, the earlier stages forming the basis of the later ones? Chomskyan linguistics does not seek a solution to this problem. It addresses the psychological problem of language acquisition only in so far as this problem presupposes an understanding of the logical problem of language acquisition.[2] In the sixties Chomskyans introduced an idealization, namely 'instantaneous language acquisition', to say that they were not

13

concerned with the temporal intricacies of real-time acquisition involved in the psychological problem of language acquisition. Chomsky and Halle (1968: 331) put the point as follows:

there is another, much more crucial, idealization implicit in this account. We have been describing acquisition of language as if it were an instantaneous process. Obviously, this is not true. A more realistic model of language acquisition would consider the order in which primary linguistic data are used by the child and the effects of preliminary 'hypotheses' developed in the earlier stages of learning on the interpretation of new, often more complex, data. To us it appears that this more realistic study is much too complex to be undertaken in any meaningful way today and that it will be far more fruitful to investigate in detail, as a first approximation, the idealized model outlined earlier, leaving refinements to a time when this idealization is better understood.

Over the years, moreover, Chomskyans have not changed these views in any essential respect, as is clear from Chomsky's more recent remark that his model of language acquisition is 'an instantaneous model of language acquisition, ignoring the role of these intermediate states attained between the initial and steady state' (1981a: 35). Specifically, Chomsky (1986: 54) still firmly believes that 'intermediate states attained do not change the principles available for interpretation of data at later states in a way that affects the state attained'.[3]

*The conceptual fork considered above, Dear Player, has been the undoing of many a player of The Generative Garden Game. Having misread it, players have stormed up the logical path armed with psychological ammunition, bent on blasting The Master into oblivion for his 'failure' to shed sufficient light on how 'in real life' children 'actually' acquire their language 'in developmental steps'. But blasting can't be done with blanks, a Law of the Labyrinth that McCawley (1980: 27) rediscovered when he shot an empty shell at the shadow of The Master: 'the programmatic accounts of language acquisition that appear in Chomsky's works (e.g., 1965; 1975a) deal only with the end-product of language acquisition and*

*have nothing to say about the developmental steps that would lead*
*to that end-product'. There was no need for taking cover. The*
*Master (1980b: 47) merely had to 'return the compliment – indeed,*
*generalize it', pointing out with respect to developmental steps that*
*'insight awaits more comprehensive and systematic analyses of stages*
*attained prior to the relatively steady state that constitutes mature*
*knowledge – a difficult research task, but one that has been addressed*
*with some success'.*
*So much for McCawley's Stand on Steps.*

2.1.2   To clarify the nature of the logical problem of
language acquisition, that is question (1) (b), from a historico-
philosophical point of view, Chomsky (1986: xxviiff) has invoked
a further distinction, namely *Plato's problem vs Orwell's problem*:

> Plato's problem . . . is to explain how we know so much, given
> that the evidence available to us is so sparse. Orwell's problem
> is to explain why we know and understand so little, even
> though the evidence available to us is so rich.

The logical problem of language acquisition (alternatively, the
problem of poverty of the stimulus) is a special case of Plato's
problem. As noted by Chomsky (1986: xxv), Plato's problem was
also raised by Russell in the form of the question 'How comes it that
human beings, whose contacts with the world are brief and personal
and limited, are nevertheless able to know as much as they do know?'
   Orwell's problem, by contrast, arises in any society, totalitarian
or democratic, in which the dominant institutions function on the
principle that Ignorance is Strength. To solve Orwell's problem,
Chomsky (1986: xxvii) observes, 'we must discover the institutional
and other factors that block insight and understanding in crucial
areas of our lives and ask why they are effective'.[4] Plato's problem
belongs to the sciences and is 'deep and intellectually exciting'
to Chomsky (1986: xxix). Its solution requires the discovery of
explanatory principles that would make sense of phenomena that
appear chaotic on the surface.

*So, Dear Player, should you get weary and worn down along the*
*way or, worse, hurt and humiliated in the hunt, then I'm afraid*

15

*you cannot get out of The Game simply by deriding it as a frivolous farce or a fracas for freaks. To do this would be to show yourself a Philosophical Philistine, mixing your Philosophical P(lato)s and Q(uine)s. Or, indeed, to make a Howler Most Unhistorical. For The Game, as we have seen, has respectable roots going back to Ancient Athens of nearly two and a half thousand years ago.*

**2.1.3** Chomsky (1980a: 65ff; 1986: xxv–vi) presents a sharper formulation of the logical problem of language acquisition by drawing the distinction *a genetic or innate component vs an experiential component in language acquisition*. This distinction is based on his view that a cognitive system such as a language results from the interaction between an organism's experience and the organism's method of dealing with the experience. This method includes what Chomsky (1986: xxv) calls 'analytic mechanisms and the intrinsic [i.e. genetic or innate] determinants of maturation and cognitive growth'. Given this distinction between experience and innate endowment, Chomsky (1986: xxv–vi) is able to say that 'The [fundamental] problem . . . is to determine the innate endowment that serves to bridge the gap between experience and knowledge [of language] attained'. Let us consider Chomsky's conception of the two poles of the distinction 'experience vs innate endowment' a little more closely, thereby erecting some scaffolding for the remaining part of this section which deals with Chomsky's answers to questions (1) (a)–(c).

The innate or genetic component, on the one hand, accounts for those aspects of knowledge of language for which there is no evidence in the data available to the child acquiring the language. These are the aspects, then, that the child does not need to 'learn' in any conventional sense of the term. Chomsky (1980a: 31ff, 241, 245) takes these innate aspects of knowledge of language to be encoded in a genetic programme that is essentially the same in different members of the human species. This genetic language programme forms the 'initial state' of a mental organ, called 'the language faculty' by Chomsky, of which the 'steady state' is the speaker's 'full' knowledge of the language. In providing for an innate or genetic factor, Chomsky adopts a 'nativist' position on language acquisition.

The experiential component of Chomsky's account of language acquisition provides for the role played by the data available to the child. This role, as we will see, is mainly (though not solely) that of a 'trigger' that at various points in time activates the various parts of the genetic programme, thus guiding its unfolding. So Chomsky considers the development of the mental organ called 'the language faculty' to be exactly parallel to that of a physical organ such as the heart or liver. This means that his solution to the logical problem of language acquisition boils down to the following: knowledge of language is on the whole not learned by a process of trial and error, conditioning, abstraction, association etc. Rather, such knowledge develops in the child by means of a process of biological growth. Chomsky's views on the nature of the genetic/innate and the experiential/evidential components of language acquisition will be spelled out in sections 2.2 and 2.3 in some detail by means of a whole range of further conceptual distinctions.

But let us briefly return to the observation that the child's linguistic experience or 'environment', as it is also called by Chomsky, does not solely serve as a trigger that activates 'language growth'. Chomsky (1980a: 33, 45, 142) in fact provides for a second function for this experience or 'environment': that of a force 'shaping' the development of the language faculty. This shaping function has to account for the fact that a child growing up in an 'English environment' acquires English and not, say, Japanese. It is in virtue of the shaping role of its linguistic experience or environment that the child acquires properties specific to a particular language. This point Chomsky (1980a: 45) illustrates with reference to English:

> The environment provides the information that questions are formed by movement of a question word and that 'each other' is a reciprocal expression; in other languages this is not the case, so that these cannot be properties of biological endowment in specific detail.

In sum: with respect to the functions of the child's linguistic experience, evidence or environment in language acquisition, Chomsky draws the distinction *triggering vs shaping*.

17

*Many a bloody battle has been fought, Prying Player, at the conceptual fork signposted as 'the innate/genetic vs the environmental component'. The neuropsychologist Luria (1975), for example, has charged that The Master's assumption that certain principles of universal grammar are genetically determined 'makes a postulate out of a problem' and that 'this means that all further study in the area can lead us nowhere'. In a counter-thrust, The Master (1980a: 210) has pointed out that these charges by Luria represent an a priori argument which, if valid, would have to hold equally for the development of physical organs:*

> *that is, it would show that the hypothesis that the growth of arms rather than wings is genetically determined makes a postulate out of a problem and guarantees that further inquiry will lead us nowhere. Since Luria would obviously not accept this conclusion, we are left with only one way of interpreting his argument: cognitive development must, on a priori grounds, be fundamentally different from physical development in that it has no genetic component.*

*This view The Master rejects as sheer dogmatism, and he twists the blade by remarking: 'One can imagine how comparable dogmatism would be regarded in the natural sciences' (p. 211).*

*The lesson, then: in attacking The Master for providing for a genetic component in language acquisition, be careful not to use The Luria Lunge. That is, avoid the use of a priori reasoning and dogmatic views to destroy a position which is intended to have empirical grounds. If you cannot show this position to be incorrect or nonempirical, but still consider The Master's nativism to be misguided, there must be more rewarding, less lethal things for you to do than trying to play The Game.*

**2.2**   This brings us to **the nature of the linguistic experience or evidence** available to the child that has to acquire knowledge of its native language. Recall that Chomsky's solution to the logical problem of language acquisition has to account for the poverty or deficiency of this experience. If the stimulus were not as poor as he makes it out to be, Chomsky's nativism would obviously collapse. So, let us consider next a constellation of conceptual distinctions

18

used by Chomsky and others to clarify the nature of this experience/
evidence.

2.2.1   To flesh out his view that the child's linguistic
experience constitutes an impoverished stimulus for language
acquisition, Chomsky draws the distinction *the poverty of the
stimulus vs the degeneracy of the stimulus*. He (1980b: 42) considers
the stimulus degenerate in that the data-base for language acquisition
contains expressions that are not well formed, including, for
example, slips of the tongue, incomplete utterances, utterances
characterized by pauses, false starts, endings that do not match
their beginnings etc. The stimulus is impoverished, however, in the
sense that it contains *no* evidence at all for certain properties
and principles of (the grammars of) the languages acquired by
children.[5] Chomsky's argument for the postulation of a genetic
component or innateness is based on (his perception of) the poverty
of the stimulus and not on (his assessment of) the degeneracy of
the stimulus.

An example, recently used by Chomsky (1986: 7–8), may serve
to clarify further the notion of 'poverty of the stimulus'. Consider
the manner in which (1) and (2) are interpreted.

(1)      I wonder who [the men expected to see them].
(2)      [the men expected to see them]

Although both (1) and (2) include the clause '[the men expected
to see them]', these forms are interpreted quite differently. In (1),
the pronoun *them* may be interpreted as referring to the people
denoted by the (antecedent) expression *the men*; in (2) this pronoun
cannot be understood as referring to these people. (In (2) the referent
of *them* is determined by what Chomsky calls 'the situational or
discourse context'.) Chomsky claims that these facts about the
interpretation of (1) and (2) 'are known without relevant experience
to differentiate the cases' (1986: 8). On Chomsky's view, that is, the
stimulus is impoverished in the sense that it contains no evidence for
the principle – currently formulated within binding theory – which
the child has to 'acquire' in order to be able to interpret (1) and
(2) correctly. Over the years Chomsky and his followers have
presented a variety of examples that are taken to illustrate the
poverty of the stimulus.[6]

19

*The 'degeneracy–poverty' fork, Dear Player, has been the cause of a number of fatalities in The Game. Certain players of a psychological or psycholinguistic bent have rather carelessly taken 'poverty of the stimulus' as resulting from the unacceptability of utterances with false starts, hesitations, slips of the tongue etc. These players have then – in the words of one of them, Cromer (1980: 16) – proceeded to*

> argue that data from mother–child interaction studies demonstrate that the input to the child is not a degenerate stimulus of this type. It is made up of short, well-formed structures and constitutes an ideal stimulus for inducing grammatical regularities (see, e.g., various contributions to Snow and Ferguson 1977). They conclude that since Chomsky's arguments for innateness are primarily based on the poverty of the input stimulus (in this sense of ill-formed utterances), his position has accordingly been falsified.

*The moral of this story is that it is a waste of energy to attack The Master's position on the poverty of the stimulus by appealing to data – such as those furnished by, for example, Labov (1970: 36–42) – which indicate that the stimulus is not as degenerate as he makes it out to be.*

*Springing, as it does, from a conflation of poverty and degeneracy (of the stimulus), this line of attack – the Poveracy Ploy – has required no real evasive action by The Master.*[7]

    2.2.2   To clarify the nature of the experiential stimulus or evidence for language acquisition, a further distinction has been drawn, namely *the simplified data offered by mothers and caretakers to children vs the actual data-base for language acquisition.* Chomsky's (1980b: 42) position is that there is no evidence that the simplified data offered to children in the form of 'motherese' constitute the stimulus on the basis of which children actually acquire their language.[8] And there is evidence, he claims, which shows that such simplified data or motherese could even make language harder for children to acquire and language acquisition more of a problem to linguists and psychologists. By avoiding apparently complex constructions, motherese could impoverish the data-base for language acquisition even further. At the same time it would turn the acquisition of such constructions into a greater problem.

*It would be a mistake, Pondering Pupil, to attack The Master by claiming that the stimulus for language acquisition is enriched by the contribution of 'motherese' and is, consequently, not anywhere near as impoverished as he makes it out to be. Not believing that linguistic mother's milk could work miracles in mental maturation, The Master just won't fall for such Mum-bo Jumbo. And as Cromer (1980: 16) and others well up on natural neonate nourishment have come to learn, mere mention of matters maternal won't mellow The Master's mood. It certainly won't mist up his glasses, making him drop his Genetic Guard. Of course had The Master, paradoxically, been himself a mother, things could have been different. Then just possibly – though perish the thought! – The Game might even have been played in a matronly manner in the serene setting of some English country garden . . .*

*Now that gender seems to be on the agenda, would I say that stalking someone single-mindedly in a maze is a sex-specific sort of sport? Well, Pupil Player, as we tour The Maze, you cannot fail to notice that those who take on The Master are mostly male members of the Sparring Species. Though we will bump into the odd Woman Warrior or Bellicose Beauty, The Garden has held few attractions for Fighters Fair (and none at all for the kind of Playmates that parade on the pin-up pages of Language and Libido, Quarterly of the Lodge of Leering Linguists). To sum it up, then, in a single statement of sociological substance:*

> *Among those who seek to meet The Master in The Maze, the majority pack a muscled mind of the male kind.*

*But before you turn yourself into a Pumped-up Pupil, stoking up on epistemic steroids, may I remind you that in Gladiatorial Grammar 'muscularity' and 'masculinity' do not map into 'mobility' in the context of 'mind'?*

2.2.3  There is another conceptual distinction that is relevant to the question of just how adequate the stimulus for language acquisition is. This is Chomsky's (1986: 31) distinction *the data available to the child learning a language vs the data available to the linguist studying the language.* Chomskyans have assumed that the data available to the child learning a language are much more limited than the data available to the linguist who studies the language. The linguist, they assume, can systematically get to know that sentences are ambiguous, are paraphrases of each other or are ungrammatical. The child, by contrast, is believed not to have (systematic) access to information about ambiguity, synonymy and ungrammaticality.[9] Such information is considered to be 'not available to preschool children and not part of their verbal experience'.[10]

On the standard view 'children have access only to sentences and pseudo-sentences uttered in appropriate context'.[11] These sentences and pseudo-sentences are assigned the status of 'primary linguistic data' and, within the framework of the idealization of instantaneous acquisition, are taken to constitute the 'totality of data available to the language learner' (Chomsky 1986: 52). So far as the availability of evidence about language is concerned, a child is therefore in a worse position than a linguist. In relation to the evidence about a language, a child cannot be viewed as a 'little linguist'.

*So The Master's position on the impoverished nature of the stimulus cannot be attacked by alluding to the extensive and varied range of data known to the linguist studying the language. Nor, Apprentice Player, would it do to claim that children, in being 'constantly' corrected by parents, receive extensive evidence about which sentences are ungrammatical and which are not. For, as observed by Baker (1978: 411),*

*Recent studies of child language use tend to suggest that such negative information in the form of corrections is not available to children in very large quantities or on a very systematic basis (n. 1). They suggest a wide variation in the ability of individual parents to notice grammatical mistakes in their children's speech and a correspondingly large variation in their propensity for making corrections. They also suggest that children quite frequently either resist a correction when it is made, or else do not understand it. There is thus some room for doubt as to whether such corrections as are made actually play a critical role in leading a child toward the system of rules that he eventually acquires.[12]*

*As regards the availability of data, then, there simply is no Little Linguist Loophole. You would be well advised, Pensive Pupil, to accept this as a fact and to look for an opening elsewhere.*

2.2.4   The notion of 'the data available to the child learning a language' may be sharpened by means of a further conceptual distinction, namely *primary linguistic data vs data about child grammars*. We have noted in section 2.2.3 above that the primary linguistic data (a) are the data available to 'preschool children', (b) include 'sentences and pseudo-sentences uttered in appropriate context', and (c) do not include (sufficient) evidence about such properties of sentences as ungrammaticality, synonymy etc. 'Data about child grammars' – an expression used by, for example, Hornstein and Lightfoot (1981c: 30, n. 8) – denotes data about developmental stages/states that interlink the initial and steady states. Such data may be gathered by observers – e.g. linguists, parents, teachers etc. – from the linguistic behaviour of children.

The effect, however, of the idealization of instantaneous language acquisition is to exclude data about child grammars from the corpus of primary linguistic data. So much is clear from Chomsky's remark that to adopt this idealization is to ignore 'the role of these intermediate states in determining what constitutes linguistic experience' (1981a: 35).

*What is the point of all this? Perhaps, Puzzled Player, you feel that The Master has exaggerated the poverty of the stimulus. Perhaps you contemplate a confrontation on the basis of his having forgotten that so-called data about child grammars/acquisitional data may be available to the child too. The counter to your charge would be that you have yourself forgotten a thing or two: the distinction between the logical and the psychological problem of language acquisition and the associated idealization of instantaneous acquisition (cf. section 2.1.1). And it might be intimated that, in your eagerness to lump primary linguistic data and data about child grammars together, you have invited a counter-charge of Instantaneous Idiocy.*

2.2.5   Even if the stimulus or data presented to a child were sufficiently rich, one still would have to keep in mind Chomsky's

(1983: 262) distinction *the child's being exposed to evidence about its language vs the child's learning the language*. This distinction – for which Chomsky credits Papert – he illustrates in the following way:

> just to present evidence isn't enough; you can sit a child in front of a television set, for example, and run well-formed sentences in front of him, and I'm sure he is not going to learn a thing. So that means that simply having the evidence presented to you is not enough for learning. Suppose that I tried to teach something to Premack's chimpanzee, Sarah; I'm sure that I could give her all the evidence – an apple, a triangle – and she wouldn't learn anything because I am not doing whatever is necessary to get the system to function. I don't know how to do this; he does. We must discover what is necessary to get the system to function; then, if we are interested in going a step further, we will ask what there is in that organism (obviously genetically determined, because there is nothing else) that brings it about that in presenting the evidence as I did, I didn't do what was necessary to make the system function.

The distinction under consideration is a special case of the more general distinction between *teaching* and *learning*, as is made clear by Bickerton (1981: 139) – in whose theory of language acquisition, as in Chomsky's, a significant role is assigned to an innate or genetic factor. Bickerton has pointed out that to equate the simplified data of motherese with the data on the basis of which children actually acquire their language is likewise to commit a logical fallacy:

> If we accept that in the vast majority of circumstances mothers do teach and children do learn, it by no means follows that children learn BECAUSE mothers teach. It would be logically quite possible to argue that there is no connection whatsoever between mothers' teaching and children's learning, any more than there is between children's walking and uncles' dragging them around the room by their fingertips.

*So, Dear Player, don't delude yourself: The Master won't be lured into a Trite Teaching Trap. Thus, he has observed (1980a: 100):*

*It is commonly argued that language is not only learned but taught by conditioning and training. Strawson and Quine, for example, have been insistent on this point (n. 13). Presumably this, at least, is a question of fact, and the facts seem to show pretty clearly that the assumption is incorrect.*

*In the note cited within this quotation (n. 13) The Master refers to his (1975a) discussion of Strawson's (1970) pronouncement that 'it is a fact about human beings that they simply would not acquire mastery [of a language] unless they were exposed, as children, to conditioning or training by adult members of a community.' The Master (1975a: 237) has found 'no reason to believe that these factual claims are true'. And, Dear Player, even if you could think of such a reason, various other dangers lurk down Learning Lane, as I will let you see in section 2.4 below.*

2.3    What we now have to consider is the nature and role assigned by Chomsky to **the genetic component in the acquisition of knowledge of language**. We will do this by considering one by one the members making up yet another constellation of conceptual distinctions on which Chomskyan linguistics is based. I will present these distinctions as they are to be found in various writings by Chomsky, warning the casual reader that some of them are partly overlapping in content and that others differ in formulation only.

2.3.1    We saw in section 2.1.3 above that Chomsky locates the genetic component of language acquisition in the speaker by postulating 'a distinct system of the mind/brain', the language faculty. With reference to this system he (1980a: 187; 1983: 109; 1986: 25–6) draws the fundamental distinction *initial state vs (relatively) stable steady state*. It is the initial state of the language faculty that Chomsky takes to be 'genetically determined'. Put another way, the initial state of this faculty incorporates the genetic language programme, or genetically encoded linguistic principles, representing the child's innate linguistic endowment.

The language faculty is in its initial state in a child that has not had any linguistic experience. Under the 'stimulating' or 'triggering' influence of such experience, the initial state – also called 'universal grammar' (UG) or 'the language acquisition device' by Chomsky (1981a: 34–5) – develops, through a number of intermediate states, into the (relatively) stable steady state, also referred to as 'the attained state'. This stable steady state of the language faculty is what Chomsky has characterized as 'knowledge of language'[13] or 'the (speaker's) mental grammar'. Accordingly, the initial state – universal grammar or the language acquisition device – is regarded by Chomsky (1980a: 65, 187; 1981a: 34) as 'a function that maps a course of experience into' the steady state, (the system of) knowledge of language or the mental grammar. The initial state of the language faculty, on Chomsky's (1980a: 65) view, constitutes an element of the (child's) genotype; the stable steady state being an element of the (mature speaker's) phenotype.[14]

The fundamental distinction drawn by Chomsky with reference to the two states of the language faculty are terminologically reflected by the following pairs of expressions:

(3)  the initial state of the language faculty  vs  the (relatively) stable steady state of the language faculty

the genetically encoded linguistic principles  vs  the attained knowledge of language

the universal grammar / the language acquisition device  vs  a (particular) mental grammar

the innate linguistic endowment  vs  the acquired / attained knowledge / grammar

the (linguistic) genotype  vs  the (linguistic) phenotype

Since Chomsky is concerned with locating the genetic component of language acquisition in the real world, the left-hand members of the *terminological* pairs of (3) are intended to have the same referent. And, in this context, all the right-hand members should denote the same object too. There are contexts within which, as we shall see in section 2.5 below, a *conceptual* distinction has to be drawn between 'language' and 'grammar' – even though in the right-hand column above they have been lumped together.[15]

*From The Garden point of view, what we have here is Treacherous Terminological Terrain. At first glance, Perplexed Player, it has the appearance of an intricate network of criss-crossing paths. 'But this is a Mentalistic Mirage masterfully created by means of terminological mirrors to confuse Players of Poor Perception', some Stray Souls would charge. Some well-meaning spirits have tried to simplify The Game by issuing special directions. Thus, at an away game played in a formal garden in France, one of the organizers suggested that 'steady state' might be conceptually distinguished from 'stable state': 'Steady states are typical of dynamic equilibria, whereas stable states are typical of static equilibria.'*[16]

*But in The Garden, there is neither a 'steady' lane nor a 'stable' lane leading from any of the forks that really matter. If I were you, Puffing Pupil, I would learn the following Lesson of the Labyrinth:*

*Don't see shapes where only shadows lurk.*

2.3.2    Chomsky uses various further conceptual distinctions to clarify his conception of the (initial state of the) language faculty, the first being *innateness vs specificity*. Thus, consider the following remark made by him in the Royaumont debate:

> On this point I agree with Premack. I think he is right in talking about two different problems that enter into this whole innateness controversy. The first is the question of the genetic determination of structures . . . The second problem concerns specificity. (1983: 179)

Innateness, then, concerns the genetic basis of language acquisition as this is embodied in the initial state of the language faculty. Specificity represents a distinct property of a mental faculty, as is clear from the following two questions that arise about the specificity of the language faculty: 'Is this faculty specific to the human species only?' and 'Is this faculty specific to the acquisition of language only?' Note that a distinction has to be drawn between species-specificity (the first question) and language-specificity (the second question).

As regards the question of species-specificity, Chomsky (1983) does indeed consider the (initial state of the) language faculty to be species-specific: a species characteristic, common to all humans and restricted to humans only. The language faculty, in other words, is taken by him to be 'a property of the mind/brain that differentiates humans from rocks, birds, or apes'. We will see below in section 2.5.16 that this view cannot be falsified by citing the existence of a couple of clever, 'talking' chimpanzees.

As regards language-specificity, the (initial state of the) language faculty represents a distinct faculty for the acquisition of language alone. It does not instantiate general/generalized learning mechanisms, a point which we will examine in section 2.3.3 below. Nor have the constitutive principles of the language faculty been found to characterize other cognitive faculties, a point to be pursued further in section 2.7.3 below. In sum: innateness implies neither species-specificity nor language-specificity. And innateness is not implied by either of these forms of specificity.[17]

*Playing The Game at Royaumont, Piaget (1983: 31) attacked The Master's postulation of innate structures or mechanisms from the angle of species-specificity. He charged that in being peculiar to the human species the mutations that might have given rise to these innate structures 'would be biologically inexplicable'. This thrust has been parried by The Master's (1983: 36) response that*

> *Although it is quite true that we have no idea how or why random mutations have endowed humans with the specific capacity to learn a human language, it is also true that we have no better idea how or why random mutations have led to the development of the particular structures of the mammalian eye or the cerebral cortex.*

*A response which, in a different context, he elaborates as follows:*

> *he [i.e., Piaget] offers no argument at all that the postulated mechanisms are any more 'inexplicable' than mechanisms postulated to account for physical development; indeed, even the most radical 'innatists' have suggested mechanisms that would add only a small increment to what any rational biologist would assume must be genetically determined. (1980a: 207)*

*And, as if this was not enough, The Master (1983: 36) has turned defence into counter-attack:*

*Little is known concerning evolutionary development, but
from ignorance, it is impossible to draw any conclusions. In
particular, it is rash to conclude either (A) that known physical
laws do not suffice in principle to account for the development
of particular structures, or (B) that physical laws, known or
unknown, do not suffice in principle. Either (A) or (B) would
seem to be entailed by the contention that evolutionary
development is literally 'inexplicable' on biological grounds.
But there seems to be no present justification for taking
(B) seriously, and (A), though conceivably true, is mere
speculation.*

*Rubbing salt into the wound, The Master (1980a: 207) remarks
that: 'Piaget's complaint would be correct if he had said "biologically
unexplained" instead of "biologically inexplicable", but then the same
might be said about current ideas concerning development of
physical organs of the body.'*

*So if ever you should attempt, Dear Player, to succeed where Piaget
failed, then do be careful to observe the distinction* biologically
inexplicable vs biologically unexplained. *But to get to the essence
of the matter: I have recounted Piaget's Plight to draw your attention
to a particular Canon of the East Coast Code of Combat:*

> *Rashness will bring rapid ruin.*

*And, in passing, you might also note that innateness cannot
easily be attacked from the angle of (species-)specificity, and
vice versa.*

2.3.3    Fundamental to Chomsky's (1983: 320ff; 1986: 4,
150) conception of language acquisition is the distinction *distinct
language faculty vs general(ized) learning mechanisms*. A child, it
has commonly been assumed, acquires its language with the aid of
the same general/generalized learning mechanism – also referred to
as 'general intelligence', 'multi-purpose learning strategies' etc. – that
it uses in the learning of nonlinguistic materials – say, physics,
history, the rules of chess etc. Chomsky, however, has rejected this
view of language acquisition, claiming that there is a distinct mental
faculty specifically for the acquisition of language. This view he bases
on considerations such as the following:

There are, in fact, striking and obvious differences between language learning and the learning (or discovery) of physics. In the first case, a rich and complex system of rules and principles is attained in a uniform way, rapidly, effortlessly, on the basis of limited and rather degenerate evidence. In the second case, we are forced to proceed on the basis of consciously articulated principles subjected to careful verification with the intervention of individual insight and often genius. It is clear enough that the cognitive domains in question are quite different. Humans are designed to learn language, which is nothing other than what their minds construct when placed in appropriate conditions; they are not designed in anything like the same way to learn physics. Gross observations suffice to suggest that very different principles of 'learning' are involved. (1983: 320)

Chomsky (1983: 110) does not deny that the language faculty, on the one hand, and, on the other hand, the learning mechanisms operative in nonlinguistic cognitive domains will turn out to 'have some properties in common'. Nor does he deny that there are forms of language acquisition – for example, the acquisition of vocabulary items, or the acquisition of a second language by an adult – in which learning mechanisms other than the language faculty play a role. His scepticism is directed at the status of general/generalized learning mechanisms, or of what he (1983: 110) also calls 'a general learning theory': 'The common assumption . . . that a general learning theory does exist, seems to me dubious, unargued, and without any empirical support of plausibility at the moment.'

*To many a Player of Power – such as Putnam and Piaget – The Master's postulation of a faculty peculiar to language acquisition has offered an irresistible target. Putnam (1983a: 295), for example, has contended that 'our cognitive repertoire . . . must include* multipurpose *learning strategies, heuristics, and so forth'. He has remarked, moreover, that 'Once it is granted that such multipurpose learning strategies exist, the claim that they* cannot *account for language becomes highly dubious . . . ' (1983a: 296).[18] Putnam's*

*Probing has failed, however, to force The Master to retreat, as is clear from the following counter-attack:*

All that Putnam has so far assumed is that $S^L{}_0$ [the genetically determined initial state for language learning], whatever it may be, contains only the general mechanisms for learning. Recall that he gives no hint as to what these are. To invoke an unspecified 'general intelligence' or unspecified 'multipurpose learning strategies' is no more illuminating than his reference, at one point, to divine intervention. We have no way of knowing what, if anything, Putnam has assumed. The point is worth stressing, since it illustrates a common fallacy in discussions of this sort. The use of words such as 'general intelligence' does not constitute an empirical assumption unless these notions are somehow clarified. (Chomsky 1983: 320)

*If you had in mind, Dear Player, using a form of offensive similar to the Putnam Probe, then do please think again. Think, specifically, about two questions. First, when challenged on the matter, what would you have to say for yourself about the general nature and specific properties of 'general/generalized learning mechanisms', 'general intelligence' or 'multipurpose learning strategies'? If the substance of your answer were to be 'Nothing of a detailed sort', then why not opt for 'divine intervention' to begin with? Second, could you show that the child acquires linguistic principles such as those involved in, say, Subjacency or Binding in essentially the same way as, for example, laws of physics, rules of chess, etc.?[19] If you couldn't, why bother at all? So, when playing on your own, do keep in mind the following Moral of The Maze:*

The Master's conception of a distinct faculty for language acquisition must be respected as a truly taunting target, simple to see, difficult to dent.

*As we will observe in section 2.4.6 below, the same experience befell the Piagetian Players who contended that language acquisition was made possible not by a distinct, specific language faculty, but rather by a more general 'sensorimotor intelligence'.[20]*

2.3.4    Returning now to the species character of the (initial state of the) language faculty, we need to note a further distinction

31

that bears on it, namely *(idealized) uniformity vs (real) variation in the species*. As is the case with other species characteristics, one would expect to find among humans some variation in the initial state of the language faculty. Chomsky (1986: 18), however, contends that

> it is plausible to suppose that apart from pathology (potentially an important area of inquiry), such variation as there may be is marginal and can be safely ignored across a broad range of linguistic investigation.

Thus, Chomsky's view of the initial state of the language faculty embodies an idealization: uniformity in the species.

*The uniformity idealization, Dear Player, has been built into The Game for the purpose of protecting The Master from Petty Pestering. No amount of juggling with data about linguistic deficiencies of, for example, children with congenital brain defects would make The Master drop his guard. Such conjuring would be no less silly, in fact, than the dumb deictic deed of pointing at an ape to ridicule The Master for his species-specificity stand, as we will come to see in section 2.5.16 below.*[21]

2.3.5    In making a critical assessment of the contents assigned by Chomsky to the genetically determined initial state of the language faculty, a basic distinction has to be observed, namely *genetically determined factors vs factors operative at birth*. Chomsky (1986: 54) draws this distinction to accommodate the assumption that the language faculty undergoes a maturation whose course (ordering and timing) is genetically determined. This provides for the possibility, noted by Chomsky (1986: 204, n. 3), 'that certain principles of UG are not available at early stages of language growth', obviously including the initial state.[22]

*How, then, does the conceptual fork signalled above affect The Game? Let us suppose, probably counter-factually I dare say, that you were to hit on a method of 'looking into' the mind of a newborn child. Suppose, moreover, that you failed 'to see' Subjacency, a genetically based principle on The Master's view, in the initial state of the language faculty. What, then, Pupil Player, would be the prudent move? I suggest: take a deep breath and refrain from hitting out at The Master for making a fallacious claim about the initial state of the language faculty. Such action would be based on a fallacy of your own, the Neonate Non Sequitur. What you should have 'looked into' is the fully matured initial state of the language faculty. The general moral of the story: Players cannot be too careful in drawing conclusions about the initial state of the language faculty from data about the properties of 'child grammars' – that is, descriptions of the knowledge that linguistically nonmature speakers have about their language.*

2.3.6 The distinction *genetic vs epigenetic* might also appear to be relevant to an appraisal of Chomsky's claims about the initial state of the language faculty. This distinction relates to two different ways of approaching innate structures. On the genetic or preformationist approach, innate structures or properties are in some sense fully formed at the beginning of development. That is, these structures or properties are in some sense directly encoded in the genes. On the epigenetic approach, innate structures arise in the development of the embryo but are not directly encoded in the genes. Factors or constraints of a mechanical and a chemical sort are held to play an important role in such epigenetic development of innate structures or properties.[23]

*The question, then, is whether The Master considers the innate principles and properties of the initial state of the language faculty to be genetic or epigenetic. Catlin (1978) contended that The Master's view of universal grammar incorporated the genetic approach.[24] This, however, has been denied by both Cromer (1980: 18) and The Master himself (1980b: 43) since, in the latter's words, 'I take no stand (here or elsewhere), agreeing [with Cromer] that there seems no current possibility of distinguishing them [the genetic vs the epigenetic approach] empirically'.*

*So, 'genetic vs epigenetic' represents a conceptual fork for future construction: at present all we have at this point in The Garden is Catlin's Cul-de-sac.*

*2.3.7*  Various conceptual distinctions drawn by Chomsky are meant to clarify the nature of the components that make up the initial state of the language faculty. Here we will consider one of those distinctions, namely the distinction *fundamental principles vs open parameters*, in order to clear the ground for dealing with the nature of the acquisition process in section 2.4 below. Viewing the make-up of the initial state of the language faculty at an abstract, mental level, Chomsky (1981a: 38ff; 1981b: 3ff; 1986: 146, 150) portrays it as a highly structured system of fundamental principles many of which have open parameters associated with them.[25]

A typical example of these fundamental principles is provided by Subjacency. Subjacency, as we have seen, implies, roughly speaking, that a phrase cannot be moved 'too far' within a sentence, where 'too far' means 'out of two bounding categories'. As a fundamental principle, Subjacency on Chomsky's view is genetically encoded, i.e., not acquired on the basis of linguistic experience. A fundamental principle such as Subjacency may, however, have one or more open parameters whose values are fixed by the child's linguistic experience. In the case of Subjacency, Chomsky (1981a: 55) takes the choice of the bounding category to be an open parameter. Whereas S̄ and NP represent bounding categories that hold good generally, S represents an optional bounding category.[26] On the basis of their linguistic experience children will select S as an additional bounding category if they happen to be acquiring English, for example, but not if they happen to be acquiring Italian. That is to say, English and Italian both use Subjacency as a fundamental principle, but they differ in regard to the way in which the open parameter of choice of bounding category is fixed. French moreover, on Chomsky's view (1981a: 55–6), differs from both English and Italian in regard to the fixing of this parameter. Unlike English (and like Italian), it does not select S as a bounding category for infinitival clauses. But, unlike Italian (though like English), it does select S as a bounding category for finite clauses.[27]

Let us, for a moment, consider the distinction between fundamental principles and open parameters in relation to the logical problem of language acquisition. As noted by Chomsky (1981b: 3), this distinction provides the basis for an account of how it is possible for the initial state of the language faculty to satisfy two apparently conflicting conditions. On the one hand, this state of the language faculty must make it possible in principle for the child to acquire any one of a wide diversity of possible human languages (or, more accurately, 'grammars' – as we will see below). On the other hand, this state must be sufficiently restrictive so as to make it possible for the child to acquire, on the basis of limited evidence, the specific language of the speech community to which it belongs. The genetically determined fundamental principles provide for the 'plasticity' to acquire any one of a wide diversity of languages; the open parameters make it possible to acquire a specific language on the basis of limited linguistic experience.

*Both the distinction 'fundamental principles vs open parameters', and the associated notion of 'the selection of values for fixing parameters', represent important features of the layout of The Garden. Failure, Dear Player, to recognize these features for what they are, may trick you into doing something superlatively stupid: charging that, say, Subjacency could not be part of an innate, genetic component of the language faculty since it did not show up in the same form in (even closely related) languages. A charge of this sort would be the result of an Errant Equation, namely the claim that 'innate' equalled 'invariable'.*

**2.4**   Having considered Chomsky's view of the genetically determined initial state of the language faculty, we can now look at his conception of the nature of **the process of language acquisition**. Generally speaking, this is the process by means of which the steady state of the language faculty, representing knowledge of language, is attained on the basis of the genetically determined initial state.[28] Over the years, Chomsky has drawn various conceptual distinctions to clarify the nature of this process. As we look at these, it will become clear that his ideas about the nature of the process of language acquisition have undergone subtle but significant changes.

*2.4.1*   A fundamental distinction drawn by Chomsky (1980a: 134–5; 1980b: 47) in an attempt to clarify the nature of language acquisition is that of *growth/maturation vs learning*. He observes that when the heart, visual system or other organs of the body develop to their mature form, we speak of growth rather than learning. Growth, then, is a process in which an organ develops (or, alternatively, by which the final structure of an organ is attained) along a course largely predetermined by our genetic programme. Chomsky takes this programme to provide 'a highly restrictive schematism that is fleshed out and articulated through interaction with the environment'. The developmental process of learning, however, takes place by means of association, induction, conditioning, hypothesis-formation, confirmation, abstraction, generalization and so on. These processes, Chomsky believes, play no significant role in the acquisition of language. He does provide for some role for 'mechanisms of association (etc.) . . . in the acquisition of idiosyncrasies (e.g., specific inflectional patterns and choice of vocabulary items)' (1980a: 139).

But knowledge of language (or grammar), on Chomsky's view, 'develops in the child through the interplay of genetically determined principles and a course of experience'. To him language acquisition represents growth, therefore, rather than learning:

> development of specialized hardware or of a specialized system that comes into operation, perhaps in the way in which sexual maturation takes place at a certain age for reasons that are probably deeply rooted in genetics, though naturally external conditions have to be appropriate. (1983: 73)

*The conceptual fork 'learning vs growth' has proved to be a hazard and, indeed, the undoing of many – including a Passionate Player such as McCawley (1980: 27), who argued:*

> *Chomsky wonders whether we can 'distinguish learning from growth in terms of the state attained'. We can, since learning and growth individuate differently. If one is given appropriate exposure to French, Flemish, and German, one develops command of all three languages but does not develop three larynxes or three pairs of ears. Your genes fix in advance the number of organs of each type that you'll develop, but they don't fix in advance the number of bodies of knowledge (e.g. languages) that you'll acquire through the use of each 'mental organ'. The possibility of acquiring several bodies of knowledge*

*of a given type is the clearest evidence that I know of for the*
*proposition that the mind involves some sort of slate.*

*Unruffled, unrattled, The Master (1980b: 47–8) responded:*

*McCawley has missed the point of my remarks on distinguishing*
*learning from growth in terms of properties of the state*
*attained. As I noted (p. 13), we might do so by speaking*
*of 'learning' in the case where the state attained is a system of*
*belief or knowledge, but 'if we do, then it is not clear that any*
*coherent notion of* learning *will remain', for reasons given*
*there. McCawley takes the criterial property of 'learning' to*
*be individuation; since our mind can acquire knowledge of*
*several languages, acquisition of language is 'learning' (so that*
*if it turned out that 'coordinate bilingualism' is impossible,*
*rather only 'compound bilingualism', in which knowledge of*
*one language is built on knowledge of another, then first-*
*language acquisition would not be 'learning'). Clearly, this does*
*not respond to the point I discussed.* [29]

*And, having blunted McCawley's attack, The Master (1980b: 48)*
*went on the offensive:*

*In fact, McCawley's proposal raises the problem discussed in*
*a more severe form than mine did. The body can become*
*accustomed to a certain style of food (say, highly spiced). But*
*it can accommodate to several such styles. When I receive*
*eyeglasses with a stronger correction, I slowly come to*
*accommodate and to see without distortion, but I continue to*
*see without distortion when the glasses are removed, so that*
*my visual system is in 'two states' in McCawley's sense. If such*
*examples constitute 'learning', in accordance with McCawley's*
*criterion, then the prospects for a coherent notion of 'learning'*
*seem even dimmer than if we identify 'learning' in the terms*
*I suggested.*

*As regards language acquisition, then, it wouldn't do you any*
*good to attack along a Learning Line if you were not equipped to*
*counter The Growth Gambit.*

2.4.2   To say that language acquisition represents a form
of growth appears to imply yet another distinction, namely *(language)*

*growth vs hypothesis-formation or abductive learning.* As noted by Chomsky (1980a: 136ff; 1980b: 13–14), abduction, in Peirce's sense, is a process in which the mind forms hypotheses according to some rule and selects the most highly valued one among them on the basis of evidence and (probably) other factors as well. Language acquisition might be construed as a process of abductive learning. In Chomsky's (1980b: 14) formulation:

> It is convenient sometimes to think of language acquisition in these terms, as if a mind equipped with universal grammar generates alternative grammars that are tested against the data of experience, with the most highly valued one selected.

Chomsky (1980b: 14) does not intend this abduction 'metaphor' to be taken too seriously, however, since he judges the distinction between the alternatives to which it gives rise to be 'far beyond conceivable research'.[30] To him, consequently, the question whether knowledge (of language) is the result of abductive learning or of growth is 'hardly worth considering'. On Chomsky's more recent formulations the distinction 'growth vs hypothesis-formation', therefore, has no empirical basis at present. It should be noted, however, that there was a time when he (1972) used the notion of 'hypothesis-formation' quite systematically when attempting to characterize the nature of the process of language acquisition. The 'growth/maturation' idiom represents an innovation, at least at the level of terminology.

*In a gruelling game, conserving one's energy is all-important, Panting Player. It would be futile to get The Master to give up his Growth Game for a bit of Abductive Action. This has been discovered, the hard way alas, by players such as Dennett (1978) and Cromer (1980). Dennett (1978: 84) presented an abductive theory of (language) learning central to which was a notion of 'self-design' that reflected Simon's (1970: 74) view of 'the design process as involving first the generation of alternatives and then the testing of these alternatives against a whole array of requirements and constraints'. Dennett views 'learning as ultimately a* process *of self-design. That process is for the purposes of this argument defined only by its* product, *and the product is a* new *design. That is, as a result of the process something comes to have a design it previously did not have.'*

For the reasons mentioned above, The Master (1980a: 136) doesn't think that the self-design/abduction 'metaphor . . . should be taken too seriously'. So let us remember the use of the notion of 'self-design' as Dennett's Decoy, a futile form of fighting.[31]

2.4.3   To sharpen his notion of 'language acquisition' further, Chomsky (1980a: 136–7; 1980b: 14) invokes a distinction drawn by the immunologist Jerne, namely *instructive theories of learning vs selective theories of learning.* On an instructive theory, change of a system takes place because a signal from outside 'imparts its character to the system that receives it'. On a selective theory, 'change of the system takes place when some already present character is identified and amplified by the intruding stimulus'. Jerne argues that from a historical point of view 'it appears that wherever a phenomenon resembles learning, an instructive theory was first proposed to account for the underlying mechanisms. In every case, this was later replaced by a selective theory'.[32]

Chomsky's (1980a: 138–9) appraisal of the distinction between instructive and selective theories of learning – and of the derived distinction between instructive and selective processes of learning – is neatly summarized by the following remarks:

I don't think that the notion of selection from preexisting materials is rich enough to provide an analysis for the large-scale interactions that are loosely called 'learning', but it may be a step along the way. It is possible that the notion 'learning' may go the way of the rising and setting of the sun.

Applied to language acquisition, Chomsky's view of the distinction between instructive and selective learning boils down to the following: language acquisition represents a further instance of those phenomena that resemble learning but whose underlying mechanisms can be accounted for more adequately by a selective theory than by an instructive theory. To put it bluntly: language acquisition is essentially a matter of selection, not instruction.

*All of this has a simple lesson for those who play The Game: you cannot score by naively invoking Learning Lore. For the term 'learning', as a rigid designator, is, in the phraseology of The Master himself (Chomsky 1980a: 138), 'commonly misapplied', being 'analogous to such terms as "witch", commonly applied at one time but always misapplied'. You could do worse, Dear Player, than to reflect for a while on the following Fact of Play:*

> *The Garden's sticks and stones*
> *may break The Master's bones,*
> *but Witch Words will not hurt him.*

2.4.4 The nature of selective growth or maturation, which is what Chomsky considers language acquisition to be, is clarified by him (1986: 151) at an abstract, mental level by means of the distinction *parameter fixing vs rule acquisition*. In section 2.3.7 above we saw that Chomsky characterizes the genetically determined, initial state of the language faculty as a system of fundamental principles, many of which have open parameters associated with them. On the basis of their experience of language, children fix the values of the open parameters to attain the (mental) grammar of their language. This brings Chomsky (1986: 150–1) to characterize the process of language acquisition as 'parameter fixing': 'What we learn are the values of the parameters and the elements of the periphery (along with the lexicon, to which similar considerations apply).'[33]

Chomsky has come to see the problem of language acquisition – (1) (b) in section 1.2 – 'not as a problem of acquiring rules but one of fixing parameters in a largely determined system'. Children have to 'learn' or 'fix' the value of the open parameter, for example, of choice of bounding category in the fundamental principle of Subjacency. As pointed out by Chomsky (1986: 151), the characterization of language acquisition as parameter fixing rather than rule acquisition forms part of the second fundamental conceptual revision or shift embodied in present-day 'generative' linguistics. Earlier, Chomsky considered language acquisition to be in essence a process of rule acquisition – in keeping with his characterization of knowledge of language as a rule system. We return to this conceptual shift in section 2.5.21 below.

40

To make the idea of language acquisition as parameter fixing a little easier to grasp, Chomsky (1986: 146) borrows an image of Higginbotham's (1983). The latter suggested that (the initial state of) the language faculty might be thought of as an intricately structured system that is only 'partially "wired up"'. 'The system', on Chomsky's (1986: 146) rendition of Higginbotham's image,

> is associated with a finite set of switches, each of which has a finite number of positions (perhaps two). Experience is required to set the switches. When they are set, the system functions (n. 8). The transition from the initial state $S_0$ to the steady state $S_s$ is a matter of setting the switches.

*The portrayal of language acquisition as being essentially a process of parameter fixing (or, metaphorically, switch setting), rather than rule acquisition, is a relatively new feature of The Garden. No direct attack on The Master has yet been made at this conceptual fork. Of course, the distinction 'parameter fixing vs rule acquisition' cannot be easily attacked or defended in isolation. It features in a more general conceptual change in which the entire status of rules – in language acquisition, in knowledge of language, in language use – has been revised by The Master. This implies that the character-ization of language acquisition as parameter fixing could be open to indirect attack: by questioning the bases of the general conceptual change. Alternatively, the more enterprising player could attempt the more direct approach of Tactical Taunting, challenging The Master to present evidence of a more specific sort which will indicate that parameter fixing and rule acquisition, as alternative characterizations of the nature of language acquisition, are empirically distinguishable. But, Dear Player, my role is that of Guide, not of Fifth Columnist.*

2.4.5 At this stage of the discussion it might be useful to set Chomsky's ideas about language acquisition in a historical perspective. So let us consider them in the context of the distinction *rationalism vs empiricism*. In Chomsky's terminology (1965: 47ff; 1980a: 234ff), rationalism and empiricism represent 'general approaches' or 'general lines of approach to the problem of acquisition of knowledge of which the problem of acquisition

41

of language is a special and particularly informative case'. The rationalist approach is based on some version of the assumption that a significant aspect of knowledge is not derived by the senses but is, as Chomsky (1965: 51) puts it, 'fixed in advance as a disposition of the mind'. On Chomsky's (1965: 48) characterization, the rationalist approach

> holds that beyond the peripheral processing mechanisms, there are innate ideas and principles of various kinds that determine the form of the acquired knowledge in what may be a rather restricted and highly organized way. A condition for innate mechanisms to become activated is that appropriate stimulation be presented.[34]

Rationalism (or innatism) in the Chomskyan mould, we saw above, provides for a distinct language faculty which has, genetically encoded in it, fundamental principles of language that grow or mature into knowledge of language under the stimulating and shaping influence of linguistic experience. As regards the intellectual tradition of rationalism, on Chomsky's (1965: 48ff) account it includes ideas and speculations of scholars as illustrious as Descartes, Lord Herbert, Cudworth, Leibnitz, Locke, Arnauld, Wilhelm von Humboldt and Plato.

In contrast, the empiricist approach is based on the view that 'all knowledge derives solely from the senses by elementary operations of association and "generalization"', as Chomsky (1965: 58–9) puts it. As to language acquisition, the empiricist approach holds that

> language is essentially an adventitious construct, taught by 'conditioning' (as would be maintained, for example, by Skinner or Quine) or by drill and explicit explanation (as was claimed by Wittgenstein), or built up by elementary 'data-processing' procedures (as modern linguistics typically maintains), but, in any event, relatively independent in its structure of any innate mental faculties.

So, on the empiricist approach, operations such as generalization, conditioning, induction etc., constitute the procedures or mechanisms by means of which language, as a system of habits or skills, is acquired. And only these procedures or mechanisms, on this

42

approach, constitute an innate property of mind, as noted by Chomsky (1965: 51).

Chomsky, of course, has rejected a variety of empiricist approaches to language acquisition. The essence of his criticism of such approaches has been that, as a matter of principle, they are at odds with the poverty of the stimulus. Such approaches cannot give an account of how children can acquire abstract principles of language, e.g. Subjacency, for which the stimulus contains no evidence at all. The poverty of the stimulus has likewise provided the basis for Chomsky's motivation – motivation considered empirical by him – of his alternative, rationalist, approach to language acquisition.

In considering Chomsky's appraisal of empiricist approaches it is of some importance to note what he has not criticized empiricism for. First, he has not criticized empiricist approaches for failing to attribute any innate structure to an organism, as Putnam (1983a) has charged. Chomsky (1983: 310) rejects this charge as 'utterly false', pointing out that he has

> repeatedly, consistently, and clearly insisted that all rational approaches to the problems of learning, including 'association-ism' and many others . . . attribute innate structure to the organism . . . The question is not whether innate structure is a prerequisite for learning, but rather what it is.

Thus, in critically considering Chomsky's appraisal of empiricism there is an important distinction to be kept in mind, namely *the question whether innate structure is a prerequisite for learning vs the question what innate structure is*. It was noted above that in Chomsky's (1965: 51) view empiricists consider learning mechanisms or procedures such as generalization, association, induction etc. to be innate properties of an organism.

Second, in rejecting empiricist approaches to language acquisition Chomsky (1980a: 139) does not wish 'to demean the content of what is learned' by means of trial-and-error, conditioning, abstraction, induction and so on. These means of learning will play a role in 'domains in which the mind is equipped with no special structure to deal with properties of the task situation', i.e. in performing tasks 'for which we have no special design'. This however, according to Chomsky (1980a: 139), implies that studying these means will 'tell us very little about the nature of the organism'.

Nevertheless, this is no criticism of the means in question, since he emphasizes the point that 'what is significant for human life is not necessarily significant for the person inquiring into human nature'. So in this quotation we find yet a further distinction, namely *something significant for human life vs something significant for the person inquiring into human nature*, that has to be kept in mind when considering Chomsky's appraisal of empiricist approaches to the acquisition of knowledge (of language).

*So, Pugnacious Player, you would like, would you, to corner The Master on the question of his reasons for taking a rationalist approach to the phenomenon of language acquisition? Others have attempted this before, including Putnam (1983a), and have found it heavy going. One line of attack has proved particularly unrewarding, namely that of accusing The Master of being committed to rationalism as a point of doctrine. In his countermove you could expect The Master to proceed along more or less the following lines:*

> As a general principle, I am committed only to the 'open-mindedness hypothesis' with regard to the genetically determined initial state for language learning (call it $S_0^L$), and I am committed to particular explanatory hypotheses about $S_0^L$ to the extent that they seem credible and empirically supported. (1983: 310–11)

*To this, Putnam (1983b: 336) had only the following lame response:*

> After twenty years of vigorously espousing this point of view in print and in conversation, it is a little unfair of Chomsky to say that he is only advocating the 'Open-mindedness hypothesis' with respect to our genetic makeup. Who could be against open-mindedness?

*Should you yourself not be able to think of some dodge less flat-footed than this, there is nothing to be gained by engaging in Doctrinaire Duelling.*

2.4.6 The historical perspective on Chomsky's ideas about language acquisition may be broadened somewhat by considering in conclusion the distinction *rationalism vs constructivism*.

Constructivism (or interactionism) represents Piaget's (1983) theory of how knowledge, including knowledge of language, is acquired. Piaget (1983: 26) considers both empiricist and rationalist (or, in his terminology, 'preformationist') theories of the genesis of knowledge to be 'devoid of concrete truth'. As an alternative, 'only constructivism is acceptable' to him. On Chomsky's (1980a: 235) reading, Piagetian constructivism (also called 'vitalism' by some) boils down to the claim that

> through interaction with the environment the child develops sensorimotor constructions which provide the basis for language, and as understanding and knowledge grow, new constructions are developed in some more or less uniform way. Thus, it is claimed, language at any stage merely reflects independent mental constructions that arise in the course of dealing with the environment, and at each stage the child develops new systems that reorganize his experience.

So, whereas Chomskyan rationalism invokes a genetically based language faculty to account for language acquisition, Piagetian constructivism places the explanatory burden on a 'general sensori-motor intelligence', a capacity not specific to language acquisition.

At Royaumont, Piaget (1983: 31) challenged The Master's pos-tulation of innate structures or mechanisms from a second, a comparative, angle as well.[35] The gist of this challenge is that, given the alternative offered by constructivism, 'the hypothesis of innateness is not mandatory in order to secure the coherence of Chomsky's beautiful [sic] system'. This expresses Piaget's (1983: 31) claim that

> the 'innate fixed nucleus' would retain all its properties of a 'fixed nucleus' if it were not innate but constituted the 'necessary' result of the constructions of sensorimotor intelligence, which is prior to language and results from those joint organic and behavioral autoregulations that determine this epigenesis.[36]

That is, Piaget claims that what can be explained on the assumption of fixed innate structures can be equally well explained as the 'necessary' result of constructions of sensorimotor intelligence. This

45

*challenge has been brushed aside by The Master (1983: 36) rather briskly in the following terms – which strike even me (an observer of some experience) as being on the brusque side:*

There are, to my knowledge, no substantive proposals involving 'constructions of sensorimotor intelligence' that offer any hope of accounting for the phenomena of language that demand explanation. Nor is there any initial plausibility to the suggestion, as far as I can see.

*And:*

the literature contains no evidence or argument to support this remarkable factual claim [about the relative explanatory power of constructivism], nor even any explanation of what sense it might have. Again, we see here an instance of the unfortunate but rather common insistence on dogmatic and unsupported factual doctrines in the human sciences. (Chomsky 1980a: 207)

*What may we learn from all this about The Game? Basically three Facts of Play:*

1  *Dogmatism will be denounced.*
2  *Bluster will be blasted.*
3  *Punches won't be pulled.*

*As for 1, we will be returning to it in section 4.3.1 below. As for 2, Boastful Bluster will bring you zero benefit. Before claiming explanatory equality – let alone superiority – for your own constructions, make sure that they are able to account for specifics. For example, could they account for the acquisition of structure-dependent rules, for the acquisition of the Specified Subject Condition, and so on?[37] As for 3, if you happen to be one who is easily wounded, you may be sure that all the way further along will see you smarting and anticipatorily starting.*

*Perhaps, before venturing deeper into The Garden, you should pause to reconsider your participation in The Game, asking yourself how you would have blocked the following bare-fisted blows, dispensed to those of the Piagetian Persuasion:*

Another factor that impedes the study of language and more generally cognitive development, in my view, is the persistence

*of certain curious doctrines that entirely lack empirical support
or inherent plausibility, for example, the Piagetian dogma that
language must reflect sensorimotor constructions, and the
refusal to consider the properties of the initial state that enter
into the postulated interstate transitions.*

*Fortunately for you, you're no Piagetian? Reckless rationalization,
but do carry on!*[38]

**2.5**  Next, we may take a closer look at Chomsky's
conception of **the nature of knowledge of language**. In section 2.3.1
we saw that on Chomsky's view such knowledge exists in the form
of a specific mental state: the steady state of the language faculty.
'To know a language', Chomsky (1980a: 48) assumes, 'is to be in a
certain mental state, which persists as a relatively steady component
of transitory mental states.' But what does it mean to say that to
know a language 'is to be in a certain mental state'? The answer
to this question is to be found in yet another constellation of
conceptual distinctions drawn by Chomsky. These distinctions are
intended to shed light on questions such as the following: 'In what
sense is knowledge of language something mental?', 'To what kind
of knowledge does knowledge of language belong?', 'What is
language?', 'What is the scope and make-up of knowledge of
language?'. Let us consider these distinctions with due care, taking
them each in turn.

*2.5.1*  A basic distinction invoked by Chomsky (1980a: 52;
1986: 9–10) to clarify the mental character of knowledge of language
is that of *knowledge of language vs the capacity to use a language*.
The latter capacity he refers to also as 'the practical ability to speak
and understand'. Chomsky (1986:9) sees the distinction under
consideration as reflecting a 'common-sense assumption' and
grounds it in a variety of common-sense considerations. Thus, he
observes (1986: 9) that, although two people may share exactly the
same knowledge of language, they may differ markedly in their
ability to put this knowledge to use. And he notes that a person's
ability to use language may improve or decline without the knowledge
itself improving or declining. Moreover, Chomsky contends, the

47

ability to use language may be impaired without a deterioration in the knowledge itself. He (1980a: 51) illustrates the latter point with the imaginary case of a person recovering from temporary brain injury:

> Imagine a person who knows English and suffers cerebral damage that does not affect the language centers at all but prevents their use in speech, comprehension, or let us suppose, even in thought (n. 5). Suppose that the effects of the injury recede and with no further experience or exposure the person recovers the original capacity to use the language. In the intervening period, he had no capacity to speak or understand English, even in thought, though the mental (ultimately physical) structures that underlie that capacity were undamaged. Did the person know English during the intervening period?

If one insisted on identifying knowledge of language with the capacity or practical ability to use language, one would have to believe that when someone like the above-mentioned aphasic lacks the ability to speak and understand, he does not know his language – a belief that seems 'perverse' to Chomsky. And one would, on Chomsky's (1980a: 52) view, be committed to the further belief that

> full knowledge of English [assuming English to be the language of this aphasic] can arise in a mind totally lacking this knowledge without any relevant experience whatsoever, as the case of the recovery shows, something that is plainly not true of the child's mind and seems an exotic claim.

There is no need, however, to hold such 'perverse' beliefs or to make such 'exotic' claims if a distinction is drawn between knowledge of language and the capacity or ability to use language. This distinction allows Chomsky to say that in the period when the aphasic lacked the capacity or ability to speak his language, he still knew this language. On Chomsky's view, during the period of impairment the aphasic's behaviour simply provided no evidence for his having knowledge of his language. Chomsky considers behaviour to be only one of the sources of evidence for knowledge. Data about electrical activity of the brain and data from autopsy are mentioned by Chomsky (1980a: 48, 52) as other possible sources of such evidence.[39]

*In The Garden, the knowledge-capacity/ability fork has been the scene of some remarkably aggressive action, Dear Player. It was here that Rachlin (1980: 31), for example – all steamed up because of The Master's remark that 'Two people might share exactly the same knowledge but differ greatly in their capacity to use it' – threw caution to the winds and let rip from the hip:*

> Here he [*i.e., Chomsky*] takes what is essentially a temporal difference and makes it into a structural (really, in the absence of physiological content, a spiritual) difference. Knowledge of English obviously involves use of English over an extended time period, whereas impaired capacity to use English involves disability over a smaller time period. To identify such dispositions with structures, like personification of the deity, may serve a psychological purpose but not a logical one.

*The retaliation was rough, The Master (1980b: 49) responding as follows:*

> Since I fail to see in what sense they are 'difficulties', I cannot respond, except to remark that his [*i.e., Rachlin's*] discussion of differences between capacity and knowledge in terms of 'temporal difference' is completely incoherent.

*This was, however, just one of Rachlin's hip shots in a whole trigger-happy salvo, which provoked The Master (1980b: 50) to continue:*

> his [*i.e., Rachlin's*] refusal to undertake the study of inner mechanisms (and his further objection to anyone undertaking it) simply amounts to a principled refusal to try to understand the behavior of organisms. I think this is an appropriate epitaph for a certain style of 'behaviorism'.

*Lone Ranger Action in the Rachlin Register of Hip and Miss evidently doesn't pay. Such Mindless Moves, Dear Player, would land you where I suspect you wouldn't particularly care to be: this ditch under the tree bearing the inscription 'Behaviorists, RIP'. (Though, between you and me, the idea of a behaviourist soul resting in peace leaves me strangely ill at ease.)*

2.5.2   Let us digress for a moment to note that Chomsky's distinction between knowledge of language and capacity/ability to use language is based on a more fundamental distinction, namely *behaviour as evidence vs behaviour as a criterion*. Chomsky (1980a: 48, 52–3) considers (linguistic) behaviour to be only one of the sources of evidence for the possession of knowledge of language. Data about electrical activity of the brain and clinical data from autopsies are mentioned by him (1980a: 48, 52) as examples of other possible sources of such evidence. And he stresses the point (1980a: 53) that linguists cannot enumerate a priori the kinds of evidence that might bear on the hypothesis that a particular person has knowledge of language.

A limitation of this nature is not, however, unique to linguistics. On Chomsky's view, the a priori enumeration of kinds of relevant evidence is never possible where the investigation being conducted is one into the internal elements and working of a complex system. Taking (linguistic) behaviour to be just one of the possible sources of evidence for having knowledge of language clearly does not warrant the equation 'no behaviour = no knowledge'. This would be a valid equation only if, by contrast, behaviour were taken as a criterion for having knowledge of language. To consider behaviour a criterion for knowledge is tantamount to assigning it the status of the sole kind of evidence for knowledge.

*The purpose of this short detour, Dear Player, is to show just how cautious you should be in using evidence from behaviour as the basis of moves against The Master. Consider in this connection Dummett's (1981) declaring by decree that we identify knowledge 'solely by its [behavioral] manifestations'. The Dummet Decree was depicted by The Master (1986: 259) as displaying a certain degree of daftness:*

> *To say that we identify knowledge (or the structure of knowledge, or the internal state of knowledge, or the system of rules constituting knowledge, etc.) 'solely by its manifestations' is true only in the sense that the nineteenth-century chemist identified the structure of benzene 'solely by its manifestations.' In fact, we identify the system of knowledge of language that accounts for facts concerning (2) [who was persuaded to like him], (3) [John is too stubborn to talk], and so forth by such manifestations of this knowledge as the judgments*

*concerning referential dependence, by judgments concerning other expressions, by behavior of speakers of other languages, and in principle in many other ways as discussed earlier.*

*The link between knowledge and behaviour is neither direct nor simple, and it is not behaviour that is basic. So Behaviour-Based Biases may backfire when they provide one with such easy equations as 'no behaviour = no knowledge'. But enough; it is time we returned to the main lane.*

*2.5.3* Closely related to the distinction between knowledge of language and the capacity / ability to use language is the distinction *knowledge of language vs the creative aspect of language (use)*. This latter phrase ('the creative aspect of language'), as Chomsky (1980a: 76) is at pains to point out, refers to 'the ability of normal persons to produce speech that is appropriate to situations though perhaps quite novel, and to understand when others do so'. He (1975a: 138) has moreover called this ability of speakers 'a mystery': a question to which there seems to be no solution within existing approaches to the study of language. Mysteries, to Chomsky, are questions in the investigation of which no progress seems to be made. And he is of the opinion that the 'creative aspect of language use' is just as much of a mystery today as it was in the heyday of the Cartesians some three centuries ago. In short, 'How do people succeed in acting appropriately and creatively in linguistic behaviour or performance?' is a question which Chomsky expressly excludes from the set of fundamental questions – cf. (1) (a)–(c) in section 1.2 – to be solved by his approach to linguistic inquiry.

And there are other, similar, questions arising in the study of mind that Chomsky (1980a: 79–80) considers 'beyond the domains of inquiry as we currently conceive them'. These include questions of free will and choice, questions that generally concern the ways in which the mechanisms of mind are creatively used. To the metascientific nature of these questions we return in section 4.1.1 below. Chomsky's study of mind, in sum, is restricted in scope: it seeks to identify only a subset of the mechanisms of mind and, moreover, it does not attempt to answer the question of how those mechanisms are creatively used.

*At this junction in The Garden, I have to recount a rather sad tale, Hunter's History. Missing the 'knowledge–creative use' fork altogether, Hunter (1973) flung himself at The Master, throwing punches as he hurtled through the air. There was a left swing, packed with power but devoid of direction: The Master's theories failed to explain 'how we talk'. This was followed by a right sweep (delivered with both eyes shut): since The Master's theories failed to explain 'how we talk', they explained nothing at all and could in principle have no psychological import. Piqued by this unprovoked onslaught, The Master threw back a quick combination. He led with a blow to the body – hitting above the belt, I hasten to add in fairness to The Master (1980a: 76–7):*

> his [i.e., Hunter's] argument is directed against proposed explanations for how we talk, that is, for what I have called 'the creative aspect of language'. It has been emphasized ad nauseam in the literature that a generative grammar is not a 'talking machine', in Hunter's sense. Virtually the whole of his argument is directed against input–output theories that purport to explain how we talk.

*This, The Master (1980a: 77–8) followed with a hook to the head, hitting out at Hunter's lack of imagination:*

> This part of the argument is in part reasonable enough but offers no support at all for his [i.e., Hunter's] conclusions, unless we accept his tacit premise that there are only two possibilities for linguistic theory: either it explains how we talk, that is, explains the creative aspect of language use, or it explains nothing, even in principle. But this dilemma merely reflects a serious failure of imagination.[40]

*If, My Dear Fellow, you have been planning some pugilistic play, do keep in mind that this particular Game demands precision punching; Hunter Haymaking will pose a hazard to no one's health but your own. Or, to quote a great Pugilistic Prophet of the Past, 'in this game you have to float like a butterfly and sting like a bee'.*

2.5.4   If to know a language is to be in a mental state, the obvious question is: 'What kind of mental state?' In answer to this question, Chomsky (1980a: 48ff) invokes the distinction *having a mental structure vs lacking a mental structure*. This allows him to reply as follows to the question under consideration: 'I assume . . . that to be in such a mental state is to have a certain mental structure consisting of a system of rules and principles that generate and relate mental representations of various types.'[41] Opposed to the idea that to be in a certain mental state is having a certain mental structure is, according to Chomsky (1980a: 49), the traditional 'concept of mental capacities as lacking structured vehicles'. One of the better known versions of this 'concept' is Wittgenstein's view that there are no processes in the brain 'correlated with associating or with thinking'. On this view, Chomsky (1980a: 50) notes 'there can be no theory of mental structures and processes that attempts to formulate the properties of the nonexistent physiological mechanisms and their operation'. This, in Chomsky's opinion, leaves us with a purely descriptive study of behaviour, potential behaviour, dispositions to behave and so on.

The choice between the 'structured' and the 'nonstructured' view is, to Chomsky (1980a: 50), not 'a straightforward empirical one'. It nevertheless has an 'empirical component', according to him (1980a: 50–1):

> In particular, success in developing a structural theory of mind, knowledge and belief would count against the picture of cognition in terms of capacities without structured vehicles, and would indicate that the prevailing concern with organization of and potential for behavior misconceives a certain category of evidence as criterial.

On Chomsky's view, considerable success has been achieved in developing a structural theory of mind, specifically in regard to knowledge of language.

*Bloody battles have been fought at the 'structured–unstructured' fork, some of them involving famous fighters such as Quine and Putnam, who have adopted a Wittgensteinian stance. Often these battles have seemed to be about peripheral positions – for example, about the nature of meaning. On closer inspection, however, they have often turned out to be fights about the essence of the matter, namely about the very existence of internal mental structures in general. Thus, harnessing Wittgenstein and Quine in support, Lear (1978: 177–8) appeared to launch an attack on the position that the meanings of words are mental objects: 'Positing interior mental objects that are named by words only gets in the way of an explanation, for it merely papers over the gaps in our understanding of how language-mastery is acquired.' The Master (1980a: 12–13) was quick, however, to spot the danger that lurked behind Lear's Leap:*

*The fact that the interior mental objects in question are 'named by words' adds no special force to the argument. If positing such interior mental objects 'merely papers over gaps in our understanding' because language-mastery must be 'explained . . . on the basis of our experience', then the same should be true of interior mental objects quite generally, whether or not they are named by words. Hence if the argument has any force it should apply as well to all types of rules and representations for language, not simply to meanings; and in fact to psychological theory quite generally. So it seems that we are presented with an argument against mental representations quite generally . . .*

*With a seemingly simple sidestep The Master (1980a: 13) moved clear of the Leaping Lear:*

*But does the argument establish anything at all? Not until something is added to explain why positing interior mental objects gets in the way of explanation and papers over gaps in our understanding of the acquisition of language-mastery, and furthermore why this must be the case. In the absence of such additional steps, what we have is a pseudo-argument against theoretical entities.*

*What you have witnessed here, Dear Player, is more than meets the eye. What appears to be a struggle about structure is in fact a match about method, manoeuvres in a metascientific mode. So, even if it seemed to you the fashionable thing to do, you'd better decline to take the Wittgenstein Line until such time as we have had a closer look at the method of the matter in section 4 below. Meanwhile, if you feel you need food for thought, here is a little something you might like to chew on: like physicists, The Master (1980a: 104) adopts 'the standard "realist" assumptions of the natural sciences in studying language, and cognition more generally'. These assumptions allow him to say that rules, principles and representations are real entities at a level, the level of mind, at which an abstract characterization is given of the properties of physical mechanisms in our brains. And so? And so, Dear Puzzled Player, you have been granted a glimpse of some of the hazards that The Garden still holds in store.*

2.5.5  Turning next to the question of the kind of knowledge that a speaker is said to have of his language, we find that the first distinction to be drawn is that of *conscious knowledge vs unconscious knowledge*. On Chomsky's view knowledge of language is unconscious, tacit or implicit knowledge (1980a: 69ff, 241ff; 1986: 270ff). A speaker of English, for example, knows in the case of the expressions 'the candidates wanted each other to win' and 'the candidates wanted me to vote for each other' that the former means that each wanted the other to win, and that the latter is not well formed with the meaning that each wanted me to vote for the other. And on Chomsky's view (1980a: 69) the speaker also knows the rules of the mental grammar of his language, the principles governing the operation of the rules, and the 'innate schematism' of the language. But, he contends, the speaker cannot become aware by introspection of what he knows specifically of the latter rules, principles and 'innate schematism'. These are 'inaccessible to consciousness'. Conscious knowledge, by contrast, is accessible, non-implicit knowledge.

To avoid terminological confusion, Chomsky (1980a: 70) introduced the term 'cognizing' to refer to tacit knowledge, reserving the term 'knowing' for conscious knowledge: 'Thus, "cognizing" is tacit or implicit knowledge . . . [and] . . . has the structure and character of knowledge, but may be and in the interesting cases is inaccessible to consciousness.' Cognizing, thus, appears to Chomsky (1986: 269) 'to have all the properties of knowledge in the ordinary sense of the term, apart, perhaps, from accessibility to consciousness'. And he would like to say that 'cognization' is 'unconscious or tacit or implicit knowledge'.

In this terminology, rules, principles governing rules and the above-mentioned 'innate schematism' are 'cognized' by the speakers of the language. Note, however, that Chomsky (1980a: 99), apparently paradoxically, 'will continue to use the term "know" in the sense of "cognize"'. Thus, wherever Chomsky uses the terms 'know' and 'knowing' to denote a relation between speakers and their language these terms should be read as 'cognize' and 'cognizing' respectively, except of course where he explicitly indicates otherwise.[42]

*A fount of fatal fascination, Dear Player, that's what the fork 'conscious vs unconscious knowledge' has been. Players have come from far and wide to attack this seemingly soft target, often railing with abusive arrogance. 'Outrageous', for example, is what McGinn (1981: 290) called The Master's view that a speaker has unconscious knowledge of his language. Many of the attacks have been launched from the assumption that one cannot attribute knowledge (of rules) to a person unless this knowledge is accessible to consciousness. Thus, Searle (1976), a Player by Profession, charged: 'It is in general characteristic of attributions of unconscious mental states that the attribution presupposes that the state can become conscious . . .' And Davis (1976: 78) declared that 'a necessary condition for someone to know the rules which govern some activity is that he must be able to say or show us what the rules are . . . we can say that someone follows a rule only if he knows what the rule is and can tell us what it is.'*

*The Master chose to defend himself with a double-barrelled gun. Firing one barrel, he shot back that he had shown that innumerable linguistic facts (concerning judgements and behaviour) were in accordance with certain rules (1980a: 130). Even more assertively, he proceeded:*

> *The critic's task is to show some fundamental flaw in principle or defect in execution or to provide a different and preferable account of how it is that what speakers do is in accordance with certain rules or is described by these rules, an account that does not attribute to them mental representation of a system of rules (rules which in fact appear to be beyond the*

*level of consciousness). If someone can offer such an account of how it is that we know what we do know, e.g., about reciprocals, or judge as we do judge, etc., there will be something to discuss. Since no such account has been forthcoming, even in the most primitive or rudimentary form, there really is nothing to discuss. (1980a: 130)*

*Aiming at Searle, The Master (1980a: 131) discharged the other barrel:*

*Searle . . . offers no argument at all. He merely stipulates that mental states must be accessible to consciousness, claiming without argument that otherwise attribution of mental states loses 'much of its explanatory power'. . . . This [i.e., Searle's condition that a person must be aware of the rules that enter into his behavior] remains sheer dogmatism, supported by no hint of argument.*[43]

*At the end of a critical survey of the history of the principles of accessibility, i.e. the belief that the contents of mind are in principle open to reflection, The Master (1980a: 244) concluded that 'there is no reason to suppose that we have any privileged access to the principles that enter into our knowledge and use of language . . . '. Here, Dear Player, we have something not to forget: in the absence of such a reason – and a strong one it would have to be – Accessibility Assaults inspire no awe.*

2.5.6   To clarify further his notion of 'cognizing' or unconscious knowledge, Chomsky (1980a: 101–2) has drawn the distinction *knowing a language vs knowing how to ride a bicycle.* Unlike knowing a language, knowing how to ride a bicycle is a skill in these terms – specifically, a skill based on certain reflex systems. Chomsky (1980a: 102) contends moreover that, in the case of knowing how to ride a bicycle, there is no factual reason to attribute a certain cognitive structure to the person who exercises the skill.[44]

It was a charge by Donnellan (1977: 720) that initially prompted Chomsky to distinguish explicitly between knowing a language and knowing how to ride a bicycle. Donnellan contended that Chomsky's concept of cognizing did not provide a basis for this distinction.

Consequently, Donnellan (1977: 720) argued, it could be said that a bicycle rider 'cognizes' 'both the rules he can articulate – push with the feet on the pedals – and those that he cannot, even though his practice is in accord with them – e.g. lean into a curve'. Chomsky (1980a: 102) conceded that there would be little point in having a concept of unconscious knowledge that could not distinguish between 'cognizing the rules of grammar' and 'knowing how to ride a bicycle'. He argued, however, that the appropriate distinction was easy enough to make:

> In the case of riding a bicycle, there is no reason to suppose that the rules in question are represented in a cognitive structure of anything like the sort I have described. Rather, we take bicycle riding to be a skill, where knowledge of language and its concomitants, for example, knowledge that reciprocal expressions have the properties I mentioned, is not a skill at all.

*On the face of it, this exchange between Donnellan and The Master represents an utterly unexciting episode in the generally tumultuous history of The Game. But, as I have warned before, Displeased Player, there is more in The Garden than meets the eye. The Bicycle Bifurcation is an example of a particularly perilous property of The Garden: a fork invisible to the naked eye. That is, when The Master built The Garden, he did not at the outset construct the fork 'knowing a language vs knowing how to ride a bicycle' for everyone to see. But this fork is an automatic byproduct as it were – hidden and hence so hazardous – of the general geometry of The Garden. The moral, Dear Player, is that for survival sensory shrewdness is simply not sufficient. Deduction and divination are part and parcel of the play.*

    2.5.7   In an attempt to clarify further the character of knowledge of language (or, rather, grammar), Chomsky (1980a: 94–5) invokes the distinction *grounded/justified knowledge vs a priori knowledge vs caused knowledge*. He argues (1980a: 93) that knowledge of grammar involves not only propositional knowledge but also belief: 'A person who knows English knows that "the candidates want me to vote for each other" is not a well-formed sentence meaning that each wants me to vote for the other, and also believes this.'[45] Thus, Chomsky considers knowledge of language/grammar to represent a case of what he calls 'knowing/ knowledge-that', to be distinguished from 'knowing-how'. He does not, however, consider such knowledge to be knowledge that is 'grounded' or 'justified' in the conventional sense. It cannot be said that speakers 'have reasons' for the beliefs involved. But Chomsky (1980a: 94) would not want to say that knowledge of language represents a priori knowledge. Some evidence or triggering experience and innate principles are required for the development of knowledge of language in the mind, a point he illustrates with reference to the English speaker's knowledge of the meaning of 'the candidates want me to vote for each other':

> presented with evidence that the phrase 'each other' is a reciprocal expression (a category presumably belonging to universal grammar, i.e., innately given), the mind develops a grammar that uses the innate principle of opacity to yield this particular case of knowledge.[46]

With reference to its genesis, then, Chomsky considers knowledge of language neither to be 'grounded or justified or supportable by good reasons' nor to be a priori: 'rather it is, in significant respects, caused'.[47] He (1980a: 94–5) proceeds to argue that the concepts of 'grounding', 'justification' and 'reasons' may be inappropriate in many instances to an analysis of the nature and origin of knowledge, citing the knowledge that enters into our 'common sense understanding' as a case in point.[48]

*Stich (1980: 39), a Polished Player of good repute, probed The Master's idea that knowledge of language shared the fundamental properties of other unproblematic cases of knowledge. He suggested that, whereas these unproblematic cases formed a highly integrated inferential system, knowledge of the rules of the grammar, as material internally represented in some other way, involved principles inferentially insulated from factual belief. The difference between inferential integration and inferential insulation would accordingly, on Stich's view, represent a significant difference between knowledge of grammar and unproblematic cases of knowledge. This gives him reason to suspect that factual beliefs and (unconscious and 'unbelieved') knowledge of grammar are 'subserved' by distinct 'mental organs'.*

*The Master (1980b: 57) cautiously responded that there were problems with Stich's distinction:*

> *Take our shared knowledge of the sample facts: e.g., that 'the men expected each other will win' is not well-formed, with the meaning that each expected the other will win. This seems to me a relatively unproblematic case of propositional knowledge – knowledge that so-and-so. But this case forms part of a system containing inferentially insulated principles, according to Stich's account. Or suppose that our knowledge that an object on a parabolic course passing behind a screen will emerge at such-and-such a point is based on an innate principle* P. *For present purposes it is enough that this might be true, that there is nothing incoherent in assuming it to be true. This case of* knowledge-that *also seems unproblematic, indeed rather typical of much of the discussion in the literature. But if matters are as just suggested, then both of these unproblematic cases form part of a highly integrated system (though perhaps not strictly an 'inferential' system) including principles (opacity,* P*) that are unconscious, innate, and perhaps inferentially insulated . . . The integrated systems may not have the properties that Stich requires. Furthermore, the elements of this system, even the unproblematic cases, might very well lack what are generally taken to be crucial features of knowledge: specifically, grounding and warrant. Thus it does not seem to me clear that the allegedly unproblematic cases have what are often regarded as typical properties of knowledge.*

*If I have devoted some space to representing The Master's response to Stich's Strictures, I have done so in order to illustrate two general features of The Game:*

1 *The Game needn't be a brutal brawl.*
2 *Exchanges can be inconclusive.*

*As regards (1), there is a category of Professional Players, cool, competent and careful, who have been playing The Game with flair and finesse, forcing The Master to measure his moves and even to modify The Maze. As for (2), the situation often is that outright victory can be claimed by neither party, the only real result being a setting of the scene for a future fixture.*

2.5.8   Implicit in Chomsky's distinction between 'justified knowledge' and 'caused knowledge' is the further distinction *'supplying good reasons' vs 'constituting triggering experience'*. The latter distinction he clarifies (1980a: 96) in the context of discussing Edgley's (1970: 28ff) presentation of the standard argument against 'innate knowledge'. On this argument, a person's belief will qualify as knowledge only if it is justified by his having good reasons for it. Innate knowledge would obviously fail this condition. On Chomsky's view of language acquisition, as presented in section 2.1.3 above, the data available to the child acquiring a language cannot be evidence supplying good reasons; rather, such data, on Chomsky's view, constitute triggering experience. As noted in section 2.1.3, Chomsky takes this experience as activating the genetic programme whose unfolding results in what he has called 'caused knowledge'. Chomsky, we saw in section 2.5.7, is not willing to concede that 'caused knowledge' is not propositional knowledge. Rather, he has rejected the idea that justification or grounding in reasons constitutes an appropriate basis for a condition for what have been considered paradigm cases of propositional knowledge. Thus he (1980b: 51) contends that

> Warrant and justification are not necessary conditions for much of what we call 'knowledge' – specifically, factual knowledge – and if the concept is narrowed to exclude these cases, then central areas of what has been called 'knowledge' will be excluded. In some respects, traditional analysis of knowledge in terms of warranted true belief may well be appropriate (apart from Gettier problems and the like); namely, instances of knowledge that do not derive from the structure of our fundamental cognitive capacities as they grow; for example, knowledge of scientific fact, which must be acquired through careful experiment and theory construction (in which, I assume, innate factors must also enter crucially, for reasons I will not

discuss here). In these cases, we must have adequate grounds for our knowledge claims, or they are worthless. Knowledge comes in many varieties, and for crucial elements of our knowledge, the traditional empiricist paradigm seems to me quite inadequate. How extensive these elements are remains to be discovered. Language seems to be one case, and if the remarks just briefly outlined prove to be somewhere near accurate, then the same is true of what are regarded as more 'typical' cases of knowledge.

*Edgley (1970: 28ff), Dear Player, argued that there is a construal on which (innate) knowledge of language could meet the condition of justification considered above. If the child learning a language were a scientist, he contended, it could cite the evidence to which it had been exposed in justification of its claim to knowledge. But The Master (1980a: 96) did not fall for this move, countering that the relation between the child's evidence and the acquired knowledge is 'a purely contingent one':*

> *Suppose that evidence that 'each other' is a reciprocal expression suffices (by virtue of the opacity principle) for the child to know that 'the candidates wanted me to vote for each other' is not a well-formed sentence meaning that each wanted me to vote for the other. To say that this case of* knowledge *is literally 'justified' by the observation that 'each other' is a reciprocal would undermine the concept of justification entirely; for a Martian lacking the principle of opacity, we would have to say that the same evidence justifies his contrary knowledge that the sentence in question is well-formed with the meaning that each wanted me to vote for the other. But then the concept of 'justification' has disappeared.*

*So, if you ever felt yourself menaced by The Master's Martian Move or none too comfortable in the presence of Prescient Preschoolers promulgated by Edgleyan Edict, then this certainly is not a fork for facing The Master. Why not move on and forget the idea of justification or grounding as a condition for 'knowing that'?*

2.5.9   A final conceptual distinction that throws light on the character of knowledge of language is the distinction *knowledge of language vs knowledge of arithmetic*. As we saw above, Chomsky considers knowledge of language to exist in the form of a mental state with a structural basis. Others, notably Katz (1981) and Bever (1982), have suggested that knowledge of language should be understood on the analogy of knowledge of arithmetic. They have taken arithmetic to be an abstract Platonic entity that does not exist in the form of a mental structure. The claim is not that there is no such thing as Chomsky's internalized language but rather that, in addition to this internalized language, there is something else: truths about language independent of facts of individual psychology. An ordinary speaker could in principle know his language in Chomsky's sense, without knowing the Platonic entity called 'language' by Katz and Bever.

Chomsky (1986: 33), however, has strongly resisted the attempts to disembody knowledge of language:

> The analogy to arithmetic is, however, quite unpersuasive. In the case of arithmetic, there is at least a certain initial plausibility to a Platonistic view insofar as the truths of arithmetic are what they are, independent of any facts of individual psychology, and we seem to discover these truths somewhat in the way that we discover facts about the physical world. In the case of language, however, the corresponding position is wholly without merit.

And:

> Knowing everything about the mind/brain, a Platonist would argue, we still have no basis for determining the truths of arithmetic or set theory, but there is not the slightest reason to suppose that there are truths of language that would still escape our grasp.

This means that knowledge of language cannot, on Chomsky's view, be profitably thought of as knowledge of an abstract, Platonistic object.

*Thus, Dear Player, The Master considers play on a Platonist Plane puerile:*

*Of course, one can construct abstract entities at will, and we can decide to call some of them 'English' or 'Japanese' and to define 'linguistics' as the study of these abstract objects . . . But there seems little point to such moves. (1986: 33–4)*

*So it is right down here in The Garden, Dear Player, that The Game will be played – in a Mundane Mentalist Mode.*

2.5.10   We have reached a natural point for taking a closer look at Chomsky's notion of language: the first conceptual distinction that bears on it is *the intuitive/pretheoretic notion of language vs the technical concept of language.* On Chomsky's (1986: 15ff) account the intuitive, pretheoretic or common-sense notion of language departs in several ways from the technical concept of language. First, the common-sense notion of language has 'a crucial socio-political dimension'. Thus, he observes, Chinese is spoken of as 'a language' despite the fact that the various 'Chinese dialects' are as diverse as the various Romance languages. Chomsky is doubtful that any coherent account of language can be given in such socio-political terms. Rather, he remarks (1986: 15), 'all scientific approaches have simply abandoned these elements [i.e. socio-political elements] of what is called "language" in common usage'.[49]

Second, Chomsky (1986:16) notes that the common-sense notion of language has 'a normative-teleological element' which is also absent from 'scientific' notions of language. This normative-teleological element is not to be identified with prescriptive grammar. Rather, the 'normative-teleological' element is present in judgements of the progress made by a foreigner or child learning English:

We have no way of referring directly to what that person knows: It is not English, nor is it some other language that resembles English. We do not, for example, say that the person has a perfect knowledge of some language L, similar to English but still different from it. What we say is that the child or foreigner has a 'partial knowledge of English', or is 'on his or her way' toward acquiring knowledge of English, and if they reach the goal, they will then know English.

Again, Chomsky doubts whether it is possible to give a coherent account of this aspect of the common-sense notion of language. In sum: unlike the 'intuitive/pretheoretic/common-sense' notion of language, Chomsky's 'technical/scientific' concept of language has no socio-political and no normative-teleological dimension.

*Jerrold Katz (1981: 79–80), a Former Friend turned Fierce Foe, has attacked The Master on, amongst other things, his view of the socio-political dimension of 'language'. Thus, Katz (1981: 79) contended, maintaining that the common-sense notions of language and dialect involved a socio-political dimension was 'like claiming that the concept of number is not a concept of mathematics but a socio-political one (or that the concept of implication is not a logical concept but a socio-political one)'.[50]*

*The Master's response (1986: 47, n. 1) to this piece of play in the Katzian Key was brief, and meant to bruise: 'There is no reason to accept this curious conclusion.'*

2.5.11    To exclude socio-political, normative-teleological and other inessential elements from his notion of language, Chomsky (1986: 16) invokes the conceptual distinction *the ideal speaker–listener vs an ordinary speaker–listener.* The ideal speaker–listener is 'ideal' in the sense that he (a) is a member of a completely homogeneous speech community and (b) knows his language perfectly.[51] The notion of an ideal speaker–listener is an instance of what has been called 'a methodologically expedient counterfactual idealization'.[52] Of course Chomsky knows as well as the next linguist that in the real world there are no ideal speakers with perfect knowledge of language and that speech communities in the real world are heterogeneous. Indeed he has recently said so, once again, in so many words:

Of course, it is understood that speech communities in the Bloomfieldian sense – that is, collections of individuals with the same speech behavior (n. 3) – do not exist in the real world. Each individual has acquired a language in the course of complex social interactions with people who vary in the ways

65

in which they speak and interpret what they hear and in the internal representations that underlie their use of language. Structural linguistics abstracted from these facts in its attempts at theory construction; we also abstract from these facts in posing questions (1) of Chapter 1 [our questions (1) (a)–(c) in section 1.2 above], considering only the case of a person presented with uniform experience in an ideal Bloomfieldian speech community with no dialect diversity and no variation among speakers. (1986: 16–17)

Chomsky sees the idealization under consideration as a methodological tool: a means of disregarding common-sense assumptions that stand in the way of assigning a coherent content to the notion 'language'. In employing this idealization he does not mean to say that the facts and considerations from which the technical notion of language abstracts away are uninteresting or do not deserve serious study. He is merely saying that progress in answering the questions (1) (a)–(c) in section 1.2 above would be impossible if these facts and considerations were included initially in the characterization of the notion 'language'. Chomsky (1986: 16) notes that in making the simplifying idealization under consideration he is perpetuating a tradition of modern linguistics and, moreover, is doing something that is normal in other sciences: 'In other scientific approaches, the same assumption [e.g. about homogeneity] enters in one or another form, explicitly or tacitly, in identification of the object of inquiry.'[53] In sum: Chomsky's notion of language is an idealized one.

*The idealization of the ideal speaker–listener has exerted a magnetic pull on Prospective Players. Agitated, aggressive, abusive, they have flocked to this fork to do The Master in. Consider a couple of the Crasser Cracks taken at The Master here:*[54]

1  *The Master, with naked naivety, believes that real speech communities are homogeneous.*
2  *The search for ideal speaker–listeners in real speech communities is a stupid stunt, fated to fail.*
3  *The Master, being blinkered or blind, has no interest in and/or understanding of linguistic variation.*

*Because these charges emanate from a major misjudgement – a methodological means being mistaken for a factual claim – they have left many a Perplexed Player entirely at the mercy of The Master.*[55]

*There have also been some Subtler Shots, such as Dummett's (1975: 134–5) argument:*

> A language, in the everyday sense, is something essentially social, a practice in which many people engage; an individual's always partial, and often in part incorrect, understanding of his language . . . needs to be explained in terms of the notion of a shared language, and not conversely.

*This argument, on The Master's (1980a: 117) interpretation, 'amounts to a denial of the legitimacy of the idealization to a homogeneous speech community that I discussed* [earlier], noting that the denial entails consequences that seem quite absurd'.

Two absurd consequences have been listed by The Master (1980a: 25–6):

1 People are so constituted that they would be incapable of learning language in a homogeneous speech community; variability or inconsistency of presented evidence is a necessary condition for language learning.

2 Though people could learn language in a homogeneous speech community, the properties of the mind that make this achievement possible do not enter into normal language acquisition in the real world of diversity, conflict of dialects, etc.

Since both of them seem to The Master 'hopelessly implausible', he cannot 'believe that anyone who thinks the matter through would really maintain either of these beliefs'. Having derailed The Dummett Drive to his own satisfaction, The Master (1980a: 26; 1986: 15–16) has reaffirmed his belief in the idealization under consideration as isolating a fundamental property of mind which is a crucial element in actual language acquisition.[56]

2.5.12 Chomsky has a second conceptual distinction bearing on the nature of speech communities and their members, namely *mixed language vs pure language*. He (1986: 17) makes the 'theory-internal assumption' that the language of the hypothesized speech community is not only uniform but also 'pure'. By means of this assumption he excludes from the speech community speakers who speak a mixture of two languages, e.g. the mixture of Russian and French spoken by the nineteenth-century Russian aristocracy:

> The language of such a speech community would not be 'pure' in the relevant sense, because it would not represent a single set of choices among the options permitted by UG but rather would include 'contradictory' choices for certain of these options.

Chomsky's technical notion thus provides for a 'pure' language: a language acquired by means of a single set of noncontradictory choices from among the options permitted by the initial state of the language faculty.

*The 'pure versus mixed language' fork holds a general lesson for Unbloodied Players anxious to remain unbloodied as long as possible. The lesson is not to make your moves in accordance with The Monkey's Maxim, i.e. the rule that says:*

*Make the obvious move, make it first, make it fast.*

*Surely even a relative newcomer to The Game cannot help wondering how the mental grammar(s) of people 'using a mixture of languages' would bear on The Master's conception of knowledge of language. Wondering will do nobody any harm, of course; but instantly and blindly to latch on to this phenomenon as a source of embarrassment to The Master would be to honour The Monkey's Maxim. Plainly, there won't be weapons lying around in The Garden for ready use against The Master. If perhaps you thought that you were the 'first' to stumble across some such 'find', chances are that you have really only been falling over your own feet. But let us move on to consider a different kind of fork.*

2.5.13  Chomsky (1986) has recently introduced a new set of terms for presenting a distinction fundamental to his conception of language: *E(xternalized) language vs I(nternalized) language*. A technical concept of language represents an instance of externalized language/E-language, according to Chomsky (1986: 20), 'in the sense that the construct is understood independently of the properties of the mind/brain'. In simple terms, an E-language is an object that exists outside the mind of a speaker–listener.

Chomsky (1986: 19) mentions, for example, structural and descriptive linguistics as well as behavioural psychology as having operated with concepts of E-language. These approaches viewed language as a collection of instances of some kind of entity – for example, actions, utterances, words, sentences etc. – or as some kind of system – of, for example, forms or events.[57] A grammar, on this approach, is, in Chomsky's (1986: 20) terminology, 'a collection of descriptive statements concerning the E-language, the actual or potential speech events'. A grammar may be selected in any way as long as it correctly identifies the E-language. If two grammars both correctly identify the E-language, that is if the two grammars are extensionally equivalent, it is senseless to argue that one is 'true' and the other 'false'.

A technical concept of language represents an instance of internalized language/I-language, on Chomsky's characterization, if it depicts a language as 'some element of the mind of the person who knows the language, acquired by the learner, and used by the speaker–hearer'. An I-language is therefore a mental object, a part of the speaker–listener's mind. Chomsky (1986: 21–2) presents Otto Jespersen's view of language as a typical instance of the concept of I-language. On this view, there is some 'notion of structure' in the mind of the speaker 'which is definite enough to guide him in framing sentences of his own', in particular, 'free expressions that may be new to the speaker and to others'. If language is taken to be I-language, a grammar would be a theory of the I-language and as such might be true or false.[58]

The study of 'generative grammar', on Chomsky's view (1986: 24), shifted the focus from the study of E-language to the study of I-language, 'from the study of language regarded as an externalized object to the study of the system of knowledge of language attained and internally represented in the mind/brain'. A grammar, on this view, is not a set of statements about externalized objects but rather a description of exactly what one knows when one knows a language.

It is because of this shift in focus – Chomsky calls it the 'first conceptual shift' associated with generative grammar – that linguists are once again being required to face such questions about the nature, development and use of language as those represented as (1) (a)–(c) in section 1.2 above.

*The conceptual fork 'E-language vs I-language', Progressing Player, is in more than one sense a fascinating feature of The Garden. So let us dwell here a little longer. On the one hand, it has been a focus of fierce confrontation. Thus Lewis (1975) once expressed the belief that it was easier to 'make sense' of the E-language notion 'language L is used by population P' than of the I-language notion 'language L is determined by internally represented grammar G'. The Master (1980a: 85) rejected this belief of Lewis's as 'quite wrong' and 'fundamentally flawed', stating that*

> *he [i.e., Lewis] presents no way to make sense of his notion, and I can imagine no reasonable way except derivatively, in terms of shared internal representation. His problem is to explain how a person can use an infinite language, or have an infinite set of expectations about sound-meaning pairings and much else, without any internal representation of that infinite object, and further, how that infinite object – a language – can be 'shared' by a population without any internal representations in the minds of members of this population.*

*And as part of a more general response to such Sans-Sense Subtleties, The Master (1986: 31) resorted to his Radical Reversal Routine:*

> *The account presented by Quine, Lewis, and others has the story backwards: E-languages are not given, but are derivative, more remote from data and from mechanisms than I-languages and the grammars that are theories of I-languages; the choice of E-language therefore raises a host of new and additional problems beyond those connected with grammar and I-language. Whether it is worthwhile addressing or attempting to solve these problems is not at all clear, because the concept of E-language, however construed, appears to have no significance. The belief that E-language is a fairly clear*

70

*notion whereas I-language or grammar raises serious, perhaps intractable philosophical problems, is quite mistaken. Just the opposite is true.*

*On the other hand, the 'E-language vs I-language' fork has arresting antecedents, including the tragic tale of Hintikka's Harakiri. Hintikka (1977), a Player Packing a Powerful Punch, thought he could provide 'a clear-cut counterexample to generative grammar' by showing that languages are not recursively enumerable.*[59] *The Master (1980a: 124ff) found the argument wanting for reasons that need not concern us here.*

*More important, he (p. 126) pointed out that*

*If the argument were valid, it might be a counter-example to the belief that a generative grammar, represented in the mind, determines the set of well-formed sentences (n. 54). It in no way impugns the belief that a generative grammar is represented in the mind, but rather implies that this grammar does not in itself determine the class of what we might choose to call 'grammatical sentences'; rather, these sentences are the ones that meet both some condition that involves the grammar and a condition lacking a decision procedure. Again, that would be interesting to know if true, but the consequences seem slight. It would be on a par with other versions of a parametrized autonomy thesis, which might well lead to various forms of ill-definedness of language, as already noted. I see no consequences, striking or otherwise, for the methodology of linguistics or psychology, once we recognize that the fundamental concepts are* grammar *and* knowing a grammar, *and that* language *and* knowing a language *are derivative.*

*We will deal presently with the distinction between a language and a grammar. For now, it is sufficient to note that Hintikka's attack on The Master was based on the assumption that The Master could be outmanoeuvred by damaging his concept of language as an instance of E-language. That is, Hintikka, having completely missed the fork 'E-language vs I-language', went for The Master down the E-language Lane, only to come to his own untimely end as a Player of The Game.*

The question, of course, is how a seemingly competent combatant of the likes of Hintikka could make such a costly miscalculation. The answer to this question might lie in the history of The Garden, for it could perhaps be contended that The Garden did not contain the 'E-language vs I-language' fork right from the beginning. This possibility, it could be argued, is suggested by the fact that in earlier works by The Master the notion 'a language' was given an E-language characterization, i.e., a characterization in terms of which a language was not portrayed as part of a speaker's mind. Consider, as an example, the following 'classic' characterization (Chomsky, 1957: 13): 'From now on I will consider a language to be a set (finite or infinite) of sentences, each finite in length and constructed out of a finite set of elements.'

Mindful of formulations such as this, various Provoked Players have hit out at The Master, claiming that he did not adopt a mentalistic or I-language concept of language at the outset. And they contended further that The Garden was not originally planned to be a mentalistic maze. Steinberg (1975: 220–1), for example, charged:

> His original conception regarding the nature of the relationship between a theoretical grammar and a speaker was actually a formalistic, not a mentalistic one. During this formalistic phase, Chomsky did not regard the rules of his theoretical grammar as representing knowledge held by speakers. Only certain aspects of the output of the theoretical grammar were regarded as psychologically significant. This formalistic type of theory was held by Chomsky until about 1959, at which time his views began to change.

The Master has been far from happy with such Historical Heresy, contending that the picture of The Garden as a nonmentalistic maze is a fake, reflecting ignorance about the circumstances under which it was constructed:

> The conceptual shift from E-language to I-language, from behavior and its products to the system of knowledge that enters into behavior, was in part obscured by accidents of publishing history, and expository passages taken out of context have given rise to occasional misunderstanding (n. 17).

*Some questionable terminological decisions also contributed to misunderstanding. In the literature of generative grammar, the term 'language' has regularly been used for E-language in the sense of a set of well-formed sentences, more or less along the lines of Bloomfield's definition of 'language' as a 'totality of utterances'. The term 'grammar' was then used with systematic ambiguity, to refer to what we have here called 'I-language' and also to the linguist's theory of the I-language; the same was true of the term UG, introduced later with the same systematic ambiguity, referring to $S_0$ and the theory of $S_0$ (1986: 28–9).*

*What we have here, Dear Player, is an important Moral of the Maze:*

*The early history of The Garden is a seductive story that could easily arouse your interest, work you up and, in the end, cause your downfall.*

No doubt, the problem in part has to do with the mechanics of mind – as time muddles our memories, tales tend to grow taller.[60] And anyway, purely as a matter of pragmatic fact, there's no way that the present-day Maze can be modified by players' scoring meticulous points about its earliest period, long since paled into irrelevance. The Genesis of The Garden, really, is a topic for relaxed raillery late at night among friends who have all had one, or more, too many.

2.5.14   A related distinction was alluded to in section 2.5.9 above, namely the distinction I(nternalized) language vs P(latonic) language. Katz (1981: 6–9, 237) and Bever (1982) have argued that apart from I-languages, in the sense characterized above, there are also P-languages.

Whereas an I-language is a mental entity, a P-language has the general nature of 'a sentence-sense correlation with unlimited expressiveness', sentences being abstract objects like numbers. Abstract objects on the Platonist conception are, in Katz's (1981: 12) words, 'objects whose existence is independent of mind and matter but which must count as real along with mental and material objects'. Such objects, being timeless and spaceless, are not ideal objects or, as Katz (1981: 56) puts it,

> abstract objects are not idealizations at all. They do not represent anything physical or psychological. They are not a means of simplifying the laws of a discipline. Rather, abstract objects are another ontological kind from the physical and psychological objects that are represented in ideal objects. Like the actual objects of empirical science, they are the things of which the statements in a science are true.

Linguistics in a Katzian Platonist mould is not a branch or form of psychology, but an 'independent' discipline.

*As indicated in section 2.5.9, Dear Player, the 'I-language vs P-language' fork is nothing but a Shifting Shadow in The Garden. The Master (1986: 33) doesn't give a fig for P-languages as abstract entities ('existing in a Platonic heaven alongside of arithmetic and (perhaps) set theory'. And we have already noted that he sees 'little point' in 'moves' by which such abstract entities as P-English, P-Japanese, etc. are 'constructed at will'. For him (1986: 33)*

> *There is no initial plausibility to the idea that apart from the truths of grammar concerning the I-language and the truths of UG [i.e., universal grammar] concerning $S_0$ [i.e., the initial state of the language faculty] there is an additional domain of facts about P-language, independent of any psychological states of individuals.*

*But this, Dear Player, is also to say that The Game is not played in a 'Platonic heaven' – which, I cannot fail to note, is a pity from the point of view of all those Plodders who have had to pay the ultimate penalty for pedestrian play.*

2.5.15   We come now to the first of the cluster of distinctions bearing on the make-up and scope of knowledge of language, namely *grammatical competence vs pragmatic competence*. This distinction is drawn by Chomsky (1980a: 59, 224) 'for purposes of inquiry and exposition'. In a nutshell, a speaker's grammatical competence is a knowledge of form and meaning; his pragmatic competence is a knowledge of conditions of appropriate use. More fully, grammatical competence is characterized by Chomsky (1980a: 59) as

> the cognitive state that encompasses all those aspects of form and meaning and their relation, including underlying structures that enter into that relation, which are properly assigned to the specific subsystem of the human mind that relates representations of form and meaning. A bit misleadingly perhaps, I will continue to call this subsystem 'the language faculty'.

Grammatical competence has also been referred to by Chomsky as 'knowledge of grammar'.

Pragmatic competence, in contradistinction, is characterized by Chomsky (1980a: 224–5) as a

> system of rules and principles [that] . . . determines how the tool [of language] can effectively be put to use. Pragmatic competence may include what Paul Grice has called 'a logic of conversation'. We might say that pragmatic competence places language in the institutional setting of its use, relating intentions and purposes to the linguistic means at hand (n. 8).

Grammatical competence and pragmatic competence constitute two of the components or modules of knowledge of language; there is also a third component, to which we will turn in section 2.5.16 below. It is important to note that in Chomsky's linguistics a mental grammar or I-language represents a speaker's grammatical competence or knowledge.

*As a feature of The Garden, the notion of 'grammatical competence' has been considered by many players to represent too narrow and straight a path. These players have clamoured for its replacement by a broad road: a more general notion of 'competence' that includes a wider range of so-called linguistic abilities. Hymes (1971: 16), for example, has coined the expression 'communicative competence' as 'the most general term for the speaking and hearing abilities of a person'. Numerous players have joined The Communicative*

*Competence Campaign to trample grammatical competence, the Heart of the Garden, to dust.*[61]

*The Master's reaction to the Communicative Competence Campaign shows why Myopic Movers won't survive The Maze. Those who can't see beyond the fork facing them would say that he had done nothing. They might even conclude that he was helpless, defenceless, at a loss what to do. This would be a costly conclusion, a deadly deduction. For, although The Master has refrained from dealing directly with the crusaders for communicative competence, he ruined their campaign by making measured moves at a deeper level of The Garden.*[62] *But this is a tale to be told in section 4.2.6 below, where it will become clear how one may perish in the play without, apparently, having been hit by a direct delivery.*

2.5.16   The make-up and scope of knowledge of language is further clarified by Chomsky's distinction *the computational system vs the conceptual system/the system of conceptual structure(s)*. Taking grammatical competence to represent the 'computational system' of the language faculty, Chomsky (1980a: 54ff; 1982: 20) distinguishes it from our 'conceptual capacity' or 'conceptual system which "permits us to perceive, and categorize, and symbolize, maybe even to reason in an elementary way"'. The conceptual system, considered by Chomsky (1980a: 57–8) to be 'more primitive' than the computational system, 'involves object reference with all of its subtleties and complexities, thematic structures, aitiational factors, and the like'.[63]

Whereas Chomsky (1980a: 57; 1982: 19) considers the computational system, i.e. grammatical competence, to be unique to humans, he believes that other species, for example chimpanzees, may have conceptual capacities:

One might speculate that higher apes, which apparently lack the capacity to develop even the rudiments of the computational structure of human language, nevertheless may command parts of the conceptual structure just discussed and thus be capable of elementary forms of symbolic function or symbolic communication (n. 14) while entirely lacking the human language faculty. Possible support for such a view derives from work indicating that humans with severe language deficit – perhaps literal destruction of the language faculty – can acquire systems similar to those that have been taught to apes (n. 15), as if, to put it very loosely, apes were in this regard like humans without the language faculty. (Chomsky 1980a: 57)

With reference to Premack's work, Chomsky observes (1982: 19–20) that great apes lack not only the computational ability of the language capacity but also the ability of humans to compute with numbers. This observation leads him to a series of interesting conclusions about what it is that uniquely differentiates humans from other species:

> What is involved is some kind of capacity to deal with discrete infinities through recursive rules which from one point of view give you the number faculty and from another point of view, together with different principles, give you the capacity to construct an unbounded range of expressions. And when that is linked to the conceptual system, which could be more primitive, then you get crucial elements of the capacity to have free thought. That could be what enters into the uniqueness of human life.

'The great step in human evolution', on Chomsky's (1982: 20) view, was the linking up of the conceptual capacity and the computational capacity: 'it is only when linked to the computational capacity that the [conceptual] system really becomes powerful.'

*Recall, Dear Player, that at a conceptual fork which we considered in section 2.3.4 above, it was noted that certain players have preached the doctrine that it is possible to hurt, if not humble, The Master by pointing at particular apes: apes of the likes of Sarah and Washoe that have been taught 'to talk'. Thus, Putnam (1983: 198), peppery as ever, has proclaimed that it would be 'surely perverse' for The Master 'to deny that Washoe's performance is continuous with language learning, and to deny that it has any interest for the study of language learning'.*

*The option offered to The Master here is dismal: a choice between perversity and suicide. For, to do the nonperverse thing The Master, by Putnam's logic, would have to concede that there existed a 'general intelligence' which allowed the acquisition of language. But the option is a fiction, given the distinction between the computational capacity of the language faculty and the conceptual system. On The Master's (1982: 20–1) own view, the conceptual system allows both for symbolic behaviour and for its acquisition:*

> *Some of the ape studies seem to indicate at least some rudimentary ability for some kind of symbolization. But what appears to be totally lacking is anything analogous to the computational facilities, which means that the conceptual capacities are more or less mute.*

*So, given the conceptual fork 'the computational capacity vs the conceptual system', 'talking' does not equal talking. If, Dear Player, my gladiatorial glory depended on a couple of Chimeric Chimpanzees, my instinct for simple survival would have seen me taking to the trees.*

Let us try, in summary, to schematize Chomsky's view of the composition of knowledge of language. Recall that knowledge of language has grammatical competence, pragmatic competence and the conceptual system as its three components.

(4)     Knowledge of language

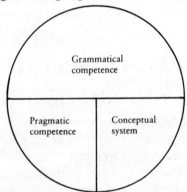

Grammatical competence, we have seen, is also referred to as 'knowledge of grammar' or 'the computational system of the language faculty'. The overarching distinction between *knowledge*

78

*of language* and *knowledge of grammar* represents a crucial conceptual component of Chomskyan linguistics, not a minor terminological trait. Notice, however, that Chomsky often uses the expression 'knowledge of language' to denote knowledge of grammar/grammatical competence. (In fact, that is just the way in which this expression has been used in the preceding sections of the present account.)

2.5.17    Implicit in the discussion of the significance of 'ape talk' is a further conceptual distinction to take note of, namely *human language vs symbolic systems taught to apes*. Chomsky (1980a: 239–40) has argued that there are fundamental differences 'at the most elementary level' between human language and 'the systems taught to apes' or, as he also calls them, 'the symbolic systems artificially induced under laboratory conditions'. The first difference is a functional one:

> From a functional point of view, human language is a system for free expression of thought, essentially independent of stimulus control, need-satisfaction, or instrumental purpose, hence, qualitatively different from the symbolic systems taught to apes. (p. 239)

The second difference is structural:

> Structurally, human language is a system with recursive structure-dependent rules, operating on sequences organized in a hierarchy of phrases to generate a countable infinity of sentences. (pp. 239–40)

The third difference pertains to physical basis:

> As far as the physical basis of human language is concerned, the very little that is known indicates that a crucial role is played by specific language centers in the dominant hemisphere that seem to have no direct analogue in other mammals. (p. 240)

The fourth difference involves acquisition by or development in the individual:

> As for development, language grows in the child through mere exposure to an unorganized linguistic environment, without training or even any particular language-specific care. (p. 240)

79

And the fifth or final difference concerns evolution or development in the species:

> Turning finally to the evolutionary level, though little is known, it seems clear that language is a fairly ancient human possession that developed long after the separation of humans from other primates. (p. 240)

Along 'each dimension of inquiry', Chomsky (1980a: 240) thus finds 'fundamental properties' that 'radically distinguish' human language from the symbolic systems taught to apes.

*The foundations of the conceptual fork 'human language vs systems taught to apes' have been a source of acrimony in the playing of The Game. Thus, the pugnacious Putnam (1983a: 293) argued amongst other things that Washoe was able to learn structure-dependent rules 'without benefit of an innate template for language'. The Master (1983: 318–20) found the argument to be without force, 'vitiated by an equivocation with respect to the notion "structure-dependent"'.*

*In support of this, The Master contended that the rules – a conjunction rule and a rule of question formation – that figured in Putnam's argument were in fact neither structure-dependent nor structure-independent since they did not modify the internal structure of a sentence. And he concluded that to his knowledge*

> *There is . . . no evidence that chimpanzees use structure-dependent (or structure-independent) rules, in the sense of my discussion. Clearly, Putnam's account involves no rules of either sort. Therefore, we can put aside the discussion of Washoe, which has no more relevance to the problem under consideration than the discussion of propositional calculus. (1983: 315–16)*

*The Washoe Wash-out recounted above should be instructive to players without much past exposure to linguistics. Unless handled with expert care, technical notions such as 'structure-dependent' should not be used as weapons against The Master. Wielded in a ham-handed manner, such notions tend to pose a greater hazard to the wielder than to the adversary. So, unless suicide is what you have in mind, don't try to trump The Master on his own Technical Turf.*

2.5.18 Turning next to the make-up of grammatical competence or knowledge of grammar, we first consider the general distinction *the component specific to the language vs the component contributed by the initial state.* Chomsky (1986: 26) characterizes this distinction – which is a function of his conception of language acquisition – as follows:

> The steady state [or I-language or grammatical competence] has two components that can be distinguished analytically, however they may be merged and intertwined: a component that is specific to the language in question and the contribution of the initial state. The former constitutes what is 'learned' [and the latter 'what is inherited'] . . .

The distinction drawn in this quotation is also commonly known as the distinction *language-specific vs language-independent or 'universal'.* In terms of the distinction considered in section 2.3.7 above, the component of a language contributed by the initial state includes fundamental principles such as Subjacency, whereas the component specific to the language reflects, amongst other things, the unique ways in which the open parameters of such principles have been set or fixed for the language.

*Not all players have recognized the fork in question for what it is – a misjudgement that has caused some futile fist-shaking at The Master. Putnam (1983a: 290, 292), for example, rejects the view, attributed by him to The Master, that 'the grammar of a language is a property of the brain of Homo Sapiens'. He suggests a different approach 'that says, in quite traditional fashion, that the grammar of a language is a property of the language'.*
*The Master (1983: 313) finds that 'Putnam's counterproposal suggests that he [i.e., Putnam] has something different in mind, and that his objection is just misstated'. Specifically, on The Master's reading, Putnam's formulation*

81

*refers to the grammar of a particular language, say English, not
to the innate constraints on possible languages and grammars.
Apparently, Putnam is confusing the grammars of particular
languages (the topic of his counterproposal) with 'universal
grammar', his notion of 'what a grammar is' (the topic of his
objection).*

*Mix-ups at the 'language-specific vs language-independent' fork
are not uncommon in the history of The Garden. The classic case,
of course, was the astonishing attribution to The Master of the idea
that all languages have the same deep structure or base rules.
Thus, referring to critics such as Jacob, Monod, Luria and Stent,
The Master (1982: 7) has remarked:*

> *When you read their comments, it is worth knowing that there
> is a systematic misinterpretation of the use of the phrase 'deep
> structure'. By and large they use the phrase 'deep structure'
> the way we use 'universal grammar'.*

*Confusing (claims about) the component specific to a language
with (claims about) the initial state constitutes what has been baldly
labelled The Basic Bungle.*

2.5.19   As regards the make-up of grammatical competence,
Chomsky (1986: 147, 221) draws the distinction *(the) core vs
(the) periphery*. This distinction must be understood against the
background of Chomsky's view of language acquisition as parameter
setting, a view considered in section 2.4.4 above. The core of
grammatical competence – also referred to as 'a core grammar'
or 'core language'[64] – Chomsky holds to be a system determined
by fixing values for the parameters of UG or the initial state
of the language faculty (1986: 147). Or, to use an equivalent
characterization by Chomsky (1986: 211),

> The core . . . consists of the set of values selected for parameters
> of the core system of $S_0$ [i.e., the initial state of the language
> faculty]; this is the essential part of what is 'learned', if that
> is the correct term for this process of fixing knowledge of a
> particular language.

In less formal terms, Chomsky (1978a: 12–13) has characterized the core (or, a core grammar) as including 'structures and rules of great simplicity' and as having

> a rigid structure which is limited in expressive devices. It incorporates principles of mental computation which interact to provide the basic skeleton on which the language is constructed, yielding in fact the basic system of constructions and the great variety in interpreted expressions, though not the full wealth of the language.

The periphery, on Chomsky's view (1986: 147), contains 'marked exceptions' added to the core on the basis of specific experience. In the periphery one will find, for example, irregular morphology, idioms, more complex rules, borrowings and historical relics of earlier stages of the language.

Chomsky (1981a: 39, 1986: 147) points out that the core (or a core grammar/language) is an idealized construct in relation to the system actually represented in the mind/brain of a speaker-hearer. Specifically, he observes:

> A core grammar is what the language faculty would develop, as a component of the steady state, under empirical conditions that depart in certain respects from those of normal life, specifically, under conditions of homogeneity of linguistic experience. (1981a: 39)

Here we have a further respect in which Chomsky's technical notion of language departs from the common-sense notion of language. The latter notion does not involve the distinction between core and periphery.

*As part of The Garden, Dear Player, the distinction 'core vs periphery' is an instance of a special kind of fork, a Fluid Fork. Such a fork is not finished, its features not fully fixed. For example, it is unclear at this stage exactly where the boundary between core and periphery runs, whether the distinction carries across over the boundaries of grammatical competence into other areas of knowledge of language, and so on. So, this fork is not an ideal spot for sparring*

*with The Master. It is simply not possible to pick up points here
by precision punching.*

2.5.20    Closely linked to the distinction between core and
periphery is the further distinction *marked (rules/structures) vs
unmarked (rules/structures)*. Unmarked rules and structures are in
some sense more simple, more highly constrained, more regular or
more basic than marked structures and rules. Chomsky (1986: 147),
in fact, provides for three notions of markedness: 'core versus
periphery, internal to the core, and internal to the periphery'. In
terms of the first notion, the constituents of the core are unmarked,
those of the periphery marked. The second notion of markedness
'has to do with the way parameters are set in the absence of evidence',
a 'way' about which Chomsky does not have much to say. He
mentions the possibility that 'the options of core grammar too, e.g.
ordering options, may be layered in accordance with some theory
of markedness' (1978a: 13). That is, not all options of the core are,
as it were, equally close to the centre of the core. The third notion
of markedness bears on the internal organization of the rules and
structures making up the periphery:

> there are, no doubt, significant regularities even in departures
> from the core principles (for example, in irregular verb
> morphology in English), and it may be that peripheral
> constructions are related to the core in systematic ways, say,
> by relaxing certain conditions of core grammar.

Chomsky (1979a: 4) expects that the less marked/more 'core-
like' structures (and the systems they form) may be related to
the more marked/less 'core-like' structures (and the systems they
form)

> by such devices as relaxing certain conditions of core grammar,
> processes of analogy in some sense to be made precise, and
> so on, though there will presumably be independent structure
> as well: hierarchies of accessibility, etc.

He illustrates this view (1979a: 20–2) with reference to reciprocals
occurring inside noun phrases (NP) in English, for example:

84

(5)  (a)  they read [$_{NP}$ each other's books]
     (b)  they heard [$_{NP}$ stories about each other]
     (c)  they heard [$_{NP}$ the stories about each other]
          (that had been published last year)

In terms of an earlier version of Chomsky's GB ( = Government Binding) theory, (5) (a)–(c) must be ungrammatical: the reciprocal *each other* is an anaphor and has to be bound inside the NP governing it. The fact that (a)–(c) are actually grammatical indicates that they are marked structures according to Chomsky (1979a: 23ff). That is, he holds that these structures fall 'under a principle that is derivable from the more general theory and applied in a case where the general theory is relaxed, to yield marked constructions' (1979a: 25).

Claims about the marked/unmarked status of specific rules or structures must, in Chomsky's (1979a) view, be empirical in principle and justified in practice.[65] Thus, commenting on the three notions of markedness mentioned above, Chomsky (1986: 147) observes that

> The problem of formulating these notions precisely is an empirical one throughout, although not a simple one, and many kinds of evidence might be relevant to determining them. For example, we would expect phenomena that belong to the periphery to be supported by specific evidence of sufficient 'density', to be variable among languages and dialects, and so forth.

*The 'marked vs unmarked' fork is located in the same murky morass as the 'core vs periphery' bifurcation with which we dealt earlier. As anyone at all familiar with the history of The Garden would confirm, the obscurity of this further fork has often been commented on in less than laudatory language.*

*Even two Faithful Friends, Huybregts and Van Riemsdijk, have ventured to remark respectfully that*

> *Reading the literature, one cannot escape the conclusion that notions such as markedness and periphery are being used as euphemistic terms to refer to phenomena that are not understood or do not fit into the core. (Chomsky 1982: 108)*

85

*To this The Master (1982: 108) has responded that all indeed is not well with the foundations of this part of The Garden:*

*The distinction is in part theory-internal, but that is unavoidable and quite reasonable. I am sure that the periphems [sic] and the theory of markedness have structure, but I just do not have any good ideas about what it should be. I suggested something in the Pisa paper (n. 2) which I do not think is correct, viz. relaxing some of the conditions of core grammar. Maybe that is somewhat the right idea, but I do not really feel that there is any evidence. I do not even think it is clear whether we should make a sharp distinction between core and periphery.*

*For the purpose of The Game, however, The Master has turned this weakness of the 'marked vs unmarked' fork into a score-building virtue. He has actually contrived to exploit it as a defensive decoy: a decoy for diverting alarming attacks away from certain areas in which he would not be able to beat off the aggressors quite so easily. Delightedly dabbing at the decoy, Pressing Players are led up the garden path that branches into the 'marked vs unmarked' fork, there to be sidetracked by a gambit to which we will presently turn our attention. First, however, we need to get a clearer idea of how the Markedness Meander, a labyrinthine loop in the Charles, is put to use. To this end, let us consider an incident in the recent history of The Garden.*

*The incident involves the prediction by The Master's GB theory that structures such as (5) (a)–(c) – i.e., structures incorporating what are known as picture noun phrases – must be ungrammatical. Contrary to the prediction, these and other similar structures are quite acceptable to native speakers. This fact indicated predictive failure on the part of the GB theory, an embarrassing state of affairs for The Master. The more so since an older theory (the 'OB' theory), rejected by him, had correctly predicted the grammaticalness of such constructions.[66] Rather than conceding the predictive failure of the GB theory, The Master (1979a: 20) deftly channelled the threat into The Markedness Meander, stating 'in summary' that 'in accordance with the GB system', structures such as (5) (a)–(c) are 'marked' and that 'it seems to me reasonable to conclude that the predictions of the GB system are in fact correct as contrasted with those of the OB system'. Thus, what went into the Markedness*

*Meander as a predictive failure of a linguistic theory came out of it as a 'marked feature' – a 'failure', as it were – of a human language. Now, the target having been suitably softened, the time was ripe for using the gambit referred to above.*

*In accordance with the requirement we have noted, The Master had to produce empirical evidence justifying the claim that the constructions under consideration were in fact marked. But he would have none of this. He coolly claimed that structures such as (5) (a)–(c) 'appear to be rare' in the languages of the world, a claim without empirical substance.*[67] *And because of the murkiness of the mud that forms the basis of the 'marked vs unmarked' fork, the rhetorical nature of this claim was difficult to detect. Resorting to refined rhetoric where empirical evidence or conceptual considerations are required, such is the essence of the Galilean Gambit, a move named after the sixteenth-century past master at 'propagandistic machinations'.*[68]

*The Master (1982: 110), to his credit I must add, subsequently admitted to having resorted to the rhetorical ploy described above:*

> *In the paper [i.e., Chomsky 1979a] I took the most extreme view with regard to their [(5) (a)–(c)] being marked, at least in anything I've written. I've always assumed they're a little odd in their behavior, but they really just didn't fall into the theory I outlined there at all, so I just had to say they're totally marked. I gave a half-baked argument about that, and there was some bad conscience, I must concede.*

*But, Dear Player, this admission, candid as it may be, is a statement about the past, and holds no promise for the future. So, be ready for rhetorical play, refined and 'reasonable', that may come your way. Do I hear you breathe the words 'Foul play'? Swallow them! And take to heart the following Facts of Play:*

> *1   The Game doesn't provide for penalties, disqualifications, yellow or red cards, and such trivialities.*
> *2   The Game isn't about playing fair or foul.*

*Surviving or succumbing, that's what it's all about.*

Before we proceed, it should be noted that the distinctions 'core vs periphery' and 'marked vs unmarked' do not bear on the make-up of grammatical competence, or on the steady state of the language faculty, only. These distinctions equally reflect the existence of distinct structural components of the initial state of the language faculty. Thus, referring to the language faculty, Chomsky (1986: 221) claims that

> There is a fixed initial state $S_0$ of the language faculty consisting of a system of principles associated with certain parameters of variation and a markedness system with several components of its own.

So, when considering the make-up of the initial state of the language faculty, one also has to take into account the conceptual distinction *a system of principles and parameters vs a composite markedness system*. It was purely for expository reasons – avoidance of duplication – that we did not do so in an earlier paragraph.

2.5.21 To conclude our survey of conceptual distinctions bearing on Chomsky's conception of the nature of knowledge of language, we have now to consider one more, namely *an abstract rule system vs a system of fixed parameters*. In earlier work, Chomsky (1986: 46) depicted knowledge of the grammar of a language as an abstract rule system that

> assigns to each expression a structure, which we may take to be a set of representations, one on each linguistic level, where a linguistic level is a particular system of mental representation. This structure must provide whatever information about an expression is available to the person who knows the language, insofar as this information derives from the language faculty; its representations must specify just what the language faculty contributes to determining how the expression is produced, used, and understood.

Recently, however, a conceptual shift – the second in the history of Chomskyan linguistics[69] – has radically changed this picture of knowledge of grammar. Specifically, Chomsky (1986: 146, 150) has come to think of knowledge of the grammar of a language as a system of principles with fixed parameters. Thus, he (1986: 150–1) states that what we 'know innately' are the principles of the various subsystems of $S_0$ and the manner of their interaction, and the parameters associated with these principles. What we learn are the values of the parameters and the elements of the periphery (along with the lexicon, to which similar considerations apply). The language that we then know is a system of principles with parameters fixed, along with a periphery of marked exceptions. What we know is not a rule system in the conventional sense. In fact, it might be that the notion of rule in this sense, like the notion of E-language (so it seems), has no status in linguistic theory. One can formulate algorithms that project rule systems from a choice of values for the parameters of UG, but it is not obvious that this is a significant move or that it matters how it is done.

The considerations which have triggered the conceptual shift from a rule-system model to a principles-and-parameters theory are of a technical linguistic sort and cannot be treated in detail here. It is sufficient to note that these considerations can be reduced to Chomsky's concern with finding a solution to Plato's problem, i.e., the logical problem of language acquisition. To solve this problem, Chomsky (1986: 83) explains, it is necessary to reduce the variety of possible rule systems and also the options the various kinds of rule systems permit. This point he (1986: 83) illustrates with reference to phrase structure rules and transformations:

Both types of rules allow a wide range of options that are never realized and are presumably unrealizable, and the availability of these options makes it extremely difficult to account for the fact that a specific language is fixed by the available evidence. The device of phrase structure rules is particularly suspect, because these rules so closely reflect lexical properties. Statement of the lexical properties is ineliminable from the grammar: For example, the grammar cannot avoid stating that *claim* takes a propositional complement as part of its lexical entry. Therefore, it is to be expected that the phrase structure rules should be eliminable insofar as they merely restate, in another form, the essential content of lexical entries. In fact, it seems that such rules are eliminable more generally, that there are no rules of this type in language. In the case of transformational

89

rules, we have no comparable reason for skepticism concerning their existence, but it seems that the variety of these rules can be significantly reduced, perhaps to Move-α or Affect-α, with some parametric variation. These steps sharply restrict the class of possible languages [available to the child] . . .

Rather than a system in which rules generate the elements of well-formed structures, it is better to have a system in which these elements have to be 'licensed', in Chomsky's (1986: 93) terminology, in one of a small number of possible ways. The conditions required for such licensing belong to components of universal grammar.

*Whatever else you may do, Dear Player, be sure you do not think of the conceptual fork 'an abstract rule system vs a system of fixed parameters' as just one more addition to or modification of The Garden. It does not simply extend The Maze in a dimension known to you. By shifting to a principles-and-parameters theory, The Master has, in fact, embarked on a Radical Reconstruction of The Maze. The topography of The Garden is, in fact, being remoulded under your very feet.*

*As noted by The Master (1986: 151–2), this conceptual revision suggests a change in the way we view the fundamental problem of language acquisition. It 'opens . . . new empirical questions for investigation' – e.g., questions of universal and comparative grammar. And it requires 'substantial rethinking' of fundamental questions – e.g., that aspect of the question of the use of knowledge of grammar known as the 'parsing problem'.*

*At the level of individual lanes and forks, The Garden has entered a transitional phase of considerable uncertainty. That is, given the conceptual shift, there are a variety of lanes and forks that can no longer be retained as they are. But exactly how they will be modified is still unclear. Even as myriad-minded a mazemaker as The Master cannot rebuild the affected stretches all at once. Which means, Dear Player, that for the foreseeable future players will need acute agility, along with a sixth sense, simply to survive. Closed-down lanes, rebuilt forks, new bifurcations – thanks to these and similar surprises, the menace of The Maze will be markedly augmented.*

*What's that? Would not I, too, care for a break to rest and recover? Unfortunately, Poor Player, this simply cannot be done. In The Game, Players don't 'take drinks', 'go to tea', 'leave the field for lunch'. Need I remind you that The Game isn't cricket?*


**2.6**  We have come to the third of Chomsky's basic questions, the question of **language use** listed as (1) (c) in section 2.1: How is knowledge of language put to use? In addressing this question Chomsky has on the whole been concerned with three aspects of language use: production of utterances (by the speaker), processing/interpretation of utterances (by the hearer), and making of intuitive judgements about the properties of utterances (by the speaker–hearer). All three of these kinds of linguistic performance or behaviour Chomsky has considered to be 'rule-guided'. He recently reiterated this view with reference to production: 'use of language is rule-guided behaviour: We have (generally tacit) knowledge of the rules of language and we use them in constructing "free expressions"' (1986: 222).

Most of the conceptual distinctions drawn by Chomsky in order to elucidate his conception of linguistic behaviour as being rule-governed apply to the production of utterances. On the other two aspects – namely, processing/interpretation and making intuitive linguistic judgements – he has had much less to say. The conceptual distinctions to be presented below accordingly bear primarily on production. Before dealing with these, however, we first have to consider a more fundamental distinction: a distinction presupposed by the idea that language use is a matter of following rules.[70]

*2.6.1*  The fundamental distinction presupposed by the idea of language use as rule following – and also underlying Chomsky's basic questions (1) (a) and (1) (c) in section 2.1 above – is that of *(linguistic) competence vs (linguistic) performance*. Whereas competence represents 'knowledge of language' (narrowed down to 'grammar'), Chomsky (1965: 4; 1980a: 205) takes performance to be 'behaviour', 'the use of knowledge of language' or 'the actual use of language in concrete situations'. Though competence is presupposed by every instance of performance, he provides for many other factors that also contribute to performance. As noted by Chomsky (1965: 3, 1980a: 225), these include the speaker-hearer's memory structure, his mode of organizing experience, his perceptual mechanisms, attention span etc. Thus, performance, on Chomsky's (1965: 3) classical formulation, is also affected 'by such grammatically irrelevant conditions as memory limitations, distractions, shifts of attention and interest, and errors (random and characteristic)' in a speaker's application of his knowledge of language. It is because of the operation of factors such as these that, as Chomsky (1965: 4) notes, 'A record of natural speech will show numerous false starts, deviations from rules, changes of plan in mid-course, and so on.' Performance, therefore, does not directly reflect competence.

Nevertheless the linguist, on Chomsky's (1980a: 225) view, has no other way of studying competence than through performance:

> Actual investigation of language necessarily deals with perform-ance, with what someone does under specific circumstances. We often attempt to devise modes of inquiry that will reduce to a minimum factors that appear irrelevant to intrinsic competence, so that the data of performance will bear directly on competence, as the object of our inquiry. To the extent that we have an explicit theory of competence, we can attempt to devise performance models to show how this knowledge is put to use.

Let us return for a moment to Chomsky's idealization of an ideal speaker–hearer. In section 2.5.11 above, a first function of this idealization was noted: to arrive at a 'pure', technical notion of language by abstracting away from inessential considerations relating to language variation. Here, now, we have a second, similar, function of this idealization: to distinguish between those aspects of performance that do and those that don't bear directly on competence or the rules followed in performance.

*So, at last, we find ourselves in Lemming Lane, the lane leading to what some take to be the focal fork of The Garden, namely the 'competence vs performance' bifurcation. About this fork a career chronicler of the history of the East Coast Court has observed: 'Probably no notion within grammatical theory has aroused more controversy than the competence/performance distinction.*[71] *This, Dear Player, is but a deliberately bloodless way of saying that over the years fuming fighters have flocked down the lane to wipe out this offensive fork and, along with it, The Master. As noted by the chronicler I have just quoted, the fork has been attacked from nearly every conceivable angle: some found the distinction in question 'incoherent', others judged it 'too confining', a third group charged that there was no clear criterion for deciding which aspects of any particular phenomenon should fall under competence and which under performance.*[72] *In their hapless haste, however, hordes have misread the fork, in their frenzy flinging themselves over the edge, and so taking the Performance Plunge into the Charles.*

*You desire some concrete evidence? The case of Kintsch and Company is as good as any. Arguing against The Master's 'strict separation' of competence and performance, Kintsch & Co. (1974) charged that this distinction*

> *permits the linguist to deal with convenient abstractions, uninhibited by psychological reality, and it provides the psychologist with the facetious argument that linguistic theories have nothing to do with processes anyway. As long as linguistic theory is strictly a competence theory, it is of no interest to the psychologist. Indeed I doubt that it should be of much interest to linguists either, but that is for them to decide.*

*The Master (1980a: 203) took these remarks to be 'not untypical', reflecting 'deep-seated confusions'. He dismissed Kintsch's charges for two basic reasons. On the one hand,*

> *Kintsch asserts that study of the abstracted competence system is 'uninhibited by psychological reality'; only processes have 'reality'. But plainly we can have no special insight into what is real apart from normal scientific practice. Adhering to these reasonable norms, we impute existence, subject to verification and test, to whatever structures and processes are postulated in the effort to explain significant facts. The enterprise is not 'uninhibited by psychological reality', but is rather concerned with specific aspects of psychological reality. Kintsch's psychologist has 'no interest' in explanatory theories, no matter how far-reaching and well-confirmed, dealing with these aspects of*

93

*knowledge of language and the basis for its acquisition (particular and universal grammar). In short, fundamental questions of cognitive psychology are to be excluded from the concern of the psychologist (or for Kintsch, the concern of anyone). Note that these positions are taken on purely a priori grounds, not on the basis of alleged empirical or conceptual inadequacies of the approach he rejects as compared with some alternatives. It is difficult to imagine comparable dogmatism in the natural sciences. (1980a: 203–4)*

In The Master's (1980a: 205) view, such a dogmatic approach 'is simply a reflection of the irrationality that has hampered investigation in the human sciences for many, many years'.

On the other hand, The Master (1980a: 205) has pointed out that Kintsch in his own work is himself concerned with the study of a certain aspect of competence. Specifically:

*Kintsch simply presupposes some system of rules that generates the representations he postulates, in particular cases. And like everyone else, Kintsch tries to gain some understanding of this 'level of representation' through the study of performance and tries to show how it figures in process models. In short, while Kintsch believes that his approach 'has no use at all for the competence-performance distinction', in fact, he invokes it in pretty much the conventional way. This is not surprising, given that no coherent alternative framework of concepts has been proposed in this domain, to my knowledge.*

You don't really care to share the watery woes of Kintsch and Company? Why not then turn an eye inwards and consider the possibility that you yourself may all along have been operating with some implicit 'competence vs performance' distinction? You're not one hundred per cent sure? Well, then you're bound to become just another Linguist Lemming, unless, of course, you leave the lane leading to the Lethal Leap.

2.6.2   The 'common-sense' view that using language to produce utterances is a matter of rule-following runs into two sorts of problems, according to Chomsky (1986: 222–3), namely *Cartesian problems vs Wittgensteinian problems*. Cartesian problems, on Chomsky's (1986: 222) reconstruction, are results of a particular conflict:

> In the Cartesian view, the 'beast-machine' is 'compelled' to act in a certain way when its parts are arranged in a particular manner, but a creature with a mind is only 'incited or inclined' to do so because 'the Soul, despite the disposition of the body, can prevent these movements when it has the ability to reflect on its actions and when the body is able to obey' (La Forge). Human action, including the use of rules of language, is free and indeterminate.

Though, in his opinion, various aspects of the formulation of such Cartesian problems may be questioned, Chomsky (1986: 223) tends to agree with Descartes that 'serious problems are touched on here, perhaps impenetrable mysteries for the human mind'.

As regards Wittgensteinian problems, these arise from Wittgenstein's sceptical paradox as reconstructed by Chomsky (1986: 225) on the basis of Kripke's exegesis:

> Given a rule R, there is no fact about my past experience (including my conscious mental states) that justifies my belief that the next application of R does or does not conform to my intentions. There is, Wittgenstein argues, no fact about me that tells me whether I am following R or R' , which coincides with R in past cases but not future ones. Specifically, there is no way for me to know whether I am following the rule of addition or another rule (involving 'quus', not 'plus') which gives the answer 5 for all pairs beyond the numbers for which I have previously given sums; 'there was no *fact* about me that constituted my having meant plus rather than quus', and more generally, 'there can be no such thing as meaning anything by any word'. Each application of a rule is 'a leap in the dark'.

Chomsky, allowing for the existence of ungrounded knowledge, is not troubled by Wittgenstein's point that 'if I follow R, I do so without reasons'.

There is, however, a Wittgensteinian question that does cause Chomsky (1986: 225) some trouble: 'How can I tell whether you are following R or R' ? Under what circumstances does it make sense

95

for me to attribute rule following to you? When is this attribution correct or justified?' The problem which these questions pose for Chomsky's account springs, in fact, from the answer (as analysed by Kripke) which Wittgenstein gave to these questions. Chomsky (1986: 235–6) summarizes Wittgenstein's answer as follows:

(6)    (I)    'To judge whether an individual is indeed following a given rule in particular applications' is to determine 'whether his responses agree with their own.'

    (II)    'We therefore reject the ' "private model" of rule following,' according to which 'the notion of a person following a given rule is to be analyzed simply in terms of facts about the rule follower and the rule follower alone, without reference to his membership in a wider community.'

    (III)    'Our community can assert of any individual that he follows a rule if he passes the tests for rule following applied to any member of the community.'

As Chomsky (1986: 226) sees it, the heart of the problem generated by this analysis of rule-following is that in terms of (II), 'There is no substance or sense to the idea of a person following a rule privately. It seems that the "individual psychology" framework of generative grammar is undermined.'


*The latter avenue of thought deserves further exploration. But, Dear Player, you would be wise to take note of your surroundings. For we have now entered a singularly strange section of The Garden: a part populated by players pretty peculiar in appearance. This is the supernatural section, where spooks and spectres stalk The Master. Here, Paling Player, he is haunted by such Cartesian Creatures as Beast-Machines, Wittgensteinian Weirdies and by sundry Dramatis Personae of plays of long ago.*

*Game as ever, The Master has shown himself to be more than a match for Garden Ghouls and Ghosts. As a case in point, consider his reaction, cited above, to the threat that the 'Classical' Cartesian problems pose for his conception of language use as rule-following. But what would be the point of having a garden, you might wonder, if part of it were for ever covered by impenetrable mists, shrouded in mystery?*

*Take care! Do not think for a moment that you will ever have The Master at your mercy by the mere mention of matters he deems mysterious. If challenged on the issue of 'impenetrable mysteries of the human mind' – which you might take as representing The Cartesian Crunch – The Master (1986: 223) would simply respond that 'There is no more reason to suppose humans to be capable of solving every problem they can formulate than to expect rats to be able to solve any maze.'*

*'Then forget about Cartesian Creatures,' you say. 'It is the Wittgensteinian Weirdies undermining The Master's "individual psychology" framework that really matter.' If you actually believe this, Dear Player, then you're bound to be caught off your guard at the fork that next confronts us.*

2.6.3   To deal with the Wittgensteinian problem of how the attribution of rules to others could be justified, Chomsky (1986: 225–6) draws a distinction between two cases of rule attribution, namely *ascription-of-rule-following by a person in ordinary life vs ascription-of-rule-following by a scientist.*

> Here we may distinguish two cases: my doing so as a person in ordinary life, and my doing so as a scientist seeking to discover the truth about the language faculty. The first case raises a question of description: When do I, in fact, attribute to you a particular instance of rule following? Both cases raise questions of justification: When am I entitled, as a person in ordinary life or as a scientist, to say that you are following a rule?

Chomsky's (1986: 226ff) discussion of these two cases of the Wittgensteinian problem of rule ascription cannot be represented in detail here. The major points will have to suffice.

As regards the case of rule ascription by a person in ordinary life, the essence of Chomsky's (1986: 227) position is that Wittgenstein's objective – that of describing language as opposed to reforming it – requires that his own solution (6) above should be descriptively adequate.

But this account is very far from descriptively adequate; it simply does not work for standard cases of attribution of rule following. Possibly, the discussion is obscured by concentrating on cases that are felt to be deep in their character and implications, and that certainly are deeply embedded in the philosophical tradition, specifically, attribution of concepts. These are, furthermore, cases where there is understood to be some normative standard of correctness.

On the basis of an analysis of 'typical cases of attribution of rule following that are less "loaded" in this sense', Chomsky (1986: 236) argues that the Wittgensteinian assumption (6) (I) is not true in standard cases: 'We regularly judge that people are following rules when their responses differ from our own.' As regards (6) (III), Chomsky (1986: 236) argues that

> it is tenable if we understand it to mean that whether or not an individual's 'responses agree with [our] own', we may assert that he or she follows rules if he or she passes the tests for rule following, not with respect to particular rules or with reference to any particular community of rule users, but more generally: He or she acts as a person, passing the tests for 'other minds' in roughly the Cartesian sense (with the provisos noted).

And contrary to (6) (III), Chomsky argues that there seems to be nothing objectionable about the 'private model' of rule-following. And he notes that no serious alternative to this model has been proposed that is relevant to the explanations and concepts involving 'competence' or 'knowledge of language' in generative grammar.

As regards the other case of the ascription of rule-following – that is, ascription by a scientist – the essence of Chomsky's position is that such ascription cannot be objectionable if it is done within the framework of an explanatory theory satisfying the usual empirical criteria of adequacy. Thus Chomsky (1986: 236–7) holds that scientists should adopt the following general approach:

> We amass evidence about Jones [the person to whom rule following is ascribed], his behavior, his judgements, his history, his physiology, or whatever else may bear on the matter. We also consider comparable evidence about others, which is relevant on the plausible empirical assumption that their genetic

endowment is in relevant respects the same as his, just as we regard a particular sample of water as water, and a particular fruit fly as a fruit fly. We then try (in principle) to construct a complete theory, the best one we can, of relevant aspects of how Jones is constructed – of the kind of 'machine' he is, if one likes.

Given that this theory meets the required empirical constraints, it may legitimately be concluded that the person (Jones) is following the rules of the particular language. This approach, in Chomsky's opinion (1986: 237),

> is not immune to general skeptical arguments – inductive uncertainty, Hilary Putnam's antirealist arguments, and others. But these are not relevant here, because they bear on science more generally. It is not clear that there are any further skeptical arguments that apply.

So, neither case of the Wittgensteinian problem of rule ascription to others leaves Chomsky with what he judges to be an embarrassing problem.


*The Master's moves against Wittgenstein (and Kripke) reveal a new dimension of The Game, namely Retroactive Retaliation. Neither Wittgenstein (1953) nor Kripke (1982) had an axe to grind with The Master. Wittgenstein posed the questions as part of his own game at a time when The Garden would have been at most a gleam in The Master's eye. Kripke, some thirty years later, was merely playing a further round in the never-ending Wittgensteinian game, taking note of The Master in passing but doing so without perceptible passion.[73] The Master, however, guards The Garden jealously. No one – whether in the spirit or in the flesh – is allowed to steal his show. And so Wittgenstein and Kripke had to be brought to book in The Maze. The meting out of punishment, even posthumously, for incidental incivilities is not paradoxical in the play. The general point, Dear Player, may be formulated as the Law of Garden Gravity:*

> *Nor time or distance, nor intent, will keep at bay
> the Maze's magnetism, the pull of Garden play.*

99

*No one, but no one, in the business of making sense of mind or language can count on escaping the consequences of the conflict on the banks of the Charles.*

2.6.4   Elaborating on observations by Kripke, Chomsky (1986: 238), with reference to the scientist's account of rule-following, draws the distinction *dispositional vs causal vs descriptive vs normative*. In Kripke's (1982: 36–7) sense, an account of rule-following would be dispositional if it said what a person would be disposed to do under particular circumstances. Such an account would be causal if it were either neurophysiological or functionalist. A functionalist account would regard psychology as given by a set of causal connections, analogous to the causal operation of a machine. Kripke argued against a dispositional account of rule-following. He argued, moreover, that such an account was causal in neither the neurophysiological nor the functionalist sense. Such an account, on his view, should be normative and not descriptive. To this Chomsky (1986: 238) has responded:

> But the account of 'competence' is descriptive: It deals with the configuration and structure of the mind/brain and takes one element of it, the component L, to be an instantiation of a certain general system that is one part of the human biological endowment. We could regard this instantiation as a particular program (machine), although guarding against implications that it determines behavior. Thus, an account can be descriptive although it is neither dispositional nor causal (neurophysiological or functional), in Kripke's sense.

A descriptive account given by a scientist must, in Chomsky's (1986: 238) view, be 'answerable to a wide range of empirical evidence, including evidence concerning the person's history and concerning speakers of other languages, and in principle much else: physiology, psychological experiment, brain damage, biochemistry, and so forth'.

*The Master (1986: 240), Progressing Player, has predicted that Kripke will be dissatisfied even with the kind of descriptive account just outlined. For instance, Kripke has noted that there might be a neurophysiological theory that would explain a person's behaviour. Kripke would consider such a theory irrelevant, however, because it would lack the necessary prescriptive force. As The Master (1986: 240) reads Kripke's argument, such a neurophysiological theory 'does not provide justification and, thus, does not answer the skeptic; and furthermore, such theories would not be relevant to ascription of rule following by others who know nothing of these matters but do ascribe rule following'. But The Master (1986: 240) knows all the steps and sidesteps in this sort of Sceptical Scuffle. To begin with, he notes that from Kripke's qualms as quoted*

> *It does not follow that we must accept the skeptical conclusion that there is no fact as to whether Jones . . . follows the rules of binding theory, or the rule that merges tense and lax /i/ before /g/. The [empirical, descriptive] approach just outlined leads to confirmable theories as to whether indeed Jones follows these rules.*

*And, pushing Kripke to the edge of a deadly drop into the Charles, The Master goes on to observe that 'the standard outlook of modern science' is that of 'constructive scepticism', which recognizes 'that absolutely certain grounds could not be given for our knowledge, and yet that we possess standards for evaluating the reliability and applicability of what we have found out about the world'.[74] In other words, the Wittgensteinian/Kripkean kind of scepticism produces the wrong kind of ammunition for firing at scientists who are engaged in setting up empirical theories of rule ascription. So, Dear Player, should you wish to launch an attack along sceptical lines against The Master's conception of language use as rule-following, be ready to beat off a countermove that exploits the distinction* Wittgensteinian/Kripkean scepticism vs constructive scepticism. *Your chances of avoiding the Charles? Pretty poor, I would predict.*

*I can now tell you, Dear Player, about a strategy of some subtlety used by The Master for cornering a quarry. My story is about a man, an Oxford man called George, who could not stand the sight of The Master cutting up conceptual kinfolk of the likes of Kripke, Quine and Wittgenstein. In the best of British bloodsport traditions, George (1987) set out to hunt The Master down and bring him to book for [carrying] out his patented demolition job on all criticisms that have been erected, or resurrected, since the last salvo. (1987: 158)*

*[being] remarkably unfair to Kripke. (1987: 159)*

*[making] remarks [in his debate with Quine] that really do obscure the main issue. (1987: 162)*

*The Master's (1987) response to being hounded in this way took on the form of a multiple-move manoeuvre. The opening move, curiously enough, was of a complimentary kind, referring to 'the interesting questions raised by Alexander George' (Chomsky 1987: 178). But the subsequent moves were intended to show just how flawed George's interpretations of Kripke and Quine really were, and so they bore a rather different complexion. As an example, consider the following thrust by The Master (1987: 185), delivered as little less than a* coup de grâce: *'In summary, my rendition of Quine's positions and criticism of them (of which this is only a part) was accurate; George's rendition is not, and furthermore, attributes to Quine a position that is completely untenable.'*

*You are wondering, Perplexed Player, how a rendition (of something) that is inaccurate and the attribution (to someone) of a completely untenable position could still allow George to raise 'interesting questions'? But herein lies the masterfulness of the opening move – the move which, from our sporting perspective, is the really interesting thing. An essentially diversionary device, The Master's opening move uses praise to side-track the hotheaded hunter. And so it turns the latter into an unwary target, suitably set up for the sting that is still to come. In Combat Code, I fear, Dear Player, this type of tenderizing of the target has been callously tagged 'Sugaring the Sucker'.*

2.6.5   A final distinction bearing on the idea that language use is rule-following[75] is Chomsky's (1986: 151) distinction *the rule-system theory vs the principles-and-parameters theory of language use.* This distinction reflects a consequence of what Chomsky presents as the second conceptual shift in generative grammar. We have already noted that, prior to this shift, the notion of a 'rule' was central to Chomsky's thinking about language: coming to know a language (or, rather, a grammar) was seen as the acquisition of a rule system, and using a language was viewed as the following of rules. Subsequent to the second conceptual shift, knowledge of language is taken to be knowledge of a system of principles with parameters fixed, and acquisition of a language is characterized as the fixing of these parameters. In the wake of the second conceptual shift, the idea of language use as rule-following will have to undergo a similarly substantial change. Thus, Chomsky (1986: 151) observes that

It [i.e., the second conceptual shift] also suggests a rethinking of the parsing problem. Parsing programs are typically rule-based; the parser, in effect, mirrors a rule system and asks how these rules can assign a structure to a string that is analysed word-by-word. The examples discussed above, and many others, suggest that a different approach might be in order. Given a lexicon, structures can be projected from heads by virtue of the projection principle, X-bar theory, and other subsystems of UG that are involved in licensing elements, which are associated with one another by these principles in the manner already illustrated. Perhaps, parsers should not be based on rules at all but should rather be based on lexical properties and principles of UG that determine structures from them. Rule-based parsers are in some respects implausible. For one thing, complexity of parsing increases rapidly as rules proliferate; for another, since languages appear to differ substantially if viewed from the perspective of rule systems, they will require quite different parsers if the latter are rule-based – an unlikely consequence. The entire question merits substantial rethinking, so it appears.

On the extent of the rethinking mentioned in this quotation and on its consequences for the Chomskyan conception of language use, Chomsky has had little more to offer than the speculative remarks quoted above. Observations such as the following by Chomsky (1986: 243) do not add much of substance to the principles-and-parameters theory of language use:

Under this [i.e., the principles-and-parameters] reformulation, we would not say, as scientists, that a person follows the rule of phrase structure (1) and the rules of passive and question-formation to yield (2):

$$VP \rightarrow V \; NP \; C \qquad (1)$$

who was persuaded to like them (2)

Rather, the person uses the lexical properties of *persuade* under the projection principle, and the principles of Case adjacency, Move-α, binding theory, and so on, with values of the parameters fixed in a particular way.

*As you couldn't possibly have failed tŏ observe, Dear Player, we are still in that area of The Garden where Cataclysmic Change is taking place. Well-known landmarks disappear under your very nose. Old forks fade away, whilst new ones appear in unexpected places. Unknown pitfalls and traps pose additional perils. Dead ends and dreadful drops, never dreamt of, are being readied in defiant disregard of your presence. But this is part of The Challenge of The Game: to stay on your feet when, in The Garden, gravity seems to have lost its grip and dimensions appear dismantled.*

*If, Panting Player, you could live only in a world where east was guaranteed to be always east and west always west, running The Maze is sure to scar your mind. What's that? Oh, you're asking yourself if radically changing The Garden without warning isn't rather like the petulant ploy of the child that tilts the chess-board to cover up its imminent defeat? No, that – I fear – is too shallow a reading of my story: so far, every major alteration has made The Garden more of a marvel, The Game more of a menace.*

2.7 Underlying the conceptual distinctions used by Chomsky in articulating his conception of language acquisition, knowledge of language/grammar and language use are a number of more fundamental distinctions concerning **the nature of mind in general**. It is with these distinctions that we will concern ourselves in the present section. They are drawn by Chomsky in his attempts to shed light on two topics in particular: the 'mental' character of mind, and the modularity of mind. Let us start with the former topic.

*2.7.1* The first distinction relevant to Chomsky's conception of the nature of mind is that of *mind vs body*. It has traditionally been assumed that mind and body represent two different kinds of entities: the former a 'nonphysical' or 'nonmaterial' entity, the latter a 'physical' or 'material' entity. Chomsky, however, does not operate with this traditional distinction between mind and body. Thus, he (1980a: 5) states that

> When I use such terms as 'mind', 'mental representation', 'mental computation', and the like, I am keeping to the level of abstract characterization of the properties of certain physical mechanisms, as yet almost entirely unknown. There is no further ontological import in such references to mind and mental representations and acts.

Chomsky, thus, uses 'mind' and other derivative expressions to talk at a certain level about properties of a physical entity, identified by himself (1980a: 31) as the brain: 'we may think of the study of mental faculties as actually being a study of the body – specifically the brain – conducted at a certain level of abstraction.'

These expressions are not intended to denote, directly or indirectly, properties or parts of something nonphysical. In fact, by using these expressions, Chomsky (1982: 34) claims not to commit himself to either dualism or monism:

> I think that there is nothing that we are doing that leads you to dualism, but there is nothing that disproves it either. We can simply understand all this talk about the mind as talk at an appropriate level of abstraction about properties of some physical systems of the brain. So it seems to me that mental talk is not inherently dualistic any more than talk about programs and computers is dualistic. I am really using that phrase to head off the assumption that since we are talking about the mind we are committed to dualism. We are not committed to its negation either; we are not committed to monism.

That Chomsky does not operate with the traditional distinction between mind and body is clear also from the way in which he (1980a: 39) extends the use of the expression 'organ' to apply to mental faculties as well:

We may usefully think of the language faculty, the number faculty, and others, as 'mental organs', analogous to the heart or the visual system or the system of motor coordination and planning. There appears to be no clear demarcation line between physical organs, perceptual and motor systems, and cognitive faculties in the respects in question.

As regards the language faculty, Chomsky (1983: 76) considers it to be a 'mental organ', hastening to warn that 'of course it is not an organ in the sense that we can delimit it physically'. 'But', he thinks, 'the growth of this capacity has the general characteristics of the growth of [physical] organs'.

*So, the traditional 'mind vs body' fork is absent from The Garden, a fact not noticed by certain Piqued Players. Hahn (1978: 136), for example, has claimed that 'Like Descartes, as [Donald Griffen] says, Chomsky implies, if he doesn't assert outright, that animals are machines.' The Master (1980a: 256) was 'surprised' by this Animalist Action, but did not experience it as a Body Blow: 'Since the inadequacies of Cartesian mechanism have been familiar for centuries, it is difficult to see why anyone should assume that animals are Cartesian automata. Surely I do not.'*

*By postulating mental faculties, The Master (1980a: 6) does not indicate that he believes 'that physics has come to an end'. In fact, he thinks:*

> *It may be that contemporary natural science already provides principles adequate for the understanding of mind. Or perhaps principles now unknown enter into the functioning of the human or animal minds, in which case the notion of 'physical body' must be extended, as has often happened in the past, to incorporate entities and principles of hitherto unrecognized character.*

*If the notion of 'physical body' could be extended in this way, the 'mind–body' problem would, on The Master's (1980a: 6) view, 'be solved in something like the way in which the problem of the motion of the heavenly bodies was solved, by invoking principles that seemed incomprehensible or even abhorrent to the scientific imagination of an earlier generation'.*[76]

*If, Dear Player, at the 'mind vs body' fork you can suggest no other move than being beastly in a mechanistic mode, it would be wise to proceed to the next bifurcation.*

2.7.2    To clarify his conception of mind and mental faculties, Chomsky draws the distinction *physical structures of the brain vs abstract structures of the mind*. According to him (1980b: 46; 1983: 81–2; 124–5; 1986: 38, 221), knowledge of language (or grammar) can in principle be characterized at either a concrete or an abstract level. At the concrete level, the initial and attained states can ultimately be characterized in a 'nonintensional idiom' by the brain sciences in terms of physical structures. These structures have a neurophysiological/neurological or genetic character, depending on the state of the language faculty that is being characterized. Since little is known about the physical structure of the brain, linguists, on Chomsky's (1983: 82) view, 'can only speak of the conditions that the physical structures must meet'. This they do at the second, abstract, level – where mentalistic (linguistic) theories, using an 'intensional idiom', attempt to describe the initial and attained states of the language faculty in terms of abstract, mental, structures.

Chomsky characterizes the relationship between the concrete, physical, structures of the brain and the abstract, mental, structures of the mind from two complementary points of view. On the one hand, he says that 'mental structures can be regarded as characterizations of certain physical systems' (1980b: 47). On the other hand, he says that neurophysiological/physical mechanisms/systems 'realize' abstract, mental, structures (1980b: 55). As noted by Chomsky (1983: 82), however, at present

> We simply don't have the kind of evidence to tell us how the abstract structures might be represented in the concrete physical system. However, that doesn't mean we should stop working on the problem. I think we can go rather far in terms of the limited sorts of evidence available to impose some fairly narrow and specific conditions on what this physical system must be doing.

Synoptically, the mutual interrelatedness of the two levels of abstract, mental, structures and physical mechanisms has recently been characterized by Chomsky (1986: 38–9) in the following way:

> We observed that it is a task for the brain sciences to explain the properties and principles discovered in the study of the mind. More accurately, the interdependency of the brain sciences and the study of mind is reciprocal. The theory of mind aims to determine the properties of the initial state $S_0$ and each attainable state $S_L$ of the language faculty, and the brain sciences seek to discover the mechanisms of the brain that are the physical realizations of these states. There is a common enterprise: to discover the correct characterization of the language faculty in its initial and attained states, to discover the truth about the language faculty. This enterprise is conducted at several levels: an abstract characterization in the theory of mind, and an inquiry into mechanisms in the brain sciences.

*Recall, Dear Player, that at the fork 'conscious vs unconscious knowledge' (section 2.5.5) we came across the blood-trail of a number of players who had launched a series of abortive Accessibility Assaults on The Master. One of them, a player of some persistence, we now find back in action at the 'mental structure vs physical mechanism' fork. It is Searle (1980: 38), of course, laying yet another Accessibility Ambush, deftly disguised this time as a Causation Challenge:*

> *Now, Chomsky's claim is that there is another level of rules beyond all possible introspection – but not neurophysiological, either. My claim is simply that any evidence for such a level would have to show its reality by showing its causal efficacy, and Chomsky has not said anything to show this – or, in this article [i.e., Chomsky 1980b], even indicated any awareness of the problem.*

*The Master, however, not exactly being Searle's sucker, was quick to spot the hidden hazard. Asked where the disagreement between Searle and himself was located, he (1980b: 56) commented as follows:*

*We can disentangle it from Searle's statement that 'Chomsky's claim is that there is another level of rules beyond all possible introspection but not neurophysiological either' (my emphasis); that is, a level of rules that is neither mental nor physiological in the sense just described. True, the rules of grammar and of UG that I postulate are not 'neurophysiological', but rather neurophysiologically realized, in the sense that both he and I agree to be legitimate. Why then are these rules not at Searle's 'mental level'? Precisely because they are 'beyond all possible introspection'; that is the only relevant property that they lack. Once again, as in his original article, Searle has been trapped by his completely unwarranted assumption that rules can be attributed at the 'mental level of characterization' only if they are open to introspection.*

*If I were a betting man, Dear Player, I wouldn't put my money on your slipping an accessibility thrust past The Master's guard. And why would anyone wish to believe that by repeated use a blunt foil develops a piercing point? Blood-sport, I think you will agree, is not about being at the wrong end of the blood-spoor.*

2.7.3   Central to Chomsky's general conception of mind and language is the conceptual distinction *modularity vs uniformity*. We will first consider the general import of this distinction and then proceed to a number of more specific distinctions that derive from it. Chomsky (1980a: 41–7, 89–91; 1981b: 7) assumes that the human mind is modular: 'I am tentatively assuming the mind to be modular in structure, a system of interacting subsystems that have their own special properties' (1980a: 89). The modularity of the mind is manifested in a variety of distinct individual modules – 'mental capacities', 'mental structures', 'cognitive faculties', in Chomsky's terminology. On Chomsky's view, the mind thus is not a single uniform, homogeneous system characterized by a single set of general principles/properties. Rather, the mind is a whole of interacting subsystems – mental faculties, capacities and structures – each with its own specific properties/principles that do not generalize to other mental modules. Taken as a whole, the mind on this view is characterized by a diversity of heterogeneous module-specific properties/principles. Uniformity (together with the associated homogeneity) represents the opposite view. For the mind to be modular in structure is, on Chomsky's view (1980a: 41), for it to be much like the body – which, after all, is a whole of distinct but interacting subsystems (e.g., the eye and the heart).

Now, in terms of Chomsky's conception of modularity as it applies to language, the mind is modular in various states or at various levels – a view reflected by some of the conceptual distinctions presented in earlier paragraphs.

First, as we saw in section 2.3.3 above, so far as language acquisition is concerned, Chomsky claims that the initial state of the mind is modular in that he (1980a: 47) provides for the existence of a distinct language faculty within the mind. In so doing, he expressly rejects the view that there are

> uniform principles of learning, accommodation, assimilation, abstraction, induction, strategy, or whatever that simply apply to different stimulus materials to provide our knowledge of the behavior of objects in physical space, our knowledge that certain strings of words do or do not have certain meanings, and so on.

Putting it another way, he (1980a: 245) rejects the 'doctrine of uniformity of mind' which claims that

> the various cognitive structures develop in a uniform way – that is, there are general principles of learning that underlie all of these systems, accounting for their development: 'multipurpose learning strategies', as they are sometimes called, that apply 'across the board'.

What, then, is the view he endorses? Here, positively speaking, is the gist of Chomsky's (1980a: 245) conception of the modularity of the mind's initial state:

> various 'mental organs' develop in specific ways, each in accordance with the genetic program, much as bodily organs develop; and . . . multipurpose learning strategies are no more likely to exist than general principles of 'growth of organs' that account for the shape, structure, and function of the kidney, the liver, the heart, the visual system, and so forth. Such

principles may exist at the level of cellular biology, but there is no reason to anticipate a 'higher level' theory of general organ growth. Rather, specific subcomponents of the genetic program, coming into operation as the organism matures, determine the specific properties of these systems. The same may well be true of the basic structures involved in our mental life.

Second, as observed in sections 2.5.15 and 2.5.16 above, so far as language is concerned, Chomsky claims that the mind is modular also in its relatively stable, steady state. In a tentative early formulation Chomsky (1980a: 58) adumbrated this claim as follows: 'we should not exclude the possibility that what we normally think of as knowledge of language might consist of quite disparate cognitive systems that interweave in normal cognitive development.' The 'cognitive systems' or modules making up knowledge of language include, as we noted above, grammatical competence, pragmatic competence and aspects of the conceptual system.

Third, on Chomsky's view both universal grammar (the language faculty in its initial state) and grammatical competence (the steady state of the language faculty) exhibit an internal structure that is modular. As for universal grammar, Chomsky (1981b: 5) distinguishes, on the one hand, a variety of interacting subsystems within (the core grammar part of) the initial state of the language faculty or universal grammar. These modules include 'subcomponents of the rule system of grammar': the lexicon, the syntax (further divided into the categorial and transformational subcomponents), the PF (phonetic form)-component and the LF (logical form)-component. On the other hand, universal grammar also includes a further class of modules, namely 'subsystems of principles': bounding theory, government theory, $\theta$-theory, binding theory, Case theory and control theory.[77] As for the steady state of the language faculty, the rules of grammatical competence exhibit a modular structure in that various subsets of them belong to the various subcomponents listed above.

A last general point that needs to be mentioned here concerns the metascientific status of Chomsky's conception of modularity. He (1980a: 47) takes the question of modularity to represent a 'relatively straightforward empirical question'. And on his judgement 'the available evidence seems to . . . favor a modular approach'.

*Perhaps, Dear Player, it is time to remind you again that not all aggressive action in The Game is of the rough-and-tumble type. The Garden has also witnessed pieces of prudent play. For example, Rosenthal (1980: 32ff) made a couple of mindful moves at the 'modularity vs uniformity' fork. He noted that a distinction may be drawn between 'initial modularity' (i.e., modularity of the initial state of the language faculty) and 'attained modularity' (i.e., modularity of the steady state). He, moreover, drew attention to 'a striking pattern of inference' in The Master's work, 'namely, the passage from "diversity in fundamental principles of capacities and mental structures attained" to some corresponding diversity in initial and innate mental structures'.*

*Rosenthal did not reject the use of this pattern of inference in the case of the language faculty. The inference from the principles governing mature mental capacities and structures to those governing initial mental structures was, however, he considered, 'far less credible in the case of the other "mental faculties" that Chomsky touches on, such as "knowledge of . . . music, of mathematics, of the behavior of objects, of social structure, of human characteristics, and so on"' (1980: 33). Rosenthal (1980: 33) aimed his scepticism specifically at The Master's treatment of the 'number faculty':*

*For he [i.e., Chomsky] claims that '(t)he capacity to deal with the number system . . . is surely unlearned in its essentials'. If Chomsky has in mind, here, either the 'second-order sense of "capacity"' that he isolates at the outset or the sense of 'capacity' as a mental faculty, his claim that our capacity to deal with the number system is unlearned will be trivial and uninformative; for it is a matter of meaning that, in these senses, capacities are unlearned. So Chomsky must have in mind the more interesting but surprising claim that our mature capacity to deal with the number system, though in many respects the product of training, is, 'in its essentials', innate. Without some idea of what the 'essentials' of this capacity are, however, even this claim would lack significant import. But Chomsky tells us that '(t)he very essence of the number system is the concept of adding one, indefinitely', presumably inviting us to infer from the 'very essence of the number system' to an understanding of what the 'capacity to deal with the number system . . . (is) in its essentials'. Chomsky is of course right that 'the concept of adding one, indefinitely' is sufficient to distinguish our number system from the rudimentary numerical abilities of other terrestrial species. But it is far from clear that understanding the essence of our number system can, by itself, help us to understand our capacity to deal with that system.*

*Despite considering these and other comments by Rosenthal to be 'thought-provoking', The Master (1980b: 52) stood his ground, apparently giving as good as he had received:*

*With regard to the number faculty, we [Chomsky and Rosenthal] agree that the concept of adding one, indefinitely, distinguishes our number system from abilities of other known species, but Rosenthal adds that understanding this does not 'by itself, help us to understand our capacity to deal with [the number] system.' I think it does help but does not exhaust the matter. It does not seem to me a 'surprising claim' that our mature capacity to deal with the number system is, in its essentials, innate. On the contrary, it is difficult to imagine by what inductive, associative, or other 'learning process' this capacity might have derived from experience (though, as I noted, it may be triggered by experience). I've heard reports that aborigines lacking any relevant experience master the number system very easily when they enter a market economy, which would suggest, if true, that the capacities are latent, ready to be put to use. The lack of diversity, which Rosenthal notes, does not seem to me to be a crucial factor; identification of common properties of a variety of diverse systems is not a necessary condition for attribution of innate structure.*

*But who was the one to draw blood? Did The Master deflect Rosenthal's main thrust as expressed in the latter's 'It is far from clear that . . . ' remark? Or did The Master merely sidetrack his attacker, deftly dealing with a different point raised by Rosenthal about innateness?[78] To be able to judge the reach of Rosenthal's Rapier, we shall have to move on to the next fork.*

2.7.4  What we have to consider next is Chomsky's distinction *modularity vs innateness*. From preceding sections it has become clear that modularity and innateness, on Chomsky's view, represent distinct aspects of mental faculties. The arguments for modularity and innateness differ accordingly, as observed by Chomsky (1980a: 41; 1980b: 3). Linguists arrive at the conclusion that 'intrinsic' or innate structure is rich by the argument from poverty of the stimulus.[79] By contrast, the conclusion that innate structure is 'diverse' or modular is based on an argument from the apparent diversity of fundamental principles of capacities and mental structures attained. But how exactly are the various positions on innateness and modularity interlinked? To this question, Chomsky (1980b: 3) provides the following answer:

> One might hold that there is rich innate structure but little or no modularity. But there is a relation between the views, in part conceptual. Insofar as there is little in the way of innate structure, what develops in the mind of an individual will be a homogeneous system derived by the application to experience of common principles that constitute the innate endowment. Such differentiation as there may be will reflect differentiation in the environment. Correspondingly, the belief that various systems of mind are organized along quite different principles leads to the natural conclusion that these systems are intrinsically determined, not simply the result of common mechanisms of learning and growth. It is not surprising, then, to find that opinions 'cluster'. Those who tend toward the assumption of modularity tend also to assume rich innate structure, while those who assume general multipurpose learning mechanisms tend to deny modularity.

Whereas rationalists such as Chomsky belong to the former of these two categories, empiricists such as Skinner and constructivists such as Piaget represent the latter category.[80]


*Having studied the layout of The Garden with considerable care, Rosenthal (1980: 33) accused The Master of mapping the 'modularity vs innateness' fork in a less than accurate way. Specifically, Rosenthal contended that The Master's conception of the conceptual distinction had more substance to it than suggested by The Master's 'clustering' formulation quoted above:*

114

*Chomsky evidently uses 'intrinsic' in a way that implies innateness; for richness of 'intrinsic structures' amounts to the richness of initial structures. But then it is these initial structures that, on the thesis of modularity, are said to be diverse; the 'diversity in fundamental principles of capacities and mental structures attained' is offered as evidence for the diversity of rich initial structures. So it is not simply that 'opinions [about modularity and rich initial structures] cluster'; modularity actually includes the assumption of rich initial structures.*

*To challenge The Master, as Rosenthal did, on the accuracy of his own map of The Garden is a daring deed. Few have got away with this kind of thing in the history of the hunt. And, judged on face value, the following response by The Master (1980b: 51–2) seems to indicate that Rosenthal has joined those who have fallen along the way:*

*Suppose we reject initial modularity and accept attained modularity. Then we are assuming that 'such differentiation as there may be [in the state attained] will reflect differentiation in the environment' (p. 3 of the target article); that is, that attained modularity reflects environmental modularity. I find this implausible in the cases mentioned, because of the argument from poverty of the stimulus. Thus, if it is true that the environment does not yield the postulated principles of UG (say, locality and opacity) or the rigidity principle and others involved in our knowledge about objects . . . , then attained modularity reflects initial modularity in these respects. While these remarks do not establish my conclusion that attained modularity in these respects reflects initial modularity, they do at least indicate how one could proceed to verify this conclusion. It is this line of reasoning that underlies the 'striking pattern of inference' to which Rosenthal calls attention, namely, from attained to initial modularity.*

*This manoeuvre by The Master, however, did not meet Rosenthal's challenge, namely that The Master's map of the 'modularity vs innateness' fork misrepresents reality. The Master's manoeuvre makes sense only if we accept that, without saying so, he conceded the point challenged by Rosenthal. (The Master, of course, would*

115

*be less than happy if in The Annals of The Game the fork under consideration were to be derisively described as The Modulateness Marshmallow.) The objective of the manoeuvre, in fact, is to defend the stronger link, established by himself, between modularity and innateness. But it is not the nature of this stronger link that was challenged by Rosenthal: he actually had no objection to its being established in the case of language. And he said so.*

*Why have I recounted this 'meaningless manoeuvring', this 'pointless play' by The Master? I have done so, Puzzled Player, to set you a tiny teaser: to see how good you have become at reading The Game. And, frankly, your misdiagnosis, signalled by the clanger 'meaningless manoeuvring', leaves me feeling rather less than encouraged. You appear to be unaware, unfortunately not 'blissfully', of the following Facts of Play:*

1  *'Meaningless manoeuvring' may mask what the beaten would bitterly brand as 'Machiavellian Machinations'.*

2  *If you can't be defeated at what you are good at, you will be beaten at what you are bad at or can be made out to look bad at.*

3  *Victory must be visible.*

*Want me to spell it out even more? Really, now . . . Well, you see, Rosenthal had gained the upper hand, albeit on a modest scale, on a minor point concerning the accuracy of The Master's mapping of The Garden. The Master, however, 'manoeuvred' in such a way as to make it seem as if Rosenthal had challenged him on a different point, a major one, and moreover, a point which The Master could be seen to be 'winning'. Never forget that The Game is very much a Spectator Sport, played in accordance with the Principle of Perceptibility:*

*Victories unseen are victories unwon.*

2.7.5   Returning now to Chomsky's view that the mind may be modular in more than one respect, let us consider this further by taking up the distinction *external autonomy vs internal autonomy*, a distinction used in the discussion between Chomsky (1982: 115) and Huybregts/Van Riemsdijk. External autonomy represents

Chomsky's view that formal grammar is autonomous from other human systems and capacities. Formal grammar, in this context, includes syntax, the abstract part of phonology, and those aspects of meaning determined by syntactic configuration. Chomsky (1982: 114) has also used the term 'syntax' in a special way to refer inclusively to formal grammar. He has moreover suggested that a better term for this system might be 'the computational component of the language faculty'. Within this framework Chomsky (1982: 114) has formulated the 'thesis of [external] autonomy of syntax' as follows:

It says that there exists a faculty of the mind which corresponds to the computational aspects of language, meaning the system of rules that give certain representations and derivations.

The parts of this autonomous system would, on Chomsky's (1982: 114) view, include: 'Presumably the base rules, the transformational rules, the rules that map S-structures onto phonological representation, and onto logical forms . . . '

The thesis of (external) autonomy has, especially on earlier formulations,[81] been stated also in terms of a notion of primitive terms: formal grammar is autonomous or forms an autonomous system in the sense that its primitive terms cannot be derived from any more fundamental or inclusive system such as one that encompasses not only language but also other human systems, capacities or faculties.

In both its earlier and the later formulation, the autonomy thesis is intended to bear on the initial and the steady state of the language faculty. Thus, having considered the question of the autonomy of the steady state, Chomsky (1982: 115) notes that 'there is an analogous question about the autonomy of the language acquisition device.' And in section 2.3.3 above, we saw that on Chomsky's view, this device – or the initial state of the language faculty – does not represent a special case of some general, non-language-specific learning strategy, device or faculty.

Among the things not implied by Chomsky's autonomy thesis, two need special mention. On the one hand, by depicting 'syntax' (in the special sense) or formal grammar as a 'self-contained', 'autonomous' system, Chomsky (1982: 115) does not mean to say that as a system it is *isolated* from all other systems: 'Undoubtedly, the system interacts with other systems, but the interaction is more or less at the periphery.' On the other hand, by calling formal grammar an autonomous system, Chomsky does not mean to say that it is without any physical basis. As noted by Newmeyer (1983: 4),

> the autonomy hypothesis does not preclude the possibility that formal grammar is rooted in neurology; far from it: generative grammarians look with pleasure on the growing evidence that there are neurological structures specific to grammar . . .

This brings us to the opposite conception, i.e., the non-(external) autonomy conception, which also has a variety of articulations. Each of these, however, attributes to the non-autonomy conception what Newmeyer (1983: 96ff) describes as 'the hypothesis that grammatical facts can, in large part or in totality, be reduced to facts derivable from the properties of some *general* human attribute (i.e., an attribute not specific to language)'. In the more recent Chomskyan idiom, the non-autonomy conception would deny the existence of a self-contained computational faculty of mind. The categories and principles attributed to such a faculty by Chomsky would on this non-autonomy view be artefacts that may be reduced to or derived from 'extragrammatical' or non-language-specific principles or attributes such as general principles of communication, cognitive functioning (including those involved in 'perceptual processing'), discourse, and so on.[82] Thus, a principle such as Subjacency would on a non-autonomy view be claimed to derive from, say, one or more general principles of perceptual processing not specific to language.

The majority of present-day linguists and psychologists would probably hold one or another version of the non-autonomy conception of grammar. With reference to the field of developmental psychology, Chomsky (1982: 115) puts this point in the following way:

> I'm sure that if you counted noses, people in developmental psychology would overwhelmingly doubt this autonomy thesis. I don't think they have a coherent argument, or a coherent alternative, but I don't doubt that they'd vote against it if asked to vote.

Let us next consider Chomsky's thesis of internal autonomy. This thesis states, on a recent general formulation of Chomsky's (1982: 114), that the rules of the autonomous computational faculty have an internal autonomy in that they have their own properties and in that, as they function, they refer just to the representations they themselves construct and not to elements outside the subcomponent of the computational faculty of which they form part. For example, Chomsky (1982: 116) considers it a good 'working hypothesis' that 'the rules mapping S-structure onto phonetic representation ought to be completely autonomous from the rules mapping S-structure onto logical form'.

The thesis of internal autonomy has a special case, put forward by Chomsky (e.g., 1957: 92ff) as a working hypothesis more than two decades ago. In regard to content it claimed that syntax was independent of meaning. This claim – referred to simply as 'the autonomy thesis' – has been put forward in two distinct versions, as pointed out by Chomsky (1975b: 178):

> We can distinguish, then, two versions of an autonomy thesis: an absolute thesis, which holds that the theory of linguistic form, including the concept 'formal grammar' and all levels apart from semantic representation, can be fully defined in terms of formal primitives, and a weaker version, which holds that this is true only conditionally, with certain parameters, perhaps localized in the dictionary.

The latter version of the autonomy thesis Chomsky (1975b: 180) has called 'the parameterized autonomy thesis'. And 'the problem' with it, he (1975b: 178) observes, 'will be to determine the specific ways in which semantic information enters into the determination of a formal grammar'. Chomsky (1975b: 178) has found the parameterized autonomy thesis more plausible than the absolute autonomy thesis. In regard to the problem of whether semantic parameters and questions of fact and belief enter into the choice of formal grammar, he noted, for example, 'that the significant question with regard to the autonomy thesis may not be a question of "yes" or "no", but rather of "more" or "less", or more correctly, "where" and "how much"'. When considering Chomsky's 'autonomy thesis', it is thus of some importance to keep in mind his distinction *the absolute autonomy thesis vs the parameterized autonomy thesis*.[83]

119

*The autonomy fork, Dear Player, presents an opportunity to place The Game in a wider historical context. Perhaps you have already wondered how The Game is related to the hostilities that marked earlier periods in the history of generative grammar in general and Chomskyan linguistics in particular. Two such periods immediately come to mind: what have been dubbed the Linguistic Wars and the Chomskyan Revolution.*

*Chomsky's autonomy thesis was one of the issues over which the Linguistic Wars were fought in the late sixties and early seventies between what Newmeyer has called the Good Guys and the Bad Guys.*[84] *The Linguistic Wars represent what Newmeyer (1980: 132) has characterized as 'the state of hostility which existed between the two rival camps of theoreticians' both of which considered themselves 'generative grammarians'. Here, we can't go either into the issues that fuelled the fighting, or into the reasons why the Good Guys, led by The Master, got the better of the Bad Guys.*[85] *For our purpose, it is sufficient to note that the Linguistic Wars represented a form of faction fighting between bands of brothers bound by blood if not brains. Although these Wars did see a number of notable duels between individuals, in essence they involved collective crusading by mobilized masses.*[86]

*The Chomskyan Revolution, likewise, was a collective campaign – fought in the late fifties and early sixties by the first generation of generativists, the Rationalist Revolutionaries, against a structuralist-empiricist Greying Old Guard.*[87] *What The Master has called 'the first conceptual shift' (cf. section 2.5.13 above) was a result of the Revolution. If the Linguistic Wars represented a period of intra-tribal trauma, the Chomskyan Revolution was one of inter-tribal turbulence. Like the former, the latter, of course, had its leaders who were not averse to man-to-man combat, but both, in essence, were manifestations of mass militancy.*[88]

*This is where The Game has been different: a form of private prowling, a sort of solitary stalking, of The Master and by The Master. The Game, as you should know by now, is a matter of mind against mind in a maze. It demands more in the way of skill and steel, craft and cool. And because its consequences are not cushioned by any collectivity, The Game is incomparably more dangerous and, indeed, more deadly than either a war or a revolution.*[89]

2.7.6    Underlying Chomsky's position on modularity and autonomy is the fundamental distinction *the form/structure of a mental faculty/entity vs the function of a mental faculty/entity*.[90] In regard to this distinction, Chomsky holds the view that structure does not reflect function in any direct way, or, in other words, function does not directly determine structure. One of the contexts that provides a good illustration of Chomsky's use of this distinction is his (1980a: 246) discussion of the belief in the 'simplicity' of mental structures. On Chomsky's interpretation, this belief – which is related to the doctrine that mental structure is uniform, i.e. non-modular – is commonly expressed by those linguists who claim that the principles of grammar cannot be 'too complex' or 'too abstract'. Such linguists take the position that these principles must directly reflect properties of sound or meaning or, significantly, that these principles must be determined in some (essentially simple) manner by 'functional considerations'.

Chomsky, however, rejects this position and along with it the belief in the 'simplicity' of mental structures. On the one hand, he notes, the matter of (non-)simplicity cannot be decided by a priori arguments. On the other hand, it seems to him (1980a: 246)

that recent work tends to support a rather different view: that rules of syntax and phonology, at least, are organized in terms of 'autonomous' principles of mental computation and do not reflect in any simple way the properties of the phonetic or semantic 'substance' or contingencies of language use.

*The 'form vs function' fork has for years been the focus of ferocious fighting in The Garden. In reviewing some of the episodes at this fork, a certain chronicler of the (pre-)history of The Game has been prompted to proclaim that*

The publication of Syntactic Structures, *besides ushering in a new era of linguistic research, also engendered a new era of belligerent polemics. Both generativists and their opponents indulged in rhetorical excesses; certainly no one would deny that some of the more vigorous defenses of generative grammar exceeded the normal bounds of partisan scholarship. But it* seems fair to say that the reactive literature has not in general balanced its belligerence with positive content.[91]

The way in which Searle (1972) stormed The Master at the 'form vs function' fork should give you some idea, Dear Player, of the verbal violence that the fork has seen. The springboard for Searle's (1972) assault was the assumption that the following represented 'the common-sense picture of human language':

> The purpose of language is communication in much the same sense that the purpose of the heart is to pump blood. In both cases it is possible to study the structure independently of function but pointless and perverse to do so, since structure and function so obviously interact. We communicate primarily with other people, but also with ourselves, as when we talk or think in words to ourselves.

Searle not only labelled The Master 'perverse' for believing in the autonomy thesis – which 'runs counter' to this 'ordinary, plausible and common-sense picture of human language'. Searle not only depicted The Master as being 'peculiar and eccentric' in insisting that the structure of language should be studied apart from its communicative function. Searle not only lashed out at The Master for having 'arbitrarily assumed' that 'use and structure . . . [do not] . . . influence each other'. He damningly proclaimed the greatest 'defect of the Chomskyan theory' to be The Master's 'failure to see the essential connection between language and communication, between meaning and speech acts'.

The Master's (1975a: 56ff) response was clinical, its consequences crushing – and far too comprehensive to be recounted here in their full complexity. A glimpse at two of the major moves made by The Master should suffice to convince you, Dear Player, of the counter-productivity of this kind of Communication Commotion. On the one hand, The Master (1975: 56–7) challenged Searle's view that the 'essential purpose' of language was communication, pointing out that

> There is, in fact, a very respectable tradition, which I have reviewed elsewhere (n. 30), that regards as a vulgar distortion the 'instrumental view' of language as 'essentially' a means of communication, or a means to achieve given ends. Language, it is argued, is 'essentially' a system for expression of thought.

*The Master observed, in addition, that the notion of 'communication' had, in Searle's scope-enlarging hands, been 'deprived of its essential and interesting character', since its scope now included 'communication with oneself', or 'thinking in words', as well as 'communication with others'.*[92]

*On the other hand, The Master (1975a: 57ff) argued that there was no way in which certain general properties – e.g. structure-dependence*[93] *– of 'an interesting class of linguistic rules' could be accounted for in terms of 'communicative purpose':*

> *let us try to account for it [i.e., 'structure-dependence'] in terms of communication. I see no way of doing so. Surely this principle enters into the function of language; we might well study the ways in which it does. But a language could function for communication (or otherwise) just as well with structure-independent rules, so it would seem. For a mind differently constituted, structure-independent rules would be far superior, in that they require no abstract analysis of a sentence beyond words. I think that the example is typical. Where it can be shown that structures serve a particular function, that is a valuable discovery. To account for or somehow explain the structure of UG, or of particular grammars, on the basis of functional considerations is a pretty hopeless prospect, I would think; it is, perhaps, even 'perverse' to assume otherwise. Perhaps Searle has something else in mind, but I frankly see no issue here, no counterproposal that has any plausibility to the picture Searle rejects.*

*Searle, of course, is by no means the only player whose curious commitment to 'communication' has caused the kind of commotion considered above. On the contrary, this is a ploy to whose attractions – fatal, I must admit – a great many players have fallen prey. Their fate, Dear Player, carries a warning carved out by The Master on a collective tombstone:*

> *Sigh here, where some Comrades of Communication lie,*
> *as this true stone engraves what they now signify:*
> *commitment triggered them to join the Garden Game;*
> *imperfect competence wrote 'finis' to their fame.*[94]

*With this, Dear Player, we have completed the first lap of our trial run through The Garden. Not without expertise, I make bold to say, you have been led along labyrinthine lanes, through fortified forks, past piked pitfalls and around deep drops. But, overwhelmed as well you might be, this is still not enough. What you have heard and seen does not yet suffice to secure survival, should you go solo. The Master's is a garden where every shadow has its surprise – its power to shock, to shake and, above all, to shatter the Presumptuous Player. So gird up your loins for a further work-out in The Garden's winding ways.*

# 3

## The Terrain of Theory

*Gardens, it is naively believed, are not designed in different dimensions. So the discovery that The Garden has a steeply sloping structure comes to some as a sobering surprise, but strikes into the hearts of others a dread of their own inevitable and imminent demise. Laid out with forks and lanes at not just one, but at several levels, The Garden is seen at last for what it is – a layered labyrinth. The lanes through which you have been led up to now, Pupil Player, all link forks at the same level: language. Let us think of this as the middle level, the Mentalistic Maze, and move one level up to the Terrain of Theory, the lofty level of superstructure from which The Master minds The Maze.*

*In taking you through the Terrain of Theory – or the Theatre of Theory, as it is called by some – I will have to be a little less lenient. You see, in proper play, Pampered Pupils tend to be turned into Pulverized Players. So, from now on I will more often insist upon your own reading of a fork, your own proposal for a piece of probing play. There is a consoling consideration, however: the penalty for committing a folly in the Theatre of Theory is less lethal than that for making a mess in the Maze of Mentalism. In The Maze the price is paid in intellectual guts and gore; in The Theatre it is paid in pride and prestige. But in the end, of course, the question of which is worse – a maiming of the mind or a pounding of the personality – is entirely 'academic'.*

To answer the questions about the nature of knowledge of language, about the acquisition of language and about the use of language (questions (1) (a)–(c) in section 1.2), Chomskyan linguists resort to theory construction. In the present section we will consider the conceptual distinctions that define the various types of theory which these linguists formulate, and we will consider the nature of the types of statement which they make in so doing. A first cluster of distinctions will bear on what are known as theories of grammar, a second on linguistic universals and a third on descriptive generative grammars.

**3.1**   Central amongst the theories constructed by Chomskyan linguists is **the theory of grammar** or **the theory of language** or **the general-linguistic theory**. This is the theory that has to provide an answer to question (1) (b) of section 1.2: 'How is knowledge of language acquired?' So let us consider the cluster of distinctions that elucidate the nature and the aims of theories of grammar/ general linguistic theories.

*3.1.1*   Let us begin with the fundamental conceptual distinction *a theory of grammar vs a generative grammar of a particular language*. The function of a theory of grammar – referred to also as 'a general linguistic theory', 'a theory of language', 'a theory of linguistic structure', 'a universal grammar' – is to provide an answer to the question 'How is knowledge of language (or, rather, grammar) acquired?'. To construct a theory of grammar is, therefore, to propose a solution to what has been called in section 2.1.1 above 'the logical problem of language acquisition'. The theory of grammar pursues this aim by using various kinds of linguistic universals to characterize or describe the initial, innate state of the language faculty. Recently, Chomsky (1986: 3) has formulated this point in the following terms:

> The nature of this faculty [i.e. the language faculty], is the subject matter of a general theory of linguistic structure that aims to discover the framework of principles and elements common to attainable human languages; this theory is now often called 'universal grammar' (UG), adapting a traditional term to a new context of inquiry. UG may be regarded as a characterization of the genetically determined language faculty.

126

A generative grammar of a given particular language – alternatively 'a descriptive grammar' – is a theory that has to present an answer to the question 'What does knowledge of this language consist of?'. A particular generative grammar – another formulation used by Chomsky (1986: 3) – attempts to answer this question by characterizing or describing the stable state of the language faculty of the (idealized) person who knows this language. In conventional terms, a particular generative grammar uses rules (which generate representations) for giving this description or characterization. Speaking in the 'rules' idiom, Chomsky (1980a: 65) has portrayed a particular generative grammar as 'a system of rules that provides representations of sound and meaning'. This conventional characterization, of course, has to be modified in accordance with Chomsky's second conceptual shift. Recall, as we saw in section 2.5.21. above, that this shift involves the replacement of the rule-system model by the principles-and-parameters theory. Within the framework of the new theory a particular generative grammar for a language L has to give an explicit description of how the open parameters have been set for L.

'A no-funk fork, child's play to negotiate.' This, Placid Pupil, is a judgement that has been made before. For more than one impetuous player, however, it has in fact been a faux pas fork. May I remind you, for example, of those who misread The Master's (grammatical) base rules of English as (general linguistic) hypotheses postulating linguistic universals. So at this 'no-sweat' fork a couple of careless combatants committed the First Folly in the Theatre of Theory: bungling the distinction between (the claims expressed by) a theory of grammar and (the claims expressed by) a generative grammar of a particular language.

3.1.2   A second basic distinction at the level of theory is *a theory of grammar vs a theory of language use*. A theory of grammar, we have seen, presents a tentative answer to the logical question of language acquisition. (And a particular generative grammar, in turn, is a theory about the knowledge of grammar or grammatical competence of an ideal speaker of an individual language.) A theory of language use, however, presents a tentative answer to (a subpart of) the question represented as (1) (c) in section 1.2 above: 'How is knowledge of language put to use?' Theories of language use, then, referred to also as 'models of performance', are theories about speech production, speech perception, the structure of memory etc. Such theories are not theories of knowledge, whether innate or acquired knowledge.

Theories of knowledge or competence and theories of use or performance are, nevertheless, clearly interlinked – as is plain from the following remarks by Chomsky (1980a: 225):

> Theories of grammatical and pragmatic competence must find their place in a theory of performance that takes into account the structure of memory, our mode of organizing experience, and so on. Actual investigation of language necessarily deals with performance, with what someone does under specific circumstances. We often attempt to devise modes of inquiry that will reduce to a minimum factors that appear irrelevant to intrinsic competence, so that the data of performance will bear directly on competence, as the object of our inquiry. To the extent that we have an explicit theory of competence, we can attempt to devise performance models to show how this knowledge is put to use.

Chomsky (1980a: 226) is at pains to stress the fact that study of competence and study of performance are mutually supportive:

> Study of performance relies essentially on advances in understanding of competence. But since a competence theory must be incorporated in a performance model, evidence about the actual organization of behavior may prove crucial to advancing the theory of underlying competence. Study of performance and study of competence are mutually supportive.

*'Why should one put up with such a proliferation of theories – theories of grammar, particular generative grammars, theories of use, production, perception and what have you? Why could we not simply have a single general system embracing every aspect of "language" – and communication to boot?' Are you implicitly*

*suggesting, Protesting Player, that theoretical superstructure, as a separate layer of lanes and forks, should be 'cut down to size', 'reduced to sensible proportions'? If so, hold your hatchet! What you suggest will be shown in section 4.2.6 below to be rather more taxing than the simple hacking job you seem to have in mind.*

3.1.3    There is a third basic distinction that is relevant to the characterization of what a theory of grammar is, namely that of *linguistic theory vs the field of linguistics*. We saw in section 2.5.11 above that Chomsky (1965: 3) introduced the idealizations of 'an ideal speaker–listener' and 'a completely homogeneous speech community' by stating that 'Linguistic theory is concerned primarily with an ideal speaker–listener, in a completely homogeneous speech community . . . '. 'Linguistic theory', in this statement, refers to theories of grammar, i.e. theories of competence or theories of knowledge of grammar. 'Linguistic theory' in this statement is not being used as a synonym for 'the field of linguistics'. Thus, Newmeyer (1983: 75) observes that

> the opening words of the paragraph are 'Linguistic theory is concerned', not 'The field of linguistics is concerned'. Chomsky has consistently used the term 'linguistic theory' to refer to theories of grammar (i.e., theories of competence) rather than to refer to *any* work (theoretical or nontheoretical) involving language study.[1]

*'Just another simple, straightforward fork,' I hear you mutter beneath your breath at the bifurcation 'linguistic theory vs the field of linguistics'. But perhaps it might be rewarding not to forget that simplicity, like beauty, is in the mind of the beholder. Many a Patronizing Player, you see, has suffered from voids of vision, a disabling if not deadly defect. This is the reason why Confident Combatants have so often overlooked this fork in its 'splendid simplicity' – an oversight that has caused them to equate 'linguistic theory' with 'the field of linguistics'.*

*And having 'confidently' conflated 'linguistic theory' with 'the field of linguistics', such players have interpreted The Master's statement that 'Linguistic theory is concerned with . . .' in a wacky way. On their reading it would indicate The Master's ignorance or even dismissal of studies of language variation. Incensed by their own disastrous deduction, they have slung terrible taunts at The Master: 'Idealizing Ignoramus', 'Homogeneity Hun' – others, I cannot move myself to mention. As noted by Newmeyer (1983: 75), there is no substance to such charges – they ruinously reflect no more than the erroneous equation 'linguistic theory = field of linguistics'. Evasive action on the part of The Master was not necessary: he (1980a: 25) signalled to everyone with the proper powers of perception that he considers the fact 'that real speech communities are not homogeneous' to be 'obvious', but 'irrelevant' as an objection to the idealization in question.*

*Incidentally, in the system of scoring, the missing of a fork altogether is about as bad a blunder as there could be. In the Mentalistic Maze it means irreversible ruin; in the Terrain of Theory, haunting humiliation. The spectators, Paling Player, you should not forget, make up a callous crowd.*

**3.2** This brings us to the basic components or building blocks of the theory of grammar, statements called **linguistic universals**. We will attempt to get a clearer idea of what such statements are by considering five distinctions that bear on the substance of the claims expressed by them.

*3.2.1* In coming to grips with Chomsky's notion of linguistic universal, a first and fundamental distinction is *linguistic universals vs statements postulating a property common to all languages*. The theory of grammar incorporates linguistic universals such as the thesis of structure-preservingness, Subjacency, the conditions of binding theory and so on. A linguistic universal in Chomskyan linguistics is a statement that attributes a property to the initial state of the language faculty. That is, as noted by Chomsky (1980a: 69), such a statement expresses a claim about the innate basis on which knowledge of language develops. A linguistic universal, in this sense, does not express a claim about a feature that is (expected to be) common to all languages. Specifically, the

130

property postulated by a linguistic universal is not being attributed to the grown or acquired grammars of all human languages.

*In arguing that no evidence at all has been provided for such specific theories of linguistic universals as those advanced by The Master, Stich (1978) seems to have stumbled at the fork of 'linguistic universals vs statements postulating a feature common to all human languages'. Given this player's generally sure-footed style of play, the following response by The Master (1980a: 69) must have caused Stich some pain.*

> *A second point has to do with his [i.e., Stich's] interpretation of the term 'linguistic universals', which is quite different from the usage of the work he criticizes, in which 'universal grammar' is taken to be the set of properties, conditions, or whatever that constitute the 'initial state' of the language learner, hence the basis on which knowledge of language develops. It by no means follows from such an account that there must be specific elements or rules common to all languages, or what he calls 'features' common to all languages, unless we take these 'features' in a suitably abstract manner, in which case, the controversy dissolves.*

*Over the years, many a player has fallen flat on his face at the fork 'linguistic universals vs statements about properties common to all languages'. And prostration, Dear Player, often puts one on the path of permanent paralysis. So, if I were you, I would try not to forget that 'linguistic universals = statements about properties common to all languages' is an Emasculating Equation.*

3.2.2   The substance of the claims expressed by linguistic universals may be further elucidated with the aid of Chomsky's (1980a: 28–9) distinction *claims about biologically necessary properties of language vs claims about logically/conceptually necessary properties of language*. Chomsky (1980a: 29) takes universal grammar to be 'a study of the biologically necessary properties of human language'. These are the genetically determined properties that are, in Chomsky's (1980a: 28) words, 'characteristic

131

of the human species'. As the basic statements making up the theory of grammar or universal grammar, Chomskyan linguistic universals thus express claims about biologically necessary properties of human language. The principle of Subjacency – roughly formulated as (1) below – is an example of a linguistic universal that attempts to capture a biologically necessary property of human language:

(1)        Nothing can be removed from more than
             a single binding category.

Chomskyan linguistic universals, by implication, do not express claims about so-called logically or conceptually necessary properties that 'language as such' must have. Properties of language are, on Chomsky's (1980a: 28–9) formulation, logically or conceptually necessary if they are properties 'such that if a system failed to have them we would simply not call it a language'.

The statement (2) expresses what on this view might, according to Chomsky (1980a: 29), be a logically or conceptually necessary property of language:

(2)     A language must have sentences and words.


*'What on earth could be wrong', you ask, 'with making statements such as (2) about languages?' 'Nothing whatsoever, Prying Player,' The Master would possibly reply. 'But, of course,' he is likely to add, 'making such statements is simply not part of my linguistics.' To make claims about biologically necessary properties of human language is to view universal grammar as an empirical enterprise, as The Master would like to do. However, to make claims about logically or conceptually necessary properties that systems must have to 'qualify' as languages is, on The Master's (1980a: 29) view, not an empirical business: 'It is not an empirical investigation, except insofar as lexicography is an empirical investigation, and must be judged by quite different standards.'*

*So, if one day you would like to try your hand at some Premeditated Play, remind yourself, Plotting Player, that The Master cannot be waylaid either in Logic Lane or in Lexicography Loop. So far as the substance of linguistic universals is concerned, he won't be beaten anywhere but in Biology Bend.*

Before proceeding: there is a secondary, but not unimportant, distinction related to that between biologically and logically/conceptually necessary properties, namely *biologically necessary properties of language vs accidental properties of language*. This further distinction Chomsky (1983: 263) presents as follows:

> As I understand it, his [i.e., Premacks's] question is, what are the universals of language? What are the necessary properties of language that hold, not only by accident, by virtue of the fact that the existing languages are what they are? That is a hard question to answer, but it is possible to proceed to answer it. At that point a move is made which I don't think has any alternatives to it, and which I hardly even regard as an inference. If I assert that certain properties are the necessary properties of language, it follows at once, if you accept what we have been calling 'the tautology', and its consequences, that these properties are rooted in the genes. Unless you are a mystic, you can't believe otherwise.[2]

As noted by Lightfoot (1982: 63) too,

> Languages may have many regularities having nothing to do with the genotype; all languages have a word for 'arm' but this has to do with the structure of our bodies and the way in which we view them and presumably nothing to do with genetically determined properties of grammars.

    *3.2.3* This brings us to the distinction *linguistic universals vs cross-linguistic generalizations*. A linguistic universal of the Chomskyan sort, we have seen, postulates a biologically necessary property of human language, a property of the genotype. Opposed to this view of linguistic universals is one that takes linguistic universals to be generalizations based on facts from a diverse cross-section of languages. Comrie (1981: 26–7) has recently characterized the cross-linguistic view of linguistic universals – as advocated by Greenberg – as the view that holds

> that research on language universals requires a wide range of languages as its data base, [that] believes that a number of language universals can be stated in terms of concrete levels of analysis, and [that] has an open mind on possible

133

explanations for language universals, considering in particular psychological and functional (including pragmatic) factors.[3]

(3) (a)–(b) represents typical cases of such cross-linguistic (Greenbergian) universals.

(3)    (a)    In declarative sentences with nominal subject and object, the dominant order is almost always one in which the subject precedes the object.

       (b)    In languages with prepositions, the genitive almost always follows the governor noun, while in languages with postpositions it almost always precedes.

Although the point is half obscured by their formulation, cross-linguistic universals such as (3) (a)–(b) are in essence generalizations that express statistical tendencies of a typological sort.

*You fail to see why, in regard to linguistic universals, one would prefer The Master's Biological Bent to the Statistical Stance of, say, Greenberg? In support of your 'open-mindedness' you quote Li (1976: x–xi), who asserted that 'One of the most productive directions of research lies in the collection of valuable facts from a diverse cross-section of languages and the discovering of generalizations based on them'.*

*The Master (1957: 17) has made no secret of his scepticism about the potential insightfulness of statistical studies and probabilistic models of linguistic structure. Thus, in considering possible explications of the notion of grammaticalness, he argued that 'statistical studies of language . . . appear to have no direct relevance to the problem of determining or characterizing the set of grammatical utterances.' And, in his view, 'we are forced to conclude that probabilistic models give no particular insight into some basic problems of syntactic structure'. With this Anti-statistics Stance, The Master long ago pre-empted the probing play planned by you and others at Probability Prong. And indeed, more recently, Newmeyer (1983: 71), adaptively amplifying The Master's stand, has cautioned combatants capable of comprehension that the 'directions of research' lauded by Li are likely not to lead them to what they would like to learn:*

*But there is no evidence that 'the collection of valuable facts' has ever led or could ever lead to the discovery of any generalizations*

134

*other than the most superficial sort. For example, the seven-year-long Stanford University Language Universals Project (whose results are now published as Greenberg, Ferguson and Moravcsik 1978) carried out Li's program to perfection yet has not led, as far as I know, to any substantial theoretical revisions. The problem is that the fairly shallow generalizations and statistical correlations described in the project's reports were far too sketchily presented to be of much use in ascertaining even the grammatical structure of the individual languages treated, much less shed any light on universal grammar (n. 9).*[4]

*What you have identified as the Li Line, Dear Aspirant Player, appears to me to be indistinguishable from the Limbo Line.*

3.2.4    As statements of the theory of grammar, individual linguistic universals form clusters that Chomsky (1981b: 5, 135) characterizes with the aid of the distinction *subcomponents of rule systems vs subsystems of principles*. As statements of the theory of grammar, some linguistic universals characterize those modules or subcomponents of rule systems that make up core grammar. Within Chomsky's (1981b: 5) *Lectures* model these subcomponents include the following:

(4)      (i)    lexicon
         (ii)   syntax
                (a)   categorial component
                (b)   transformational component
         (iii)  PF-component
         (iv)   LF-component

The following is Chomsky's (1981b: 5) brief characterization of these subcomponents:

The lexicon specifies the abstract morpho-phonological structure of each lexical item and its syntactic features, including its categorial features and its contextual features. The rules of the categorial component meet some variety of X-bar theory. Systems (i) and (iia) constitute the base. Base rules generate D-structures (deep structures) through insertion of lexical items into structures generated by (iia), in accordance with their

135

feature structure. These are mapped to S-structure by the rule Move-α, leaving traces coindexed with their antecedents; this rule constitutes the transformational component (iib), and may also appear in the PF- and LF-components. Thus the syntax generates S-structures which are assigned PF- and LF-representations by components (iii) and (iv) of [4] respectively.[5]

Chomsky (1981b: 17) uses the following diagram to represent schematically the way in which the 'three fundamental components' of universal grammar are organized:

(5)

Other linguistic universals characterize the subsystems of principles provided for by Chomsky. Calling these subsystems of principles 'theories', Chomsky (1981b: 5) provides for the following:

(6)　　(i)　　bounding theory
　　　　(ii)　　government theory
　　　　(iii)　　θ-theory
　　　　(iv)　　binding theory
　　　　(v)　　Case theory
　　　　(vi)　　control theory

The following remarks by Chomsky (1981b: 5–6) give some indication of the claims expressed in these theories:

Bounding theory poses locality conditions on certain processes and related items. The central notion of government theory is the relation between the head of a construction and categories depending on it. θ-theory is concerned with the assignment of thematic roles such as agent-of-action, etc. (henceforth: θ-roles). Binding theory is concerned with relations of anaphors, pronouns, names and variables to possible antecedents. Case theory deals with assignment of abstract Case and its

136

morphological realization. Control theory determines the potential for reference of the abstract pronominal element PRO.[6]

*As for 'subcomponents of rule systems vs subsystems of principles', it has all the appearances of a basic bifurcation in The Garden. But only Nervous Novices would allow themselves to be cajolled into combat at this conceptual cleft. Why? The reasons, really, are simple: it is not clear at all that The Master could be embarrassed at this bifurcation. And it is even less clear how such embarrassment could be caused. That is, Impolitic Pupil, take note of the following Principles Underpinning the Pragmatics of Prudent Play:*

1 *No prospect of profit, no point in play.*
2 *No plan of play, no point in pugnacious posturing.*

*Without the guidance of principles such as these, I fear, your involvement in The Game is bound to bring you no more than a series of close encounters of the nerd kind.*

3.3   We turn next to a series of distinctions that bear on the nature and properties of (**generative**) **grammars** as theories of particular human languages. It was noted in section 3.1.1 above that a generative grammar of a particular language is a theory that has to give an answer to the question 'What does knowledge of this language consist of?'. At this point of our survey, the useful distinctions are those that will give us a clearer idea of what such grammars are not.

3.3.1   Basic among the distinctions in question is that of *a descriptive/linguistic grammar vs a mental/internalized grammar*. A descriptive grammar, on a recent formulation by Chomsky (1986: 3), is 'a theory concerned with the state of the mind/brain of the person who knows a particular language'. Such a theory has to present a certain type of description or characterization of the relatively stable state of the language faculty of the person who knows the particular language.[7] A descriptive grammar, therefore, is a theory about an object that – in the terminology of

137

section 2.5.13 – may be called a specific I-language. Returning to the essential point: a descriptive grammar of a language is a metascientific object of the linguist's own making: a theory that has to have the attribute of 'being scientific'. What 'being scientific' means to Chomsky will become clear in chapter 4 below.

A mental grammar, by contrast, is a property of the (ideal) speaker–listener's mind/brain: the state of the language faculty described or characterized by a descriptive grammar. That is, the mental grammar of a language constitutes the relatively stable steady state of the ideal speaker–listener. A mental grammar therefore, on Chomsky's view, is not a metascientific object created by the linguist, but a physically based cognitive system 'out there in the real world'. In his earlier writings, Chomsky (e.g. 1965) often used the expression 'linguistic grammar' as an alternative to 'descriptive grammar' and 'internalized grammar' as an alternative to 'mental grammar'.

To sum up, we consider Chomsky's (1980a: 220) characterization of the distinction between a descriptive/linguistic grammar on the one hand and a mental/internalized grammar on the other hand:

> We must be careful to distinguish the grammar, regarded as a structure postulated in the mind, from the linguist's grammar, which is an explicit articulated theory that attempts to express precisely the rules and principles of the grammar in the mind of the ideal speaker–hearer. The linguist's grammar is a scientific theory, correct insofar as it corresponds to the internally represented grammar.

*'As easy as pie, a piece of cake'? Is this, Optimistic Player, your considered judgement of the fork in question? But, then, how would a novice know about The Master's cultivated capacity to complicate, his astonishing ability to make the frivolous fighter choke on even a piece of cake. The Master – in his wilful and wily way, some would say – has created a confusing complication: he (e.g. 1980a: 220; 1980b: 54) has – and a deft touch it is, one has to admit – with 'systematic ambiguity' used the expression 'a grammar (of a language)' to denote both the metascientific object and the mental state. 'It is standard practice to use the term "grammar" ambiguously, referring to the linguist's theory or the system of rules attributed to the mind*

*in this theory (similarly, "universal grammar").'[8] And he proceeds to warn: 'But one must be careful not to be misled by the practice.'*

*This warning, alas, has come too late for many an unwary warrior. In fact, it forms part of The Master's beating off of yet another sally by Searle who, The Master intimates, committed the Grand Grammar Goof by failing to distinguish between metascientific object and mental capacity.*

3.3.2  The nature of particular grammars as theories may be further elucidated by considering Chomsky's (1986: 6–7) distinction *a generative grammar vs a traditional/pedagogical grammar*. A particular generative grammar has to give a fully explicit and complete characterization of a mental capacity, a speaker-hearer's tacit knowledge of his language. A traditional or pedagogical grammar, on Chomsky's (1986: 6) view, has a complementary concern:

> a good traditional or pedagogical grammar provides a full list of exceptions (irregular verbs, etc.), paradigms and examples of regular constructions, and observations at various levels of detail and generality about the form and meaning of expressions.

A traditional or pedagogical grammar, however,

> does not examine the question of how the reader of the grammar uses such information to attain the knowledge that is used to form and interpret new expressions, or the question of the nature and elements of this knowledge . . .

This is to say, according to Chomsky, that a traditional or pedagogical grammar does not attempt to provide an answer to the question 'What constitutes knowledge of the specific language with which it is concerned?'. Chomsky (1986: 6–7) would, 'without too much exaggeration', rather describe a traditional or pedagogical grammar as 'a structured and organized version of the data presented to a child learning a language, with some general commentary and often insightful observations'. Such a grammar, unlike a generative grammar, does not aim to specify the speaker–listener's 'full knowledge' of the language.

*In days gone by, when The Garden was still young, the lane leading to the 'generative vs pedagogical grammar' fork had a strangely slippery surface. Actually it was the scene of the sort of sliding and slithering that resulted, most unfortunately, in flat-footed fighters taking the Pedagogical Pitch by uncomprehendingly criticizing The Master for constructing generative grammars that stated the obvious, unproblematical things which learners/speakers already knew about their language.*

3.3.3   As regards the nature of generative grammars – specifically as this was seen by Chomsky before the second conceptual shift – a technical distinction has to be drawn, namely *the generation of sentences vs the production and interpretation of sentences*. This distinction ties in with Chomsky's (1980a: 220) earlier E-language view that

> The grammar of the language determines the properties of each of the sentences of the language . For each sentence, the grammar determines aspects of its phonetic form, its meaning, and perhaps more. The language is the set of sentences that are described by the grammar.

Against this background Chomsky (1980a: 220) introduces the technical term 'to generate' to say that

> the grammar 'generates' the sentences it describes and their structural descriptions; the grammar is said to 'weakly generate' the sentences of the language and to 'strongly generate' the structural descriptions of these sentences. When we speak of the linguist's grammar as a 'generative grammar', we mean only that it is sufficiently explicit to determine how sentences of the language are in fact characterized by the grammar.

Note, in passing, that the quoted remarks by Chomsky clarify a further, secondary distinction bearing on the properties of generative grammars, namely *weakly generate/weak generative capacity vs strongly generate/strong generative capacity.*[9]

From the very beginning of his work on generative grammar, Chomsky has been at pains to make it clear that a sharp distinction has to be drawn between the generation of sentences by a grammar,

140

in the technical sense elucidated above, and the production and interpretation of sentences by speakers of the language. Recently, he (1980a: 222) has once more stated that

> It is important to bear in mind the fundamental conceptual distinction between generation of sentences by the grammar, on the one hand, and production and interpretation of sentences by the speaker, making use of the resources of the grammar and much else, on the other. The grammar, in whatever form its principles are represented in the mind and brain, simply characterizes the properties of sentences, much as the principles of arithmetic determine the properties of numbers.

> We have some understanding of the principles of grammar, but there is no promising approach to the normal creative use of language, or to other rule-governed human acts that are freely undertaken. The study of grammar raises problems that we have some hope of solving; the creative use of language is a mystery that eludes our intellectual grasp.

A generative grammar, then, is not a device modelling or characterizing the speaker's ability to produce and/or interpret sentences.


*For those concerned about the quality of the combat, 'generation vs production/interpretation' is a fork with a rather sad history. The blunders, bloomers and boners committed over the years at this bifurcation by aggressors from all over the gaming globe add up to a number causing despondency, if not dismay, about the keenness of the contest. A recent episode – involving a member of a certain AI clan – should show you what I have in mind. Schank (1980: 35–6) – who purported to speak for 'those of us who work in artificial intelligence' – declared by decree that*

> *A theory of language must explain how people can comprehend sentences that they read or hear, and how they respond appropriately. In my view, a theory of language must embody a theory of comprehension, a theory of production, a theory of memory, a theory of motivation and behavior, and much more.*

*From this platform Schank showered The Master's position with all sorts of shells, setting his sights on, among other things, the latter's informal account of how questions such as* Whom did John see? *may be generated by a grammar.*[10] *Carelessly taking 'generated by the grammar' to be the same as 'formed by people', Schank (1980: 36) hurled conceptual cocktails such as the following in the general direction of the Garden Guru:*

> *Chomsky postulates an important 'general property of language' from the fact that people do not actually attempt to transform this sentence into an interrogative that questions 'the class'. Actually, he does think that people are silly enough to try it, but he allows that they are also smart enough to realize that such a question would be more than cumbersome, and thus somehow they are able to 'block' that question!*

*Neither shocked nor shaken by Schank's Shelling, The Master, distinctly dismissively, shot back: 'Schank misunderstood my account of these facts [i.e., that the question (1)* Which class did the teacher think his assistant had told to study the lesson? *is well-formed but that the question (2)* Which class was the lesson harder than the teacher had told that it would be? *is not well-formed], but that is unimportant.' And, as if this were not sufficiently shattering, The Master went on to take Schank to task for an attitude that would reap riotous ridicule in the natural sciences:*

> *Consider, rather, his own reaction to them. He does not propose an explanation for such facts. Rather, he denies that an explanation should be sought, since 'we do not form questions apart from our desire to know something.' Such facts as these are not worth considering (or perhaps are not facts) because people are not 'silly enough' to produce such sentences as (1) and (2). It is therefore of no interest to him that such sample facts about our knowledge provide evidence bearing on the structure of comparatives, on general principles of locality, and so on, in English and other languages. His attitude is like that of someone who objects to physics on the grounds that in normal life one doesn't find balls rolling down smooth inclined planes, let alone more exotic facts. (Chomsky 1980b: 53)*

142

*So, Dear Player, if you have to rely on intelligence of the Artificial Ilk that shines at superficial simulation, on brilliance that boasts more bytes than brains, on cleverness of the cloddish class exclusive to computers, then making mincemeat of The Master is most likely not your métier.*

3.3.4   The second conceptual shift in Chomskyan linguistics has made it necessary to draw the distinction *sentence generation vs parameter fixing and element licensing.* Before the second conceptual shift in Chomskyan linguistics, a generative grammar was technically characterized as a device for generating sentences in the sense considered in section 3.3.3 above. Following this shift, however, we saw in section 2.5.21 above, Chomsky's (1986: 150–1) conception of knowledge of grammar has changed in an essential way. He no longer sees such knowledge as being represented in a rule system:

> What we know is not a rule system in the conventional sense. In fact, it might be that the notion of rule in this sense, like the notion of E-language (so it seems), has no status in linguistic theory.

Chomsky now believes that 'The language that we . . . know is a system of principles with parameters fixed, along with a periphery of marked exceptions.' And in regard to the setting up of rule systems – after all, the linguist's conventional activity in pre-shift days – he contends that 'One can formulate algorithms that project rule systems from a choice of values for the parameters of UG, but it is not obvious that this is a significant move or that it matters how it is done.'

In line with this contention, as we have noted, Chomsky (1986: 83) argues for the elimination of phrase structure rules, the status of transformations being less clear. Following the second conceptual shift, consequently, grammars are no longer formal systems of explicitly formulated rules for the generation of sentences. Grammars of the post-shift sort must contain devices specifying how the values of open parameters are fixed in the language. In doing this, such devices, in terms of a recent statement by Chomsky (1986: 93), are to perform a sort of 'licensing', the assumption being that 'Every element that appears in well-formed structure must be *licensed* in

143

one of a small number of available ways.' It is not clear in what format (maximally explicit, of course) such 'parameter-fixing' or 'licensing' devices are to be represented.

*We have moved again into an area of The Garden where purposeful play is not possible. You feel strongly, do you, that you would like to lodge a complaint about the absence of proper paths and fully formed forks? But with whom? The Master? Complaining to The Master about being unable to foil him at a phantom fork?! Appealing to The Spectators? Derision, ridicule, even raspberries perhaps – that's all you would get for your trouble. And, of course, angry admonitions to get on with The Game at one of the places – and there are plenty! – where proper play is possible. No, there is no canon in the East Coast Code of Combat to call on in this case. There is only the Garden Guru's Court with its rough jungle justice.*

*And so we have traversed the relatively tame Terrain of Theory, that level of elevated lanes from which The Master manages his Mentalist Maze. Compared with the tumultuous tussles and fierce fracas we saw in The Maze, the dust-ups in the Theatre of Theory have been rather dull, you will agree. This is as good a reason as any to move on to that awesome area of The Garden where fights are fought to the finish.*

# 4

## The Marshes of Method

*So we are approaching, in pursuit of more passionate play, the arena where old scores are settled – where running battles are brought to a bitter end. You have the sickening sensation of dropping down into depths, dark and dank? So you should. But how is this possible in a garden, of all places? Well, as I have said before, it is not the garden variety of garden that one is playing in. It is a sloping structure, a multi-levelled labyrinth. And we are descending from the level of theoretical superstructure through the middle level of language/mind, down into the Marshes of Method, the lowest level of the labyrinth. We are moving into the bowels of The Garden, a philosophical substructure of slippery paths and poorly lit prongs, crisscrossed by maelstroms of (mentalistic) method. It is here, in this web of winding ways of doing (linguistic) science, that many an interchange which starts out as a 'linguistic' game is decided as a metascientific match. It is at this level of philosophically fluid forks that The Master is at his barely beatable best.*

In chapter 2 we considered the essence of Chomsky's answers to the three basic questions represented as (1) (a)–(c) in section 1.2, i.e., the questions: 'What constitutes knowledge of language?', 'How is knowledge of language acquired?', and 'How is knowledge of language put to use?' Subsequently, in chapter 3, we looked at the various kinds of theories within the framework of which these answers are proposed by Chomsky. In the present chapter we come to the philosophical principles and methodological practices that appear to govern the ways in which Chomsky sets about answering the questions (1) (a)–(c), and also the ways in which he sets about justifying the theories that express these answers. In short, we come to the metascientific assumptions of Chomskyan linguistics. Specifically, we will consider some of the more fundamental conceptual distinctions on which these assumptions are based. The distinctions that will be elucidated below cluster around Chomsky's conception of a number of matters: the aims of inquiry, the relation between linguistic theories and reality, the kinds of descriptions and explanations given by such theories, the empirical status and testing of linguistic theories, the role(s) (not) played by simplicity and other conceptual considerations in the justification of such theories, the nature and weight of the empirical evidence used in the justification of linguistic theories, and the major sources of linguistic evidence.

**4.1**   To start off with, let us consider a cluster of conceptual distinctions that underlie Chomsky's views of the sort of **problems, aims and idealizations** that should guide (linguistic) inquiry.

*4.1.1*   Fundamental to Chomsky's scientific concerns is his distinction *problems vs mysteries*. Linguistic inquiry in the Chomskyan mould is initiated and guided by the desire to find answers to questions of a sort called 'problems' by Chomsky. Problems, in Chomsky's (1980a: 6) sense, 'lie within these limits [i.e., the limits and scope of human minds as fixed biological systems] and can be approached by human science with some hope of success'. Thus problems concern unknown 'operative principles' that are not, because of limitations on human intellectual capacities, 'humanly unknowable'. Mysteries, by contrast, according to Chomsky (1980a: 6), are questions that

> simply lie beyond the reach of our minds, structured and organized as they are, either absolutely beyond those limits or at so far a remove from anything that we can comprehend with requisite facility that they will never be incorporated within explanatory theories intelligible to humans.

Questions about the nature and acquisition of knowledge of language (or grammar) are considered by Chomsky to represent 'problems' in the sense considered above. Questions about 'the

146

normal creative use of language', the 'creative aspect of language', he (1980a: 76, 222) takes to be 'mysteries': questions in the investigation of which no progress seems to be made. As we noted in section 2.5.3 above, it is for this reason that the question 'How do people succeed in acting appropriately and creatively in linguistic behaviour or performance?' is a question which Chomsky expressly excludes from the set of fundamental questions to be addressed by his approach to linguistic inquiry.

*At the point where the 'question' passage splits into the 'problems vs mysteries' prong you may find it profitable to pause, Dear Peripatetic Player. Yes, let us make a halt here as you think back: try to recall the History of one Hapless Hunter, recounted in section 2.5.3 above. That Pitiable Player, as we saw, committed a faux pas at the fork 'knowledge vs creative use' when he hit out at The Master because the latter's theories failed to explain 'how we talk'.*

*Observe now that what The Master did in retaliation highlights a fundamental feature of The Game: the switching of the action from one level to another, whereby a seemingly simple scrap is turned into a multi-levelled battle. Thus in the Mentalistic Maze, if you will recall, The Master let Hunter have it for missing the fork 'knowledge vs creative use' altogether. But there was more to The Master's retaliative move: with devastating deftness he drew Hunter down into a metascientific maelstrom foaming in the Guts of The Garden. Here The Master promptly further faulted Hunter for being so blinded by the question 'how we talk' that he had, at this deeper level, overshot the 'problems vs mysteries' fork as well.*

*Now, carrying on about someone's inability to explain 'how we talk' instantiates a special kind of exercise, namely making much of mystery. This may well win the day in the field of fiction, but in The Garden other principles obtain:*

1 *By Mystery-mongering that misses both muscle and menace, you will neither score nor scare.*
2 *Play proceeds from problems.*

*And problems have to be probes into principles, as we will see below in section 4.1.2.*

*4.1.2* Chomsky's conception of the aims of (linguistic) science is based, ultimately, on the distinction *depth of insight vs gross coverage of data*. He (e.g., 1978a: 9ff; 1980a: 9ff; 1980b: 49; 1982: 82-3) has repeatedly stated the aim of his form of linguistic inquiry to be the attainment of depth of insight or understanding in (restricted areas) of the human mind in general and man's language capacity in particular. Depth of insight is pursued through the construction of theories that attempt to explain observations about problematic phenomena in terms of underlying principles. Chomsky (e.g. 1982: 82-3) regards gross coverage of data that fails to go further than arbitrary classification or inventorization as being of restricted intellectual significance, not an aim to be pursued in serious inquiry.

> I certainly feel that explanation is much more important than gross coverage of data. The reason is, very simply, that gross coverage of data is much too easily obtained, in too many different ways. There are a million ways in which you can give a kind of rough characterization of a lot of data, and therefore you don't learn anything about the principles at all.

And he (1980b: 49) considers observation useful 'only insofar as it provides evidence for an explanatory theory, and [he has] therefore no interest in catalogues of observations, which can easily be constructed on a massive scale'.

Chomsky's (1982: 83) pursuit of depth of insight rather than gross coverage of data also forms the basis of his judgement that whereas certain problematic (linguistic) phenomena are 'interesting' as 'good probes', other phenomena are not:

> There are certain phenomena, like anaphora, which have just been extremely good probes; they've raised questions that have to be answered, and there are other things that also do, but I haven't seen many. Most phenomena simply do not make good probes. They are really just puzzles which are unexplained. It seems to me to make good sense to work intensively in those subareas where sharp questions seem to arise that can be answered in ways that have an explanatory character.

For the linguist who lacks the inclination to bring observations and data to bear on the construction of explanatory theories, there is in Chomsky's (1978a: 10) opinion only one, not particularly attractive, alternative: 'a kind of butterfly collecting or elaborate taxonomies of sensations and observations'.

*Over the years, The Master has often been attacked at the 'insight vs coverage of data' fork for his pursuit of insight and his concern with explanatory theories. Thus Rachlin (1980: 30–1) – stung by The Master's 'contempt for the other side' – again raised the question why it is 'necessary' to develop explanatory theories – of the sort proposed by The Master – as true of the mind/brain. And matching 'contempt' with contempt, he fired a couple of metaphorical missiles at The Master:*

> *Why is it necessary to (so to speak) hold a behavioral function hostage in the body? Where does this get us? Do we need to fear that this imprisoned function (in the case of language) will escape and lodge itself in a dolphin or a chimp or even, God forbid, a pigeon?*

*Rough stuff, you would agree, Perturbed Player. Predictably The Master readily resisted Rachlin's Rush (of blood to the head), repulsing it by refined ridicule:*

> *The answer [to Rachlin's 'necessary' question] is that it is not necessary. One need not be concerned to understand or explain observations of behavior, just as some person might be interested in collecting insects or rocks with no further concern in mind; or one can conceive of an uncurious engineer who might simply be concerned to predict what some mechanism will do without caring how or why it does it. A child is different from a pigeon or a chimpanzee in that, presented with certain data, it will come to know the sample facts and myriad others like them. Presumably this is because the internal structure of the child is somehow different from that of the pigeon or chimpanzee, surely not merely at the level of sensory mechanisms, since the same results hold if the language input is recoded for a different system. It is not 'necessary' to be*

149

*interested in these properties of the child – that is, in psychology and biology – or to try to discover and understand them. But someone who is interested in these questions will proceed to construct theories of hypothetical inner mechanisms and will find observations 'useful' insofar as they contribute to these theories. (Chomsky 1980b: 49)*

*Thereby we have uncovered a Garden Truth:*

> *To take up arms about aims is to risk the performance of an asinine act.*

*Unless the attacker has firm philosophical footholds, that is. Why? Because, lacking firm philosophical footholds, it is all too easy, Puzzled Player, to be swept off one's feet by ridicule, whether reasoned or merely rhetorical.*

4.1.3  In the pursuit of insight and explanation it is, on Chomsky's (1978a: 16) view, essential to draw the distinction *(deep) explanatory principles vs (superficial) empirical generalizations*. To arrive at the required insight – which would make it possible to answer the questions (1) (a)–(c) of section 1.2 insightfully – it is necessary to discover unifying principles (of language/mind) of considerable deductive depth. A proposed principle has the property of being unified if it governs a wide range of phenomena; it has the property of deductive depth if it does not follow from other 'deeper' principles but if less 'deep' generalizations and other kinds of claims may be reduced to it.[1] (Superficial) empirical generalizations, though 'covering' a certain range of data, neither unify (or govern) a wide range of phenomena nor exhibit the required deductive depth.

Chomsky (1978a: 17) illustrates the distinction between (deep) explanatory principles and (superficial) empirical generalizations with reference to the ways in which Subjacency – repeated as (1) below – differs from the 'island' conditions/constraints known as the Complex Noun Phrase Constraint (2), the WH-Island Constraint (3), the Sentential Subject Constraint (4), the Phrasal Subject Constraint (5) and the Upward Boundedness Constraint (6).

(1)  Nothing can be removed from more than a single binding category.

(2)  No element can be removed from an appositional clause.[2]
(3)  No element can be removed from a clause introduced by a (*wh*) question word.[3]
(4)  No element can be removed from a sentential subject.[4]
(5)  No element can be removed from a nominal subject.[5]
(6)  No element can be removed to the right from the minimal sentence containing it.[6]

Chomsky (1978a: 17) considers Subjacency to be 'a genuine unifying principle . . . , that is, a number of island constraints can be deduced from it'. These island constraints, according to him (1978a: 16), 'express empirical generalizations over observed linguistic structures'. The status he assigns them is, moreover, that of 'descriptive catalogues'. Clearly the data covered by these empirical generalizations are related to the principle of Subjacency only by means of a complex inferential chain. That makes this principle 'abstract' in relation to these data. Note the unifying nature of this principle: by means of the fundamental notion of 'binding category' it expresses the deeper regularity which underlies a variety of island constraints formulated in terms of a set of apparently disparate notions.[7]

So: to have explanatory power, principles (and the theories incorporating them) must have both unifying power and deductive depth. On Chomsky's (1981b: 7) view, it is highly desirable for such principles (and theories) to have another metascientific property, namely a certain kind of simplicity. What this involves, we will see in section 4.5 below where we consider a number of distinctions underlying the various notions of 'simplicity' and 'complexity' distinguished by Chomsky.

*I know of no recent clash at or about the bifurcation '(deep) explanatory principles vs (superficial) empirical generalizations'. However, Disappointed Player, as you will see in section 4.2.6 below, a number of pitched battles were fought on topographically closely related terrain in the Linguistic Wars mentioned in section 2.7.5 above.*

*'Not another balladeering band of Footloose Fellows!', I hear you exclaim, Exasperated Player. But no, those you won't find marching*

*in the mud of metascientific marshland – it's too miserable a milieu for merrymaking. Content to indulge in hand clapping and back slapping, they are more than happy to stay on the stands. Except for an enterprising few whose innate inclination for investment has led them to lobby The Master for the licence to market his modules of mind. Just recently they set up shop in the entrance lane to The Labyrinth, and so this is where Fans flashing fistfuls of florins and mighty marks find on offer an amazing medley of Mentalistic Merchandise, Master's Memorabilia, Players' Paraphernalia and other Garden Goodies: from scarves, stickers and similar corporeal consumer commodities to ethereal thetas and other theoretical things. Dealers by descent, traders by tradition, these mercantile men make you pay a packet for all sorts of nothing, including intangible traces and other kinds of empty spaces.*

*But what, then, is it that you hear? Ah, Dear Player, it's the Cambridge Mass Choir, and it's rehearsing against the dreaded day when into The Garden there may venture a Prodigious Player, a Martial Man in The Master's mould, able to do unto him as once he did unto the unsuspecting Skinner, now close on thirty years ago. If ever this did happen, the choir would be ready to recite Jay S. Bach's Requiem for a Ravaged Rationalist in fittingly funereal fashion. ('The Master is dead, long live the Master!') But this is a scenario, I hasten to add, that has the sort of substance one associates with science fiction.*

*Who Skinner is? Surely you have heard of the Big Boss of the behaviourist breed – the clan who conditioned themselves to believe the curious creed that language was no more than habit, its learning and use a mechanical matter to Mindless Man.*

4.1.4    In order to make progress in the search for unifying explanatory principles it is vital, on Chomsky's (1980a: 9, 11, 218) view, to observe the distinction *idealization vs inventorization*. Specifically, to uncover the kind of principles under consideration, the linguist must be willing to make radical idealizations, idealizations such as that of an ideal speaker–listener, that of a completely homogeneous speech community, that of instantaneous language acquisition, that of core grammar and so on.[8] As a source of problematic phenomena and data, therefore, linguistic performance /

language behaviour constitutes a highly complex phenomenon with a variety of facets or features that are determined by a diversity of internal systems interacting under poorly understood conditions. Knowledge of language/grammatical competence represents just one of these systems.

To find the principles [of core grammar] that jointly constitute grammatical competence it is necessary, on Chomsky's view, to abstract away from the contribution made by the other, 'non-competence', systems to linguistic performance. This the Chomskyan linguist does by making radical idealizations such as those of the ideal speaker–listener and a completely homogeneous speech community. In other words, he/she looks upon idealization as a means of *initially* simplifying the complex linguistic reality of problematic phenomena in order to gain a first grip on a world of sensations and observations that appears to be chaotic and overwhelmingly complex.

Not every idealization, however, is a good one. There are clear conditions of adequacy that idealizations have to meet in Chomsky's (1980a: 224) opinion: 'The discovery of such principles, and that alone, will justify the idealizations adopted and indicate that we have captured an important element of the real structure of the organism.' Moreover, as progress is made in the uncovering of deep explanatory principles, specific idealizations lose their initial usefulness. Chomsky (1980a: 224) makes it quite clear that, ultimately, his aim is to try to understand linguistic reality in its full complexity:

> To account for the confused and disorderly phenomena of the 'ordinary world of sensation', we will, in general, have to move from the idealizations to systems of greater complexity, considering variation of languages and grammars, the interaction of cognitive systems, and the use of language under specific conditions of human life.

As was noted above in section 4.1.2, Chomsky (1978a: 10) sees only one alternative to idealization, namely inventorization: 'a kind of butterfly collecting or elaborate taxonomies of sensations and observations'. Inventorization, obviously, is not geared to uncovering the 'deep, unifying principles' that Chomskyan linguists are after in their pursuit of insight.

153

*As we moved through the Mentalistic Maze, Patient Player, I drew your attention to quite a few pieces of provocative play that involved The Master's idealization. There was The Master's eruptive encounter with McCawley triggered by the notion of 'instantaneous language acquisition' (section 2.1.1); there were the dismal dealings with Dummett about the idea of a 'completely homogeneous speech community' (section 2.5.11); there was the comprehensive clobbering of Kintsch & Co. about the 'strict separation between competence and performance' (section 2.6.1).*

*On the surface, confrontations such as these appear to be about individual idealizations; they appear, as it were, to be incidental incivilities. But deep down, The Master (1982: 12–13) has sensed them to be about the way in which science ought to be done:*

> *There are people who are worried about abstraction and want to keep close to the data. It is like doing descriptive phonetics or descriptive semantics, I think. If you look at intellectual activity in the humanities and the natural sciences, with very rare exceptions, it is highly data-bound. There are only a few areas of intellectual endeavor where people have really gone beyond to develop theoretical work which is not a kind of data arrangement, in the humanities as well as in the natural sciences.*

*Why, then, are so many players of The Game – including scholars of some standing – so deeply attached to data-bound description, so aggressively averse to studying systems in abstraction, so incurably intolerant of idealization? The Master (1982: 70) has given these questions some thought, Dear Player, and has suggested certain reasons for the use of Anti-idealization Invective, reasons that make one think. These are the reasons, he intimates, that do not have rational roots. The Master was struck by the fact, for example, that a certain book about language acquisition was lauded by so respected a scholar as Jerome Bruner.*

> *It was a book about the growth of the mind of a child, or something like that. It was very critical of language acquisition device (LAD) type approaches to language acquisition because it said that they dealt with the child as if it was an abstract entity, there was no blood flowing through its veins, as if it*

*was just a mechanism, so it was very heartless. That represents an extreme form of anti-intellectualism that holds that if you try to abstract to a system with certain properties, and you do not look at the whole complexity of reality, there is something fundamentally wrong with what you are doing, and that it is just the phenomena of the world that we ought to be studying and that it is wrong or immoral to look for explanatory theories and systems, abstract systems that enter into them somehow.*

*These observations, Dear Player, if correct, say something about the metascientific motives that make certain players attempt The Maze. But even if these remarks were false, they would still be instructive for what they tell you about The Master and his multifarious modes of play: he is in The Game not merely as an agent of aggressive action, but also as an acute analyst of the philosophical prejudices that propel people into play. So, if you are concerned about your fighting future, it would be foolish not to note that:*

1  *Major Movers are put under a microscope, both their manoeuvres and their motives being meticulously monitored by The Master.*
2  *If The Master judges your motives malignant (or merely murky, for that matter), your prejudices perverse, there will be a proportionate penalty for you to pay.*

*You are incensed by what you call The Master's Anti-intellectualist Insult? I urge you to keep your cool: agitated action has not proved to be particularly profitable in putting pressure on The Master.*

Before we move to the following cluster of conceptual distinctions, note that the distinctions bearing on Chomsky's conception of the aim(s) of (linguistic) science reflect his commitment to the more fundamental and comprehensive philosophical position known as 'rationalism'. This point will be taken up again when we come to the distinction 'rationalism vs empiricism' in section 4.2.6.

**4.2**  We consider next a cluster of distinctions that forms the basis of Chomsky's conception of the relationship between linguistic theories – both particular grammars and the general theory of language / grammar – and those parts of linguistic reality of which they are theories. That is, we will take a closer look at the notions – **description and explanation** used by Chomsky to characterize the ways in which his theories bear on linguistic reality. As our point of departure we will take Chomsky's view – mentioned in section 3.1.1 above – that, whereas the general theory of language provides a characterization or description of the initial state of the language faculty, a particular grammar gives a characterization or description of the relatively stable steady state of the language faculty. So, on the one hand, we will be concerned with the metascientific distinctions that underlie the relationship referred to as 'characterization' or 'description'. On the other hand, we will consider the field-specific notion of 'explanation' that Chomsky has introduced into the discussion of the 'tasks' and 'conditions of adequacy' of linguistic theories.

4.2.1 Chomsky's position on the relation holding between a (linguistic) theory T and the objects / phenomena of which T is a theory may be clarified with reference to the philosophical distinction *realism vs non-realism*. Chomsky (1980a: 15, 18, 104; 1982: 31; 1986: 252) has repeatedly stated that he judges it to be 'legitimate to adopt the standard "realist" assumptions of the natural sciences in studying language, and cognition more generally' (1980a 104). That is, Chomsky (1986: 252) proceeds 'in practice by taking a realist stance toward theoretical discourse'.

The essence of the 'standard "realist" assumptions' or the 'realist stance', as seen by Chomsky, is:

(7)     (a)    that the questions (e.g., (1) (a)–(c) in section 1.2) to be answered by a theory are questions of fact;

        (b)    that in trying to answer these questions the theory postulates and tries to describe 'real' entities or mechanisms at a deeper, not directly observable, level of reality;

        (c)    that the claims made by the theory about these entities can in principle be true.

As regards the truth of a theory, however, Chomsky (1980a: 104) cautions that

Of course, we expect that the theory is probably false, and even if on the road to truth, that it does no more than describe at some appropriate level of abstraction properties alleged to be true of whatever the real elements of the world may be when considered at this level of description . . .

To show what the realist position on the ontological status of linguistic theories involves, Chomsky (1980a: 191) has compared his investigation of the language faculty to the investigation of the thermonuclear reactions that take place inside the sun:

Our investigation of the apparatus of the language faculty, whether in its initial or final steady state, bears some similarity to the investigation of thermonuclear reactions in the solar interior that is limited to evidence provided by light emitted at the periphery. We observe what people say and do, how they react and respond, often in situations contrived so that this behavior will provide some evidence (we hope) concerning the operative mechanisms. We then try, as best we can, to devise a theory of some depth and significance with regard to these mechanisms, testing our theory by its success in providing explanations for selected phenomena. Challenged to show that the constructions postulated in that theory have 'psychological reality', we can do no more than repeat the evidence and the proposed explanations that involve these constructions. Or, like the astronomer dissatisfied with study of light emissions from the periphery of the sun, we can search for more conclusive evidence, always aware that in empirical inquiry we can, at best, support a theory against substantive alternatives and empirical challenge; we cannot prove it to be true.[9]

Non-realist 'stances toward theoretical discourse' – such as those known as 'nominalism' or 'instrumentalism' – deny some version of the assumptions (7) (a)–(c).[10] As noted in section 2.5.14 above, Katz (1981) has proposed a Platonist ontological interpretation of linguistic theories as an alternative to Chomsky's realist (called 'conceptualist' by Katz) and Harris's nominalist positions. On Katz's (1981: 12) view 'it is preferable, on scientific grounds, to interpret theories of natural language and theories of language Platonistically (as theories of abstract objects) rather than nominalistically (as

157

theories of disturbances in the air) or conceptualistically [i.e. 'realistically'] (as theories about the human mind or brain)'.

*The 'realist vs non-realist' bifurcation has for many years been the scene of serious strife. We have, in fact, already seen some mêlées – in the multilevelled mode – that involved The Master's realist position, e.g. The Master contra Lear (section 2.5.4) and Katz (section 2.5.14). But the major battle at this bifurcation has been a war of attrition waged by Quine – and the fraternity of philosophers following him – against The Master. In essence, Quine's Quarrel with The Master springs from the question of how one could choose between two extensionally equivalent grammars – i.e., grammars generating the same sentences – the one which 'guides' and not merely 'fits' the behaviour of the speakers of the language.*

*Quine (1972: 442) queries The Master's 'doctrine' that extensionally equivalent systems of grammatical rules need not be equally correct. He contends that, since the two grammars are both underdetermined by the evidence, it is not possible to determine which rules are 'the right rules', 'the right rules' being those that native speakers have 'somehow implicitly in mind'. And Quine's more general conclusion – derived in part from his thesis of the indeterminacy of translation[11] – is that there is 'no fact of the matter', 'no question of right choice'. On Quine's view, that is, because of what he calls the 'indeterminacy' of linguistic theories their truth cannot be determined. Of course, this conclusion strikes a blow at the very heart of The Master's realist position, represented in (7) (a)–(c) above.*

*No attack at the base of one's beliefs, Dear Player, can be brushed off as a bagatelle. So, whenever Quine has aired his qualms – and he has done so with some monotony – he has found The Master raring to respond. Giving tit for tat, The Master (1975a: 183) on one occasion, for example, retorted as follows:*

> *when Quine asserts that there is no fact of the matter, no question of right choice, he is once again merely reiterating an unargued claim which does not become more persuasive on repetition. If the underdetermination of physical theory by evidence does not lead us to abandon the 'realistic point of*

*view' with regard to physical theory, then the comparable underdetermination of grammatical theory by evidence does not support Quine's claim that there is no fact of the matter in this domain to be right or wrong about.*

And not being one to play for a draw, The Master (1975a: 183–4) went all out to see Quine's qualms well and truly quelled:

*Neither here nor elsewhere has Quine given any argument whatsoever to justify his assertion that statements about language that go beyond his notion of 'ordinary induction' (with its uncertainties) are subject to some methodological doubts that do not hold (in principle) in any nontrivial empirical study. His thesis of 'indeterminacy' thus has no support beyond the truism that theory is underdetermined by evidence in empirical research.*

So, Dear Fellow, if you really feel that you have made some headway towards more Perceptive Play, here is a test for you. How do you read The Master's repartee? The punch, I trust you appreciate, is in the way the Quinian rejection of Realist Religion is portrayed as a slightly silly denial of the self-evidently reasonable.

4.2.2 A certain distinction, namely *psychological reality vs truth*, has played an important role in the discussion of the ontological status of linguistic theories. In terms of this distinction the evidence for linguistic theories falls into two epistemological categories. On the one hand, there is 'linguistic evidence'. This simply makes the theory on which it bears a 'good (or better) theory'. On the other hand, there is 'psychological evidence'. This allows a (good) theory on which it bears to claim 'psychological reality', a 'higher' epistemological attribute. This kind of evidence is called 'evidence for psychological reality'. Over the years it has been contended that Chomskyans have failed to adduce the proper kind of (psychological) evidence for the psychological reality of their theories.

Chomsky (1980a: 189ff; 1980b: 12), however, has rejected all three distinctions mentioned above, i.e. 'truth vs psychological reality', 'evidence for truth vs evidence for psychological reality' and 'linguistic evidence vs psychological evidence'. The following, for example, are his (1980b: 12) remarks about the distinction 'truth vs psychological reality':

> As has been evident throughout, I am not convinced that there is any such distinction. I see no reason not to take our theories tentatively to be true at the level of description at which we are working, then proceeding to refine and evaluate them and to relate them to other levels of description, hoping ultimately to find neural and biochemical systems with the properties expressed in these theories.

And, having posed the question 'What is psychological reality?', he (1980b: 12) contends that

> Presumably, it is to be understood on the model of 'physical reality'. But in the natural sciences one is not accustomed to ask whether the best theory we can devise in some idealized domains has the property of 'physical reality', apart from the context of metaphysics and epistemology, which I have here put aside, since I am interested in some new and special problem that is held to arise in the domain of psychology.

As for the distinction between linguistic and psychological evidence as two kinds of evidence, Chomsky (1980b: 12) has observed that

> What we should say, in all these cases, is that any theory of language, grammar, or whatever, carries a truth claim if it is serious – though the supporting argument is, and must be, inconclusive. We will always search for more evidence and for deeper understanding of given evidence, which also may lead to change of theory. What the best evidence is depends on the state of the field. The best evidence may be provided by as yet unexplained facts drawn from the language being studied, or from similar facts about other languages, or from psycho-linguistic experiment, or from clinical studies of language disability, or from neurology, or from innumerable other sources. We should always be on the lookout for new kinds of evidence, and we cannot know in advance what they will be. But there is no distinction of epistemological category. In each case we have evidence – good or bad, convincing or

not – as to the truth of the theories we are constructing; or, if one prefers, as to their 'psychological reality', though this term is best abandoned, as seriously misleading.

In essence, then, what Chomsky (1986: 253) rejects is the distinction 'the best theory vs a theory better than the best theory': 'we cannot obtain more evidence than all the evidence [which would make a particular theory 'the best theory'], or find better theories than the best theory.' So, although the distinction 'truth vs psychological reality' may be useful as a tool for gaining a better understanding of Chomsky's view of the ontological status of linguistic theories, it is a distinction held by him to be fallacious.

*Despite The Master's having declared it a fabricated fork, the 'truth vs psychological reality' bifurcation has been the scene of some surprisingly pulsating play. In the ways winding through this poorly charted part of The Garden, The Master has had to summon all his strength, use his every skill, simply to survive and fight another day. You want proof of this, Dear Player? Well, you shall have it. Have you ever heard the name of Harman, a craftsman known for his cool and class? No? Then, let me give you an account of one of the most memorable matches in the metascientific morass at the base of The Maze.*

*With deceptive self-depreciation, Harman (1980: 21) approached The Master with 'a quibble about psychological reality'. His 'quibble' turned out to be, both quantity- and quality-wise, something of substance:*

Chomsky claims that it is pointless to distinguish the question of psychological reality from that of truth, and he asserts that no similar distinction is made in the natural sciences. But, given any theory we take to be true, we can always ask what aspects of the theory correspond to reality and what aspects are mere artifacts of our notation. Geography contains true statements locating mountains and rivers in terms of longitude and latitude without implying that the equator has the sort of physical reality the Mississippi River does. Similarly, we can describe some part of the universe, given a choice of spatio-temporal coordinates, recognizing that the special role of that choice of

161

*coordinates in our description is an artifact of our notation. And we might present a theory in axiomatic form without assigning any physical significance to the distinction between axioms and theorems.*

*Sometimes we are not sure about the physical reality of some aspect of a theory, even given strong evidence for the truth of the theory. A different sort of evidence may be needed. The postulation of quarks gives a structure to the proliferation of subatomic particles, but physicists demand a different sort of evidence in order to establish the physical reality of quarks.*

*And moving in, he (1980: 21-2) manoeuvred The Master into a corner where there was no room for retraction, no space for sidestepping:*

*Chomsky implicitly recognizes the point as it applies to linguistics when he acknowledges that one linguistic theory may be a 'notational variant' of another. Aspects of a true theory not shared by its notational variants are not taken to have psychological reality. The 'linguistic evidence' for a given linguistic theory is like the evidence that led to quark theory – namely that the theory brings order to a given domain. That by itself may not indicate what aspects of the theory correspond to reality and what aspects are artifacts of notation. We might wonder, for example, whether the grammatical structures of sentences have psychological reality or are mere artifacts of our notation, so that a notational variant of our theory could assign different structures to sentences.*

*Recognizing the hacking power of Harman's Hatchet – honed to be handled like Occam's Razor or Einstein's Chopper[12] – The Master (1980b: 45) made the following candid concession:*

*The points that Harman makes are well-taken . . . With regard to psychological reality, my main point is that no new problems of principle arise in the study of language that are not familiar in the 'hard sciences', and that evidence does not come in two epistemological categories: 'linguistic evidence' bearing on 'good theories', and 'psychological evidence' bearing on 'psychological reality'. Harman and I agree, I believe, on these points. As for the first, as I noted, there are serious questions about what*

162

*is meant when we take a theory to be true: 'what is the status of its theoretical entities, its principles, its idealizations', and so on. Harman points out some of these questions, quite appropriately – though, I think, as his final example shows, it is misleading to say that 'linguistic evidence' merely shows that 'the theory brings order to a given domain' in any sense that does not hold as well for a theory of click experiments and the like. He is also right to emphasize that we may ask about the physical reality of elements of a theory that we take to be true, and that psychological reality is on a par with physical reality in this respect. In this connection, he correctly points out an error in my formulation: there is a question of physical (or psychological) reality apart from truth in a certain domain, as Harman explains.*

*I hear you cry out in admiration 'Game, set and match to Harman!'. Hold your horses! The Game, you still have not fully understood, represents a curious kind of contest in which The Master is never wholly whipped, never comprehensively clobbered, never completely crushed. And his powers of regeneration and recovery are remarkable, so remarkable that recently he (1986: 274, n. 19) was able once again to renounce 'psychological reality':*

> *On some confusions about the nature and force of the evidence, and the belief that only some categories of evidence serve to confer a mysterious property called 'psychological reality', see Chomsky (1980b). See also Gilbert Harman's comments in the reference of note 14.*

*Had I not told you so, Perplexed Player, I bet you wouldn't have guessed that in the quotation above The Master is referring to the match in which Harman seemed clearly to have had the upper hand. 'What happened in between?', you wonder. Was there by any chance a rematch in which The Master turned the tables on Harman? Nothing of the sort, Dear Player. You will have to learn to live – the alternative is so utterly unattractive – with yet another Fact of Play:*

> *However trenchant the trauma, The Master has remarkable powers of recuperation.*

163

*And I am sad to say, the operation of The Master's Mechanism*
*of Miraculous Mending is aided in no small way by the memory*
*capacity, modest as it is, of the standard sort of spectator.*[13]

*4.2.3*   There is yet another dubious distinction that has
featured prominently in discussions of the ontological status of the
rules postulated in Chomskyan linguistic theories: the distinction
*hypotheses describing behaviour vs rules constituting part of the*
*structure of AS* (i.e., 'the attained state of the language faculty').
This is a distinction that has been used by Searle (1980) and others
to criticize Chomsky's position on the ontological status of linguistic
theories. In terms of this distinction, the rules postulated by
Chomskyan linguistic theories remain 'mere hypotheses describing
behaviour' unless a particular condition of independent evidence
is met. On this condition, a particular sort of evidence has to be
adduced in support of the rules in order to be able to claim that
they do not merely have explanatory power but are also in fact
followed by speakers of the language. If such evidence were
available, the rules could, in Chomsky's terminology, be attributed
to the structure of the attained or steady state of the language faculty.
In this event the rules could be claimed to have psychological reality.

The 'independent evidence' that Searle seems to have in mind may
be derived from speakers' intuitions or introspective judgements
about the rules that they in fact follow. Chomsky (1980b: 55)
rejected Searle's line of argument:

> To Searle, none of the evidence that I have provided is evidence
> that the person is following the postulated rules. Something
> else is required in principle, some 'independent' evidence over
> and above the explanatory power of the hypotheses. What else?
> Suppose that the rules could miraculously be made accessible
> to consciousness, as in the case of the rules that Searle has in
> mind, which are part of what Moravcsik calls a 'shallow theory'
> of the mind (and which, of course, do not bear on the kinds
> of empirical problems that I have been discussing, as I take
> it Searle would agree). Then Searle would agree that we have
> evidence that the rules are being followed; in his paper, which
> I discussed in my target article, he went further, but now he

states, more reasonably, that such introspective judgment would simply provide inconclusive evidence for the hypothesis that the postulated rules are part of the state attained. But why is this particular kind of evidence of such significance? Why would the speaker's obviously fallible and uncertain intuitions and judgments about the rules he allegedly follows provide evidence that the rules are being followed, whereas the kinds of evidence I discuss (namely, explanation of the sample facts on the basis of the hypothesis that the rules are being followed) in principle are not evidence at all? To this question Searle still offers no response, perhaps because of the confusion with regard to the status of the rules: not hypotheses describing behavior, but rather attributed to AS as part of its structure in hypotheses that purport to explain behavior on the assumption that the rules attributed to AS are followed in behavior ('cause' behavior).

*If your memory is better than that of the standard sort of spectator – and if you are to stand a chance of surviving in The Garden, it has to be, Dear Player – the thrust of Searle's attack will seem familiar. What we have here, in fact, is a watery version of the types of Accessibility Assaults seen at the fork explored in section 2.5.5 above. Having survived the Mentalistic Maze, you should be able to see that no amount of watering down or, for that matter, souping up could turn a Searle Sally of the Accessibility Sort into a profitable procedure of play.*

4.2.4   At this juncture, it is necessary to consider the distinction *abstract description/characterization vs concrete description/ characterization*. By doing so, we will gain a better understanding of, on the one hand, the nature of the descriptions provided by Chomskyan linguistic theories of the language faculty and, on the other hand, the nature of the entities or mechanisms postulated by such theories. Chomsky (1980a: 5; 1982: 32; 1983: 82, 124–5; 1986: 38) has argued that the language faculty, in both the initial and the attained state, may be studied and characterized at several levels, two of which are of special significance. At one level abstract characterizations may be given of it. The theory of language or grammar, characterizing the initial state, and particular grammars characterizing the various attained states, constitute such abstract characterizations. Such characterizations are abstract in the sense that they do not describe the language faculty 'in terms of physical mechanisms or properties of the brain' because, as Chomsky (1983: 82) puts it:

> we cannot speak of the physical structure of the brain because of our ignorance, and therefore we can only speak of some of the conditions that the physical structures must meet, however they meet them. We simply don't have the kind of evidence to tell us how the abstract structures might be represented in the concrete physical system.

To give an abstract characterization of the language faculty, in positive terms, is to 'impose some fairly narrow and specific conditions on what this physical system must be doing'. For example, in formulating the syntactic rule 'Move alpha', Chomsky (1982: 32) does not think there is a particular neuron corresponding to the rule.[14] Rather, he (1982: 32) is

> talking somehow about general structural properties of the brain, and there are real nontrivial questions about what it means to say that the brain, or any system, has general properties. It is like saying, what do we exactly mean when we say this computer is programmed to do arithmetic? We say that, and we understand it – it certainly has some meaning. But we do not mean there is a neuron in there that says 'Add 1' or a diode or something that says 'Add 1'.

At the level of concrete characterization, by contrast, linguistic theories would (have to) describe the language faculty by attributing physical mechanisms to the brain. Thus, Chomsky (1983: 124) doesn't see why someone couldn't, *in principle*, 'spell out' the genetic program for human language – i.e. give a description of the initial state of the language faculty – 'in terms of nucleotides'. That this can't be done at present does not indicate to Chomsky (1983: 125) that it is impossible in principle:

> We can say what the genetic program must look like (of course this is a scientific and not a mathematical 'must' – we are dealing

166

with a hypothesis about reality) but we cannot yet say what the genetic program is – which does not mean that we *could not* in principle say what it is. One has to make a sharp distinction between notions like 'inexplicable' and notions like 'unexplained'. At the moment there is no explanation, in terms of the biological structure of the organism, for the genetic program for this particular human language, and of course that is true of any other organ as well. To say that there is no explanation at the moment means, to me, that there is no set of principles by which we can deductively conclude this or that. There is no explanation at the moment for the fact that the heart is what it is, or the liver. That is not to say that it is inexplicable. It is possible that the principles are actually known but we don't know how to draw the conclusions because it is too complicated.

Notice that fundamental to the views expressed in this quotation is the metascientific distinction *inexplicable vs unexplained*, a point to which I will return below.

*Challenges of The Master at the 'abstract vs concrete characterization' fork have been plentiful, scoring shots scarce. To give you some idea of the diversity of the duels recently fought at this fork: Searle (1980: 37–8) vs The Master (1980b: 55–6) about the 'artefact-like' character of the mechanisms of UG; Katz (1981) vs The Master (1986: 36) about the (non-)Platonic character of postulated linguistic entities, and Piaget (1983) vs The Master (1980a: 207; 1983: 125) about the biological basis of postulated linguistic entities.[15] What each of these encounters evidences is just how hard it is to extend The Master on a metascientific mat.*

*The idea of a mat, involuntarily, makes one think of cricket. This, in turn, brings to mind an incident in which your Guide ventured into The Garden as a player planning to bowl The Master a bumper – a bumper being a bouncing ball directed at the body to bruise the batsman, thereby cracking his nerve, breaking his spirit. (This, incidentally, is cricket. I fear that what follows will be meaningful mostly to players of English extraction. There has to be some compensation, you would agree, for having ovals rather than diamonds as part of your culture.)*

167

*The ball bowled by Botha (1980: 20ff) was to derive its bump from the argument that the abstract entities – e.g. rules and conditions on rules – postulated by Chomskyan linguistic theories were not uniquely identifiable as mental entities, and therefore were ontologically indeterminate, unlike entities such as the protons, alpha particles and neutrinos postulated by theories of physics.[16] Hence the claims made about the former entities are not testable as mentalistic claims, the argument ran.*

*If, in cricket, you are at the striker's end, there are basically two ways of dealing with bumpers: hostile hooking or defensive ducking. The Master chose neither option, however. As a matter of fact, he appeared not to notice the threat of the bouncing ball at all. Of course, how could someone who did not know cricket from croquet entertain the right sort of respect for bumpers, yorkers, googlies and other devious deliveries with philosophical spin? There is, I admit, another possibility, one that I don't particularly care to contemplate: that the Bowler miserably misread the pitch, overestimating his ability to derive the necessary bounce from a soggy metascientific surface.*

*To accommodate players knowing nothing about cricket, let me restate the moral of this mini-story in a duelling idiom:*

*Offering to fence against The Master with a philosophical foil of which, rightly or wrongly, he has no fear is futility in its most refined form.*

*By the way, the (non-)incident at the Bumper Bifurcation provoked some by-play of an instructive nature. Incensed by the slinging of bumpers at The Master, Slezak (1981), a fervent follower of the Great Guy, rushed on to the pitch to hit the Bowler for a six. In his fury, however, Slezak threw his bat to the wind and, not having padded up properly, had to play the bowling with the proverbial bus ticket – which, even for a player from Down Under who knows his cricket, is too taxing a task. The outcome was utterly unavoidable: on the score book, the entry 'retired hurt' next to his name.[17]*

*The general point, Dear Player, may be remembered as the Fan Fury Factor:*

*When going flat out for The Master, be ready for some impulsive intervention by frothing fans who cannot face even the potential prospect of their Skipper being stumped (or, if you prefer, bumped) on his own wicket.*

4.2.5   The distinction *descriptive adequacy/descriptively adequate vs explanatory adequacy/explanatorily adequate* is at the root of what Chomsky (1986: 51) takes to be 'the central task' of his linguistics – namely, the task of 'finding the basic elements of I-language'. This distinction he (1986: 53) draws as follows:

> Continuing to think of a grammar as a theory of a language [i.e., an I-language], we may say that a grammar is *descriptively adequate* for a particular language to the extent that it correctly describes this language. A theory of UG meets the condition of *explanatory adequacy* to the extent that it provides descriptively adequate grammars under the boundary conditions set by experience. A theory of UG that meets this condition will, then, permit relevant facts about linguistic expressions to be derived from the grammars it selects, thus providing an explanation for the facts.[18]

In order to claim descriptive adequacy (for a grammar), one has to show that the descriptive devices provided for by the (associated) theory of UG are rich enough to account both for what Chomsky (1986: 51) calls 'the attested variety of languages' and for what he calls 'their possible variety'. To claim explanatory adequacy (for the associated theory of UG), one has to show that 'these devices are meager enough so that very few languages are made available to the language-learner, given data that, in fact, suffice for language acquisition'.

It is in order to meet this condition of 'meagreness' that Chomsky and other generative grammarians have over the years made strenuous attempts to restrict the formal power of, especially, syntactic transformations. The more powerful such devices are, the larger is the class of possible grammars provided for by UG, and the less likely the language-learner is to be able to arrive at the grammar of his language on the basis of insufficient primary linguistic data. As Chomsky (e.g. 1986: 52) has noted again and again, there is a certain tension or conflict between the 'task' of attaining descriptive adequacy and that of attaining explanatory adequacy:

169

To achieve descriptive adequacy, it often seems necessary to enrich the system of available devices, whereas to solve our case of Plato's problem we must restrict the system of available devices so that only a few languages, or just one, are determined by the given data. It is the tension between the two tasks that makes the field an intellectually interesting one, in my view.

To conclude: as pointed out by Chomsky (1986: 83), the 'problem of (attaining) explanatory adequacy' is a variant of Plato's problem (cf. section 2.1.2 above). And it is his concern for this problem which has 'led to efforts to reduce the variety of rule systems of this format [i.e., the phrase structure rule and transformational rule format]'.

*To some extent, 'descriptive adequacy vs explanatory adequacy' merely reflects a more basic fork – a bifurcation in the philosophical foundations of The Garden. The action that has taken place at the 'upper' of these two forks can therefore best be viewed from the vantage point of the 'lower' one, to which we turn next.*

4.2.6   Chomsky's pursuit of depth of insight, his defence of idealization, his concern with explanatory adequacy, his efforts to restrict the formal power of the theory of grammar, and his thesis of modularity have been placed in a more general philosophical perspective with reference to the distinction *rationalism vs empiricism*. For a convenient nutshell characterization of this distinction, we may turn to Katz and Bever (1977: 23).

'Empiricism' is the name of a metatheory. It is a theory about theories of how knowledge is acquired. It claims that the proper theory of how knowledge is acquired says that it comes from sensory experience by means of inductive principles. On empiricist theories, innate mental mechanisms are restricted to procedures for inductive generalization, and therefore contribute nothing to the content of our knowledge. 'Rationalism' is the name of the opposing metatheory. It claims that the general form of our knowledge comes not from experience but from innate schemata. On rationalist theories, much of the content of our knowledge is fixed as a biological disposition of our

170

mind; the function of experience is simply to activate this disposition and thereby cause the innate schemata to be realized and differentiated.

Chomskyan linguistic theory, as Katz and Bever (1977: 12) see it, is rationalist

because it allows for unobservable grammatical properties (which in the taxonomic model have no linguistic reality) to be stated as part of the rules of the linguist's theory about the speaker's internalized linguistic competence. Thus, the shift from a conception of grammar as cataloguing the data of a corpus to a conception of grammar as explicating the internalized rules underlying the speaker's ability to produce and understand sentences introduces 'deep structure' levels of grammar, which provide the linguistic reality that unobservable features otherwise lack.

Rationalism is further characterized by Bever (1974: 178) as the philosophical position that makes, amongst other things, the following assumptions:

(8)    (a)    Specific factual phenomena are often the result of interactions among different (physical, psychological, biological) systems.

        (b)    The formal theory of each of these systems should be as limited as possible in order to be as testable as possible.

        (c)    When a new fact can be described by the existing formal theories of both of two systems, but its description would require elaboration of one of these theories and not of the other, the fact is interpreted as due to the system whose formal theory requires no such elaboration.

These assumptions are made in order to provide explanations for the factual phenomena mentioned in (8) (a). If the phenomena or 'facts' or data to be accounted for by particular grammars are taken to include the linguistic judgements which native speakers make about expressions of their language, the essence of the rationalist position may be formulated as follows:

171

(9)     Intuitive linguistic judgements result from the operation
        of a number of factors. Only those intuitive linguistic
        judgements which result from the linguistic factor of
        grammatical competence fall within the domain of
        grammatical inquiry.[19]

Empiricism, as a general metascientific position, does not have the
explanatory concerns of rationalism and, consequently, does not
make the assumptions of (8) (a)-(c). The empiricist view of the data
to be accounted for by particular grammars may be characterized
as follows:

(10)    *All* intuitive linguistic judgements which can be studied
        systematically fall within the domain of grammatical
        inquiry.

The consequences of this view for the domain of 'linguistic inquiry'
have been spelled out by Lakoff (1974: 151):

I take linguistics to be the study of natural language in *all* its
manifestations. This is a broad conception of the field, and
I think it is an appropriately broad one. It includes not just
syntax-semantics, phonetics-phonology, historical linguistics,
anthropological linguistics, etc., which form the core of
most academic programs in this country, but also the role
of language in social interaction, in literature, in ritual, and in
propaganda, and as well the study of the relationship between
language and thought, speech production and perception,
linguistic disorders, etc.

An empiricist grammarian is required, therefore, to be able to
give an account of all intuitive judgements which the native speaker
is capable of systematically making about the utterances of his
language. Within the empiricist approach to linguistic inquiry a single
theory, namely a grammar, is assigned the whole of the function
which, within the rationalist approach, is assigned to the interaction
of several theories, including a grammar, a theory of speech
perception, a pragmatic theory of context and speech acts, a theory
of dialectal variation, a theory of social variation and possibly other
theories as well.

*The final battles in the Linguistic Wars, mentioned in section 2.7.5 above, were fought at the rationalist-empiricist front.*[20] *Fighting under the banner of interpretive semantics, the Chomskyan army got the upper hand by severely pounding the generative semanticist, empiricist enemy for its lack of explanatory concerns – for its urge to establish a New Taxonomy. To establish their New Taxonomy, it was challenged, the empiricists needed such powerful descriptive devices that it became impossible to solve the logical problem of language acquisition. The power of these devices made possible the construction of infinitely many grammars compatible with the primary linguistic data. Hence it would remain a mystery how children learning any particular language could be 'driven' to a unique grammar by the impoverished data.*

*Recently, The Garden saw a further piece of rationalist-versus-empiricist action. Trying his hand at The Game, a Wars-scarred George Lakoff (1980: 23) ventured into The Garden, questioning The Master's motives for reducing the class of possible syntactic transformations. It was his perception that The Master was reducing this class in order to uphold modularity, specifically to shore up his belief in an autonomous syntactic component. On Lakoff's own linguistic view, considerations of meaning and use 'affected virtually every rule of syntax'. In these terms it followed that, in order to preserve modularity, and specifically to preserve the autonomy of formal grammar, it was necessary for The Master to redefine and narrow down the domain of syntax. This The Master did, as Lakoff saw it, by getting rid of scores of troublesome transformations.*

*As earlier in The Wars so now in The Game, however, The Master was unmoved by Lakoff's Lament: 'His [i.e., Chomsky's] views on modularity are extreme and, I think, fundamentally mistaken' (Lakoff 1980: 23). Pulling Lakoff up for 'completely misunderstanding' the developments in question, The Master (1980b: 46) rather disdainfully declared:*

*Lakoff seems completely unaware of the actual character of the technical work to which he refers. Furthermore, where I have proposed restrictions on the scope (rather than the variety) of transformations – e.g., with regard to nominalization – the motivation was completely different from what Lakoff suggests, and in fact was internal to the language faculty, largely syntactic.*

*Of course a major consideration, reflected here in the phrase 'internal to the language faculty', was to restrict the class of possible transformations – an aim wholly consonant with the rationalist pursuit of explanatory adequacy as articulated in the logical problem of language acquisition.*

**4.3**  Having considered the ontological status of Chomskyan linguistic theories, we turn next to their epistemological nature. In particular we will consider a number of distinctions that shed some light on the **empirical status** of these theories.

*4.3.1*  The fundamental distinction in this context, repeatedly invoked by Chomsky, is *empirical vs a priori*. Chomsky (e.g. 1978a: 9; 1980a: 3, 48, 185ff) has always maintained that mentalistic linguistic theories must be empirical. This is to say that he 1978a: 9) requires both particular grammars and the theory of grammar to be 'falsifiable in principle'. Commenting on Lenneberg's work, Chomsky (1980a: 211) has stated the basic point as follows with reference to the theory of grammar:

> Lenneberg was quite right to take the trouble to emphasize that 'the discovery and description of innate mechanisms is a thoroughly empirical procedure and is an integral part of modern scientific inquiry' and to insist that there is no room here for dogmatism or *a priori* doctrine.

To undertake the study of innate mechanisms in an empirical manner is, on Chomsky's (1983: 65) view, to proceed 'not by philosophical discussion, but by looking at specific properties of the fixed nucleus [i.e., universal grammar] and asking how they might arise'. And Chomsky (1983: 80) insists that the claims made about the 'fixed nucleus' have been refutable hypotheses:

> An innatist hypothesis is a refutable hypothesis. Any hypothesis which says that such and such a property of language is genetically determined is subject to the most immediate refutation of the strongest kind. Such hypotheses have been refuted over and over again in the past by just looking at the next phenomenon in the same language or the next language.

174

That is why it has been so hard to formulate specific hypotheses about genetically determined structures.

A precondition for adopting such an empirical approach, Chomsky has stated (e.g. 1983: 65, 310–11), is an attitude of non-dogmatic open-mindedness.

*In our tour of The Maze, we came across quite a few forks – e.g. in sections 2.4.5 and 2.4.6 – where the fighting had broken out as a struggle about the nature of mind, but had ended as a clash about the empirical nature of mentalistic inquiry. Let us consider a further case in point.*

*As champions of Piagetian constructivism, Inhelder, Sinclair and Bovet (1974: 10) rejected the neonativist approach attributed by them to The Master because it 'does not help to solve any problem; all it does is to transfer the question from the psychological to the biological level by formulating it in terms of biological development'. The Master (1980a: 208–9) countered that no one would take such an argument seriously if Inhelder and Associates advanced it in the case of physical development, say that of the general structure of binocular vision. Moreover, he argued, if extensive evidence were found that the principles underlying, say, the* wh-*island constraint are acquired by the learner in the absence of relevant experience, it would be rational, not only to suppose that these principles are genetically determined, but to search for a further account in terms of biological development. Going for the kill, The Master (1980a: 209) continued:*

*The Geneva school doctrine seems to be that no matter how substantial the evidence in favor of such a thesis may be, and no matter how weak the argument for ontogenetic development, nevertheless we must maintain the thesis that the principles in question are derived by 'regulatory or autoregulatory mechanisms' in accordance with the hypothesis of 'developmental constructivism'. At least, I see no other way to read their proposals, since the arguments they put forth are in no way empirical but rather purely a priori. All of this again simply constitutes another chapter in the history of dogmatism.*

175

*So, Dear Player, The Master is not one to be won over by mere dogma, however winsome or worldly-wise its presentation, not even by dogma generated in the genre of a Geneva Gospel.*

4.3.2   Chomsky's conception of the empirical nature of linguistic theories may be clarified further with reference to the distinction *naive falsificationism vs sophisticated falsificationism.* Suppose that a grammatical analysis of a certain language presented data that appeared to conflict with a relatively deep, simple and unifying explanatory principle such as Subjacency. In such a case naive falsification would insist that the principle in question is to be rejected as falsified. However, according to Chomsky (1978a: 10) a linguist subscribing to a (more) sophisticated falsificationism would be willing to retain this principle, rather setting aside the 'falsifying' data as incorrect or irrelevant.

Chomsky (1978a: 10); 1978b: 14; 1980a: 10) furnishes two considerations in support of the attitude of epistemological tolerance adopted by sophisticated falsificationists towards threatened theories. The first is historical: this attitude has paid off in the case of the natural sciences, Galileo being a notable exponent of it. Consider the following characterization by Chomsky (1978b: 14) of Galileo's epistemological tolerance:

> If you go back to the time of Galileo, and you looked at the array of phenomena that had to be accounted for, it was prima facie obvious that the Galilean theory, the Copernican theory could not be supported. That is, there were just masses of refuting data. And, Galileo sort of plowed his way through this, putting much of the data aside, redefining what was relevant, and what was not relevant, formulating questions in such a way that what appeared to be refuting data were no longer so, and in fact, very often just disregarding data that should have refuted the system, and did this, not simply with reckless abandon, but because of a recognition that explanatory principles were being discovered that gave insight into at least some of the phenomena.

The second consideration adduced by Chomsky (1978a: 10) in justification of the attitude of epistemological tolerance, he derives

176

from the current state of development of linguistic theory. Linguistic theory, in Chomsky's opinion, is so underdeveloped that it is often not clear which data are relevant to the appraisal of individual theories and which are not. Often, moreover, the apparently negative evidence is not fully understood by linguists. For instance, Chomsky (1980a: 10) contends as follows:

> As for the matter of unexplained apparent counterevidence, if someone were to descend from heaven with the absolute truth about language or some other cognitive faculty, this theory would doubtless be confronted at once with all sorts of problems and 'counterexamples', if only because we do not yet understand the natural bounds of these particular faculties and because partially understood data are so easily misconstrued.

In the case of a conflict between a relatively deep unifying principle and some poorly understood negative data Chomsky, in a spirit of sophisticated falsificationism, is willing to practise epistemological tolerance, giving the principle the benefit of the doubt.[21] To pursue depth of insight by making radical idealizations and by practising epistemological tolerance is, according to Chomsky (1980a: 8, 218), to operate in the 'Galilean style' of inquiry.[22]


*The Master has been vehemently attacked, more than once, for preaching and practising an attitude of epistemological tolerance. Recently, Brame (1985) has intolerantly suggested that the adoption of this attitude by The Master amounts to the 'immunization' of The Master's 'idealizations' against refutation. This attitude, on Brame's analysis, creates 'escape hatches' which make it impossible to hold The Master 'responsible' for misanalyses and to refute his theories 'on any grounds'. Not yet scraping the bottom of his barrel of barbed brusquerie, Brame (1985: 346) branded The Master's epistemological tolerance as part of 'a last ditch stand to defend transformational grammar before it falls of its own weight'. Then, dipping still deeper, Brame (1985: 346) denounced The Master's (1980a: 10) defence of epistemological tolerance as 'designed to impress upon us that counterevidence must be tolerated for the very reason that the theory to which these counterexamples are being posed is on the verge of collapse'. So, to Brame, The Master's tolerant position on the impact of counterevidence implies the message that 'the ordinary canons of rationality' are to be 'kissed goodbye'. Strong stuff, you would agree, Dear Player.*

*As for The Master's reaction to this Brame Brand Brusqueness, we will have to wait for it a little while longer. In the meantime, why not contemplate the following Playful Poser:*

> *If you could command conviction by invoking clinically cool considerations, why brew your rhetoric to some red-hot recipe?[23]*

4.3.3   The distinction *empirical vs notational* provides additional aid in determining the sense in which Chomskyan linguistic theories could be considered 'empirical'. This distinction is implicit in Harman's (1980) attempt to distinguish between the truth of a linguistic theory and the psychological reality of such a theory. From the discussion in section 4.2.2 it seems clear that not only Harman, but also Chomsky himself, finds it necessary to draw a distinction between aspects of a theory that 'correspond to reality' and aspects of a theory that don't. The former aspects express refutable claims about reality and may consequently be characterized as 'empirical'. The latter aspects are 'mere artifacts of our notation', to use an expression of Harman's, and consequently are non-empirical or notational.

Chomsky (1980b: 45–6) appears to have accepted the correctness of Harman's basic distinction. He has even extended the distinction 'empirical vs notational' to a class of more interesting cases:

> There are interesting examples that go beyond notational variants in a narrow sense. Thus, suppose we assume the trace theory of movement rules (cf. Chomsky 1975; 1977). Consider two theories: (1) generate base structures, which are mapped to abstract S-structures including trace by transformations, with S-structures mapped to phonetic representations by the rules $R_1$ and to 'logical form' representations (LF) by the rules $R_2$; (2) base-generate S-structures directly, mapping them to phonetic representation by $R_1$ and to LF by rules $R_2$ and $R_3$, where $R_3$ have the properties of the transformational

movement rules (properties distinct from $R_2$, I believe). These two theories are not notational variants in a narrow sense, but it is not entirely clear whether they have different empirical content within the domain of 'linguistic evidence', and it might be argued that on such evidence one should not attempt to choose between these theories but only to aim at a more abstract theory of which these are two specific realizations . . .

*The fork 'empirical vs notational' has not lately been the scene of serious strife; yet it is very much part of The Garden. Indeed, in The Linguistic Wars, The Master's men made clever use of this very fork to ambush the generative semanticist guard. But all that is ancient history now.*[24]

**4.4** This brings us to Chomsky's view of what is involved in furnishing **justification** for linguistic theories. This view may be explored by considering some basic distinctions relating to the notions 'evidence', 'data', 'demonstration', 'proof', 'plausibility' and so on.

*4.4.1* Fundamental to Chomsky's view of what is involved in the justification of linguistic theories is the distinction *evidence vs demonstration*. Because he considers linguistics an empirical science, Chomsky (1983: 80) notes that one cannot 'prove' or 'demonstrate' that a particular linguistic property is innate:

In science [as opposed to mathematics] you don't have demonstrative inferences; in science you can accumulate evidence that makes certain hypotheses seem reasonable, and that is all you can do – otherwise you are doing mathematics.

The linguist, like the astronomer, must on Chomsky's (1980a: 191) view be 'always aware that in empirical inquiry we can, at best, support a theory against substantive alternatives and empirical challenge; we cannot prove it to be true'.

Chomsky (1983: 80) thinks it possible, nevertheless, to 'find a lot of evidence that is convincing', even though he (1980a: 198) sees the conditions on evidence as being themselves 'subject to

179

doubt and revision'. Nor, in his (1980a: 198) opinion, is there any ground of certainty when it comes to assessing the import of evidence:

> Even if we were to grant that there is some set of observation sentences that constitute the bedrock of inquiry and are immune to challenge, it nevertheless remains true that theory must be invoked to determine to what, if anything, these pure and perfect observations attest, and here there is no Cartesian ground of certainty.

Chomsky's (1980a: 18; 1986: 13, n. 5) view of the justification of empirical (mentalistic) theories is, in essence, that such theories are 'underdetermined by the evidence'. This view he considers to be that of a 'moderately sophisticated realist'.

*Recall, Dear Player, that at the fork 'realism vs non-realism' we found lots of evidence – not to say 'proof'! – of a protracted battle between The Master and Quine about the ontological status of (linguistic) theories. This battle, in fact, has spilled over to the 'evidence vs demonstration' fork. Thus, Quine (1972), and Putnam (1981) in his wake, have charged, in The Master's (1986: 13, n. 5) words, that 'there is a very severe, in fact, insuperable problem of underdetermination affecting all aspects of language and grammar; and much of psychology more generally'. The 'severe problem' is the alleged lack of evidence on the basis of which a choice could be made between (extensionally) equivalent theories. The Master (1986: 13, n. 5) has stood his ground, however:*

> *I do not think that he [i.e., Quine] succeeded in showing that some novel form of indeterminacy affects the study of language beyond the normal underdetermination of theory by evidence; his own formulations of the thesis furthermore involve internal inconsistency . . .*[25]

*The Master (1975a: 181) was unable to find in Quine's problem 'anything enigmatic . . . apart from the inescapable problems of empirical uncertainty'. And, demonstrating his dexterity, The Master (1975a: 181–2) depreciatingly deflated Quine's Quandary: 'Quine's sole point reduces to the observation that there will always be distinct theories that are compatible with all the evidence at hand.' This observation by Quine does not distinguish linguistics and psychology in principle from the natural sciences, as we will see in section 5.5 below.*

4.4.2 To understand the way in which Chomskyans proceed to justify claims about the genetic basis of the language faculty – what are termed 'nativist claims' – we have to consider the distinction *direct methods/tests vs indirect argumentation*. The evidence needed for the justification of nativist claims cannot be obtained by direct methods for, as noted by Chomsky (1983: 80), 'we [cannot] deal with humans the way we deal with fruit flies', a point that he (1980a: 197) elaborates on as follows:

> If we were able to investigate humans as we study other, defenseless organisms, we might very well proceed to inquire into the operative mechanisms by intrusive experimentation, by constructing controlled conditions for language growth, and so on, thus perhaps narrowing the gap between the language example and the astronomical example. The barriers to this direct investigation are ethical.[26]

Chomskyans, therefore, 'must be satisfied with quite indirect evidence' (1980a: 197). According to Chomsky (1983: 80–1) they 'are forced to have arguments that are much more indirect and complex, inferences that are only partially supported, open questions that we know how to investigate in principle but are barred from investigating'.

To find arguments of the indirect sort is certainly possible on Chomsky's (1983: 113) view:

> The natural way to proceed, if we are trying to determine the nature of $S_0$, is to try to find some property of the steady state that is minimally affected by experience, a property for which E (experience) is reduced as close to zero as possible.

This type of indirect argument is what Chomsky (1980a: 34) has referred to as the 'argument from poverty of the stimulus'. It is, in his own words (1980a: 36), the argument proceeding from the

181

assumption 'that what the stimulus lacks is produced by the organism from its inner [genetically endowed] resources'.[27]

*The fork 'direct methods/tests vs indirect argumentation' – I predict, Dear Player – is going to witness progressively Pugnacious Play. A couple of preparatory moves have already been made. Thus, appraising Lightfoot's (1982: 51ff) map of this area of The Garden, Botha (1985: 110–11) has contended that, as used by certain followers of The Master's, the so-called argument from poverty of the stimulus may be more aptly characterized as 'the argument from ignorance of the stimulus'. These are fellow fighters of The Master's who fail to furnish any specific facts about the poverty of the stimulus, i.e., about the primary linguistic data to which children did or did not have access in their acquisition of certain universal elements of grammar.*

*Showing an acute sense of anticipation of possible action to come, The Master (1983: 113) has hinted at one line of defence that could be tried in response to the Ignorance Incursion:*

> *Of course, in order to demonstrate that there is no relevant experience with respect to some property of language, we really would have to have a complete record of a person's experience – a job that would be totally boring; there is no empirical problem in getting this information, but nobody in his right mind would try to do it. So what we can try to do is to find properties for which it is very implausible to assume that everyone has had relevant experience.*

*These remarks, Duly Impressed Pupil, reveal the existence of yet another weapon in The Master's already awesome arsenal of means of aggressive action aimed at adversaries: Rhetorical Riposte Doing Deterrent Duty. Do you, by any chance, know a self-respecting scholar who would stick out his neck to defend the notion of doing 'a job that [is] totally boring' or of toiling at a task 'nobody in his right mind would try to do'?*

4.4.3    The nature of the evidence used in the justification of Chomskyan theories may be considered further with reference to the distinction *internal (linguistic) evidence vs external (linguistic) evidence*. On one characterization, internal (linguistic) evidence consists of data about the objects internal to the linguistic reality of the Chomskyan linguist as this reality is delimited by means of the abstractions and idealizations used by him. The primary source of internal evidence is the linguistic intuitions which native speakers of a language are claimed to have about the properties of utterances of the language.

External (linguistic) evidence, by contrast, consists of data about objects and phenomena outside the idealized linguistic reality of which Chomskyan linguistic theories have to provide an account.[28] External evidence may include, for example, data about the physical basis of the language capacity, data about the actual use of grammatical competence in performance, data about linguistic change, data about language variation, data about speech pathology, and so on. External evidence may also be denoted by means of Chomsky's (1986: 34) expression 'extralinguistic data'. While we are dealing with terminology, note also that the terminological pairs 'introspective–nonintrospective', 'intuitive–nonintuitive' and 'judgemental–nonjudgemental' have been widely used as sloppy synonyms for 'internal–external'.

Over the years it has been often contended that the distinction 'internal evidence vs external evidence' is essential to the justification of the claims of Chomskyan linguistic theories if these are to have mentalistic import. Specifically, it has been argued that neither mentalistic claims about the structure of the language faculty nor markedness claims about the distinction between core and periphery can be adequately justified without recourse to external linguistic evidence.[29]

Chomsky's position on the epistemological status of external evidence is not entirely perspicuous. On the one hand, he (1981b: 9) has clearly recognized the need for external evidence in the justification of markedness claims:

How do we delimit the domain of core grammar as distinct from marked periphery? In principle, one would hope that evidence from [real-time] language acquisition would be useful with regard to determining the nature of the boundary or the propriety of the distinction in the first place, since it is predicted that the systems develop in quite different ways. Similarly, such evidence, along with evidence derived from psycholinguistic experimentation, the study of language use (e.g., processing), language deficit, and other sources should be relevant, in principle, to determining the properties of UG and of particular grammars.

And, invoking the notion of 'I-language', Chomsky (1986: 36–7) has observed that

In principle, evidence concerning the character of the I-language and initial state could come from many different sources apart from judgments concerning the form and meaning of expressions: perceptual experiments, the study of acquisition and deficit or of partially invented languages such as creoles (n. 25), or of literary usage or language change, neurology, biochemistry, and so on.

On the other hand, Chomsky (1980b: 45) has repeatedly rejected the idea that, for establishing the psychological reality of (an aspect of) a theory, a distinction has to be drawn between 'two epistemological categories: "linguistic evidence" bearing on "good theories", and "psychological evidence" bearing on "psychological reality"'.

Recall, however, that in section 4.2.2 above we saw that Chomsky did agree with Harman's (1980: 21) contention that the evidence required for the (physical) reality of some aspect of a theory may be different from the evidence required for the truth of the theory:

Sometimes we are not sure about the physical reality of some aspect of a theory, even given strong evidence for the truth of the theory. A different sort of evidence may be needed. The postulation of quarks gives a structure to the proliferation of subatomic particles, but physicists demand a different sort of evidence in order to establish the physical reality of quarks.

Chomsky (1980b: 45) has emphatically noted that he and Harman 'agree' on there not being two categories of evidence, namely 'linguistic evidence' and 'psychological evidence'. But, italicizing the word 'experiments', Harman (1980: 22) in fact was saying something different – namely, that he 'completely agree[s] with Chomsky that

184

this does not mean we have to appeal to psychological *experiments* to provide evidence for psychological reality'. Chomsky, moreover, has not brought his epistemological stance in line with his concession that the evidence needed for psychological reality may be *different* from that needed for truth.

*So, quite frankly, Dear Player, the 'internal vs external' fork, immersed as it is in the mists of a Metascientific Marshland, forms a somewhat indefinable feature of The Garden. Unfortunately, that is, The Master's style in striving to sustain his stand on this soggy and unstable soil leaves us with a patently murky perception of the problem. And so it would be prudent, Peering Player, to take notice of the Marksman's Maxim:*

*A mote of methodological mud in the marksman's eye makes the mark all the easier to miss.*

Before proceeding to the next major metascientific distinction, let us briefly reflect on the nature of internal (linguistic) evidence. This kind of evidence is often described as comprising 'judgements of native speakers' or 'informant judgements'. As pointed out by Chomsky (1986: 36), informant judgements 'do not reflect the structure of [I-]language directly'. Because of the intrusion of a variety of factors, such judgements often provide evidence merely about the properties of utterances and fail to provide direct evidence about the I-language structures that underlie the utterances. Thus, a given judgement may provide evidence about the acceptability of an utterance without furnishing direct evidence about the grammaticality of the underlying structure of the utterance.

Notice that implicit in Chomsky's remarks on the import of native speaker judgements is the distinction *grammatical vs acceptable*. In earlier studies, Chomsky (1965: 10) used the term 'acceptable' to denote a property of utterances 'that are perfectly natural and immediately comprehensible without paper-and-pencil analysis, and in no way bizarre or outlandish'. 'Grammatical', by contrast, denotes the property that sentences have if they are formed, technically 'generated', by the rules of the grammar of the language. The grammaticalness of a sentence is just one among the many factors that jointly determine the acceptability of the utterances by means of which the sentence may be 'performed'. Thus, to take Chomsky's (1957: 15) classic example, the sentence *Colorless green ideas sleep furiously* is at once grammatical and unacceptable. It is grammatical in having been formed in accordance with the grammatical rules of English, but it is unacceptable in not having a coherent literal interpretation. Chomsky (1965: 11), considered 'Acceptability [to be] a concept that belongs to the study of performance, whereas grammaticalness belongs to the study of competence'. And, technically, generative grammars had to draw a distinction between grammatical and ungrammatical sentences – by generating all and only the former – and not between acceptable and unacceptable sentences.

Returning to native speaker judgements, native speakers are claimed to arrive at their linguistic judgements by means of two 'methods' or 'processes': intuition and introspection. Pateman (1987: 135) has recently characterized intuition as a process that 'gives us causally related indexical or symptomatic evidence for the character of underlying psycholinguistic (or, more generally, psychological) processes'. He, thus, takes intuitions to be 'reports of appearances' that provide 'causal evidence' of a subjective sort about our minds. Introspection represents to Chomsky (1980a: 140ff) the 'reflection', 'analysis' or 'careful thought' to which 'accessible' elements of the contents of the mind may be subjected.

Pateman (1987: 135), moreover, has made an interesting attempt to establish a link between the distinctions *intuition vs introspection* and *I-language vs E-language*:

In Chomsky's terms (Chomsky 1986, ch. 2), intuition provides evidence for the character of I-languages (internalized languages), whereas introspective judgement – exercised, for example, when a foreigner asks me whether you can say P in English – provides evidence for the character of E-languages (externalized languages).

In sum: there is a distinction *intuitive evidence vs introspective evidence* that is a useful tool for giving some structure to the notion of 'internal (linguistic) evidence'.

186

*4.4.4* A further distinction bearing on the nature of linguistic evidence is *evidence from a single language vs evidence from a diversity of languages*. Traditionally, it has been believed that in order to test or justify claims about linguistic universals a large number of languages, preferably genetically unrelated, must be analysed in order to obtain what is termed 'cross-linguistic evidence'. This view ties in with the idea – examined in section 3.2.1 above – that linguistic univerals are statements about properties common to all languages. On the Chomskyan view, however, linguistic universals are claims about biologically necessary properties of language. For this reason, Chomskyans have chosen – to use the words of Newmeyer (1983: 69) – to concentrate on a single language, 'their native languages (which, again, has typically meant English) because they believe that the *intensive* study of one language will yield far more insights into the basic nature of linguistic processes than the *superficial* study of many'.

The form of argument within which 'intensive' analyses of single languages are used to furnish evidence for (genetically based) linguistic universals is, of course, that of poverty of the stimulus. A biologically necessary property of language, we have seen, is one that cannot be acquired on the basis of the impoverished stimulus. And as we have also seen, in order to justify a hypothesis postulating such a universal, it is sufficient to provide evidence from a single language showing that the stimulus is impoverished in the appropriate sense. There is, furthermore, a general methodological problem with analysing a diversity of non-native languages, as noted by Newmeyer (1983: 69): 'the principles found to constrain grammars [i.e., linguistic universals in the biological sense] are in general too complex and abstract to be discovered by a superficial look at a nonnative language.'

*Hiż (1967) is one of the Past Players who tried to lock The Master in a stranglehold at the 'single language vs diverse languages' fork. He (1967: 71) observed that The Master's proposals concerning linguistic universals were not based on an 'examination of many cases' but rather on an analysis of a few languages: 'Chomsky presents no more than English and an isolated property of Mohawk to substantiate some grammatical universals.' The Master (1972: 188) had no difficulty in breaking the Hiż Hold, however, agreeing that one should study as many languages as possible but entering a 'caveat':*

> It would be quite easy to present enormous masses of data from varied languages that are compatible with all conceptions of universal grammar that have so far been formulated. There is no point in doing so. If one is concerned with the principles of universal grammar, he will try to discover those properties of particular grammars that bear on these principles, putting aside large amounts of material that, so far as he can determine, do not. It is only through intensive studies of particular languages that one can hope to find crucial evidence for the study of universal grammar.

*The history of Hiż – who was hauled up for other howlers too – contains a lesson that you would be wise to heed: never put your trust in a hold that has been tried but that failed to hurt.*

4.4.5    Chomsky's new position on the usefulness of evidence from a diversity of languages can be further elucidated with reference to the distinction *evidence from genetically related languages vs evidence from genetically unrelated languages*. This distinction ties in with the more basic one between fundamental principles and open parameters considered in section 2.3.7 above.

Evidence derived from genetically unrelated languages provides an additional, independent basis for appraising claims that postulate fundamental universal principles. Such claims, we have seen, are initially justified with reference to the poverty of the stimulus. In his *Lectures on Government and Binding* Chomsky in fact uses evidence from a variety of genetically unrelated languages to test claims postulated initially on the basis of an analysis of English (and a few other genetically related languages). For example, on the basis of an analysis of English, Chomsky (1981b: 210) at first believed that opacity could result from the occurrence of tense in a particular domain. In time, however, he abandoned this idea because it had failed to be borne out by evidence from genetically unrelated languages:

> But this is not true in certain other languages. George and Kornfilt show that in Turkish, where tense and agreement are dissociated, it is agreement rather than tense that determines

opacity. The same is true in Portuguese, as observed by Rouveret . . .

Turning to the import of evidence from genetically related languages, Chomsky (1981b: 6) considers the study of languages that differ in regard to their clustering of properties most useful. The comparative study of genetically related languages makes it possible to identify open parameters of fundamental principles and, moreover, to determine the possible range of variation in these principles. Chomsky (1981b: 6) puts his position as follows:

> study of closely related languages that differ in some clustering of properties is particularly valuable for the opportunities it affords to identify and clarify parameters of UG that permit a range of variation in the proposed principles. Work of the past several years on the Romance languages, some of which will be discussed below, has exploited these possibilities quite effectively.

As indicated in section 2.5.21 above, the study of genetically related languages has, for example, led to an increase in our understanding of the parametric variation in Subjacency.

*No, Protesting Player, there is no inconsistency here between The Master's earlier handling of Hiż and his subsequent use of evidence from a diversity of languages. The Inconsistency Injunction, that is, is not decisive in itself. The Master has invariably insisted that a crucial condition governs the analyses of fragment grammars which provide the evidence for or against general linguistic claims about universal grammar. This is the condition of descriptive adequacy, formulated below in terms of a notion of 'convincingness':*

> *To find evidence to support or to refute a proposed condition on rules, it does not suffice to list unexplained phenomena; rather it is necessary to present rules, i.e. to present a fragment of grammar. The confirmation or refutation will be as convincing as the fragment of grammar presented. (Chomsky 1977: 74)*

**4.5** In Chomskyan linguistics, more than one notion of **simplicity** plays a role in theory appraisal. Since it is of some importance to keep the various Chomskyan notions of 'simplicity' apart, we turn next to a network of distinctions in which they are involved. The discussion will be brief, setting up signposts rather than drawing a detailed map.

4.5.1 To begin with, there is Chomsky's distinction *conceptual simplicity vs messy systems*. In pursuing depth of insight, Chomsky (1982: 30-1) values theories that are conceptually simple in the sense that they do not incorporate redundancies. This kind of simplicity – also called '(conceptual) elegance' or 'beauty' – is the product of conceptual unification. The reason why scientists value such attributes of theories, Chomsky (1982: 30) speculates, is 'an almost mystical belief that there is something about our concept of elegance that relates to truth'. Chomsky (1982: 30) also notes, however, that this linking of elegance and truth

> is certainly not logically necessary. Our brains might have been devised in such a way that what looks elegant to them is totally off base. But you really have no choice but to try to use the resources of your mind to find conceptual unification and explanation and elegance, hoping that by some miracle that is the way the world works.

Up to a point, Chomsky (1982: 30) further observes, the pursuit of truth via conceptual simplicity or elegance has been successful in the study both of biological systems and of language. But at the same time he (1982: 30) seriously considers the position that the world might be messy:

> it might be a fundamental error to search for too much elegance in the theory of language, because maybe those parts of the brain developed the way they did in part accidentally. For example, what has been so far a very productive leading idea, trying to eliminate redundancy, could be argued to be the wrong move, because in fact we know that biological systems tend to be highly redundant for good reasons. Suppose it does turn out that biological systems are messy, either because of historical accident or maybe because they work better when they're messy. They may provide many different ways of doing the same thing. If something fails, something else will work. To the extent that that is true. [*sic*] The theory of these systems is going to be messy too.

190

If this turned out to be the case, it might, in Chomsky's (1982: 31) opinion, 'be a really fundamental error to be guided too much by an effort to eliminate redundancy in developing explanatory theories'.

*You find that 'Pupil' has become a misnomer, a paternalistic appellative? Having practised hard, you present yourself as a candidate for the predicate of 'Proper Player'? To assist you in appraising your playing powers, I will set you a couple of posers at some of the 'simplicity vs complexity' forks in this part of The Garden. Your test is to tell how good my questions/statements will be as probes in profitable play.*

Poser Number One
*Finding (conceptually) elegant theories to account for the apparent messiness of systems – isn't that what science is really about?*

OR

*Saying that the system is messy is just a roundabout way of conceding that your theory is flawed.*

4.5.2    In outlining his view of simplicity, Chomsky (1981b: 7) invokes, moreover, the distinction *simplicity of principles and rules vs (apparent) complexity of phenomena and structures*. Chomsky's modular conception of the human mind in general and language in particular – cf. section 2.7.3 above – makes it possible to formulate simple principles for the explanation of apparently complex phenomena. The apparent complexity of a given problematic phenomenon may on deeper analysis reflect the interaction of several essentially simple principles belonging to various modules of core grammar. In Chomsky's (1981b: 7) words: 'The full range of properties of some construction may often result from interaction of several components, its apparent complexity reducible to simple principles of separate subsystems.' And with reference to mental representations at the level of sound structure, Chomsky (1986: 43) has recently observed that 'The systems of rules and principles that form and modify them [i.e., the mental representations] are fairly

191

simple and natural, although they interact to yield structures of considerable complexity and to determine their properties in quite a precise fashion.'

In *Lectures on Government and Binding*, Chomsky illustrates this 'modular character of grammar' with a variety of typical cases, a classic one being his analysis of sentences such as *John is certain to be here, John seems to be here* etc. (1981b: 79). Recall that – as explained in section 4.2.6 above – Chomsky's modular approach reflects the fundamental philosophical position of rationalism.

Poser Number Two
*Measured in terms of the messiness of the system(s) described, what would be the cost of having a variety of (minute) mental modules, each with its own make-up and mode of organization?*

4.5.3    A further distinction involving conceptual or theoretical simplicity is that of *simplicity of principles and theories vs complexity of argument*. This distinction is mentioned by Chomsky (1986: 45) when he draws attention to 'a characteristic and important feature of the shift from the earlier conception of UG in terms of rule systems to a principles-and-parameters model':

Argument is much more complex, the reason being that the theory is much simpler; it is based on a fairly small number of general principles that must suffice to derive the consequences of elaborate and language-specific rule systems.

Chomsky (1981b: 15) considers this form of complexity, moreover, to be a 'positive merit':

Insofar as we succeed in finding unifying principles that are deeper, simpler and more natural, we can expect that the complexity of argument explaining why the facts are such-and-such will increase, as valid (or, in the real world, partially valid) generalizations and observations are reduced to more abstract principles. But this form of complexity is a positive merit of an explanatory theory, one to be valued and not to be regarded as a defect in it. It is a concomitant of what Moravcsik (1980) calls 'deep' as opposed to 'shallow' theories of mind, and is an indication of success in developing such theories. It is important to distinguish clearly between complexity of theory and complexity of argument, the latter tending to increase as theory becomes less complex in the intuitive sense.

Note that these remarks by Chomsky reflect his acceptance of another metascientific distinction, Moravcsik's (1980: 28) distinction *deep theories (of mind) vs shallow theories (of mind)*:

> I shall label as 'deep' (without implying any depth in a normative sense) the theories that refer to many layers of unobservables in their explanations, and I shall regard even some of the fundamental facts to be accounted for as lying beneath the level of observability. Such theories are guided by the intuition that the observable appearances can be explained adequately only by the examination of the underlying unobservable aspects of nature. ('Nature does not wear its essence on its sleeves.') What I label 'shallow' theories are those that try to stick as close to the observable as possible, aim mostly at correlations between observables, and posit something unobservable only when this seems unavoidable – even then, such theories demand some direct relationships between the observable and the unobservable.

We have isolated, then, two further metascientific consequences of Chomsky's second conceptual shift: an increase in the depth of theories and a concomitant increase in the complexity of argument.

Poser Number Three
*Welcoming inferential complexity that arises from theoretical simplicity – isn't this a little like both eating one's cake and having it?*

OR

*Complexity of argument that is not a sign of deductive depth is metascientifically neither a virtue nor a vice.*

4.5.4 Crucial to an understanding of the Chomskyan conception of theory appraisal is the distinction *conceptual simplicity vs notational simplicity*. The nature of conceptual simplicity has received some measure of clarification in the paragraphs immediately preceding. Conceptual simplicity represents a general metascientific notion; however, notational simplicity is a technical notion specific to generative grammar. Specifically, notational simplicity was embodied in the 'simplicity measures' or 'evaluation metrics' which Chomsky (1965: 37ff) (at one time) looked upon as the devices by which a particular grammar within the set of possible grammars compatible with the data would be selected as the 'most highly valued' one. This kind of simplicity was 'notational' in the sense that it was taken by some generative grammarians to be reflected by the simplicity of the notation used in the formulation of fragments of grammar. Thus, Newmeyer (1983: 41) observes that

> the idea of a 'simplicity measure' is often implicit in the choice of notational conventions. The parentheses notation for collapsing rules is a good example. This notation was devised so that, given two analyses – one employing parentheses and one not – the former would be more directly reflective of linguistic generalizations and also be shorter.

Ultimately, the choice of the best simplicity measure or evaluation metric was, on Chomsky's view (1965: 37ff), an empirical matter. The correct measure or metric would be the one that accurately characterized the way in which the child in acquiring its language 'selected' the grammar of its language on the basis of impoverished data. Chomsky's principles-and-parameters approach, however, makes no explicit provision for a form of simplicity that is 'notational' in the above sense. In place of a simplicity metric, this approach incorporates a concept of 'markedness' that has to provide a basis for drawing a distinction between more highly valued (or less marked) and less highly valued (or more marked) grammars (cf. section 2.5.20 above for this equation).

*You're pained by my posers, playful or otherwise, and concede that Practising Pupils and Practising Professionals are related by homonymy and not much more. At your request, then, I am of course willing to let you have some more of the Lore of the Labyrinth. If ever, Fledgling Fighter, you should wish to analyse the anatomy of Barren Bellicosity, the 'conceptual simplicity vs notational simplicity' bifurcation would be an excellent place to start. It is a fork that has seen much in the way of profitless play by opponents of The Master's who failed to keep the two kinds of simplicity apart.*

*Consider in this connection Baron's (1981: 84) rejection of the 'Chomskian cost–benefit analysis of language'.*

> *The Chomskian school, developing an economic metaphor, has implied that exceptions to grammatical rules should be very 'costly', and therefore, rules should be constructed so as to yield the smallest number of exceptions possible. Like latter-day counterparts of Karl Verner, transformational grammarians have implied that actual language can be wholly generated by rules; our task is to find them. There have, however, been many schools of linguistics which have [correctly] rejected the Chomskian cost–benefit analysis of language.*

*Baron's Broadside, as correctly noted by Newmeyer (1983: 84), was triggered by a confusion of the Chomskyan technical simplicity metric with a field-independent general notion of simplicity that is an essential building block of the metascientific foundations of 'scientific linguistics'. Thus, Newmeyer (1983: 42) observes that:*

> *Baron's phraseology suggests that she is opposed to some particular evaluation metric internal to grammatical theory. But consider the content of the rejection of the idea that 'rules should be constructed so as to yield the smallest number of exceptions possible'. It is no less than the rejection of the goal of finding as much systematicity as exists in language.*

*And Newmeyer proceeds to point out that the rejection of this goal entails 'the abandonment of a scientific perspective on language'.*

*So in the Simplicity Sector of The Garden, Dear Player, you will need to watch your step no less warily than elsewhere. It is a minefield of apparent contradictions, I can tell you, which – when prodded in imprudent play – could blast you into oblivion.[30] Having picked our way through the pitfalls of this perilous part of The Garden, we have come to the end of our march through the Marshlands of Method. To have survived at all is a philosophical feat of formidable format, which you will appreciate all the more keenly when you return to engage The Giant Generative Jouster in single combat.*

# 5

## Locus in the Landscape of Learning

*Where in the wider World of Wisdom is The Garden to be found? What Site in Science does it occupy?*

*Yes, indeed, Pondering Player, these questions now press for a proper reply. If you couldn't locate The Garden in the Landscape of Learning, how would you ever be able to return there – propelled by your appetite for perilous play in the Mind-mapper's Marvellous Maze? Or, how could you be sure that you were hot on the heels of the Generative Genius and not pottering around in some other Arboreal Area of Academe, far removed from the channels of the Charles?*

*So, what I will give you, as a parting gift, are a couple of coordinates for locating Noam's Land on the Globe of Ologies and Isms. And for an encore, I will tell you the tempestuous tale of a holy war that was fought between the Lord of the Labyrinth and a Phylum of Philosophers at a purportedly basic bifurcation in The Garden.*

We have considered Chomskyan linguistics from the point of view of its basic questions, guiding aims, fundamental ideas, types of theory and metascientific means. We come now to a final question: How does Chomskyan linguistics relate to what have been considered to be adjacent but separate fields of study? The sections that follow provide the outlines of an answer to this question. These outlines are drawn with the aid of a set of distinctions linking

Chomskyan linguistics to philosophy, mathematics, psychology, the brain sciences and biology on the one hand, and to the harder natural sciences on the other hand.

**5.1**  With reference to the distinction **linguistics vs philosophy**, Chomsky (1982: 5) has observed that 'the interactions with philosophy are very tight and many-layered. They occur in all sorts of places.' The 'levels' or 'points of contact' between linguistics and philosophy singled out by Chomsky (1982: 5–6) include: (a) the work by 'people' such as Vendler 'who have looked to linguistics to try to answer philosophical questions';[1] (b) the work of ordinary-language philosophers such as Austin who 'are really just doing linguistics', or, more accurately, 'philology';[2] (c) the work that certain philosophers have done on semantics – for example, 'model theoretic semantics of a natural language'; (d) the 'philosophical work' that has been done by certain philosophers on the methodological problems of the sciences, e.g. the question of what explanation is in linguistics; (e) the work by philosophers who have explored 'what the study of language has to say about questions of epistemology'.

As regards works of the latter sort, Chomsky (1982: 6) is of the opinion that

> one can conceive of the study of language as being one possible paradigm for the investigation of the nature of knowledge, the nature of human knowledge, and the problems of a priori knowledge (n. 6). In my view, here is where the most interesting connections lie, but only a very small number of philosophers are interested in these questions.

The 'points of contact' mentioned above, however, should not obscure the fundamental methodological difference between Chomskyan linguistics and philosophical analysis proper. The former is claimed by Chomsky to be an empirical enterprise – cf. section 4.3 above. The latter is not. And Chomsky has insisted that to conduct his kind of inquiry into the nature and properties of the language faculty is to engage neither in 'conceptual analysis' (1980a: 28–9) nor in 'philosophical discussion' (1983: 65).

*Something suitable to stimulate your memory, Dear Player? What about a maxim or two?*

Maxim Number One
*To do linguistics in the Chomskyan style, forget your philosophical flair once and for all, lay all a priori argument aside for good.*

**5.2**   Turning to the distinction **linguistics vs mathematics,** Chomsky (1982: 14) is of the opinion that 'there was a period of fairly fruitful contact between automata theory and linguistics in the late fifties and early sixties'. This contact, which 'mostly had to do with the properties of context-free grammars', turned up, in Chomsky's (1982: 15) opinion, 'one result (n. 18) which had linguistic interest, namely the fact you can think of a context-free grammar as a certain kind of automaton that takes symbols from left to right and prints out tree structures for them'.

Chomsky (1982: 16) also finds it useful to compare the study of language to the study of arithmetic considered from an intuitionist point of view. Commenting on this point of view, Chomsky (1982: 16) speculates that

One could perhaps take the intuitionist view of mathematics as being not unlike the linguistic view of grammar. That is, grammar does not have an independent existence apart from the functions of the human mind, but they are in fact precisely systems of principles that the human mind is capable of constructing, given the primary linguistic data.

As noted in section 2.5.9 above, however, Chomsky (1986: 33) has rejected the suggestion that knowledge of language should be understood on the analogy of knowledge of arithmetic, arithmetic being taken to be an abstract 'Platonistic' entity that exists apart from mental structures.

He has found this analogy to arithmetic 'quite unpersuasive' since

In the case of arithmetic, there is at least a certain initial plausibility to a Platonistic view insofar as the truths of arithmetic are what they are, independent of any facts of individual psychology, and we seem to discover these truths

198

somewhat in the way that we discover facts about the physical world. In the case of language, however, the corresponding position is wholly without merit. (Chomsky 1986: 33)

As an intellectual enterprise, moreover, Chomskyan linguistics differs from mathematics in a fundamental metascientific respect. Because it is a form of empirical science, Chomskyan linguistics cannot demonstratively prove its claims about the language faculty. In Chomsky's (1983: 80) words:

You can't demonstratively prove it is innate – that is because we are dealing with science and not mathematics; even if you looked at genes you couldn't prove that. In science you don't have demonstrative inferences; in science you can accumulate evidence that makes certain hypotheses seem reasonable, and that is all you can do – otherwise you are doing mathematics.

*To guide you on your way, Dear Player, here is*

Maxim Number Two
*To do linguistics in the Chomskyan style, disown all desire for demonstration, foreswear any passion for proof.*

5.3   As regards the distinction **linguistics vs psychology**, Chomsky (1986: 34) rejects it if it implies that 'there is any reason to establish a discipline of "linguistics" that restricts itself on *a priori* grounds to some particular data [so-called 'purely linguistic' or 'non-psychological' data] and constructs a concept of "language" that can be studied within this choice of relevant data'. In fact, Chomsky (1980a: 2) has never been willing to 'draw a line separating the two disciplines, linguistics and psychology, in terms of the kinds of evidence they prefer to use and the specific focus of their attention'. Accordingly, he has resisted attempts to define linguistics as the field 'that relies on informant judgments in order to study competence' *vis-à-vis* psychology as the field 'that is concerned with performance rather than competence'. 'This distinction has always seemed quite senseless' to Chomsky.[3]

Rather, of course, Chomsky (1972: 1) has characterized his form of linguistics as 'a psychological science', 'a particular branch of cognitive psychology'. The following formulation (1980a: 4) is representative of this perspective:

> I would like to think of linguistics as that part of psychology that focuses its attention on one specific cognitive domain and one faculty of mind, the language faculty. Psychology, in the sense of this discussion, is concerned, at the very least, with human capacities to act and to interpret experience, and with the mental structures that underlie these capacities and their exercise; and more deeply, with the second-order capacity to construct these mental structures, and the structures that underlie these second-order capacities (n. 2).

And, as is well known, Chomsky rightly deserves the credit for establishing this view of linguistics/psychology as an intellectually respectable and heuristically fruitful alternative to behaviourist psychology.[4]

*This, Dear Player, brings us to*

Maxim Number Three
*To do linguistics in the Chomskyan style, be ready for traditional boundaries between ologies to get abolished as a matter of course.*

5.4   The distinction **linguistics vs the brain sciences** is useful in further locating Chomskyan generative grammar within a wider disciplinary context. Recall that the distinction between mind and brain has been seen – e.g. sections 2.7.1, 4.2.4 – as crucial in understanding the aims of the Chomskyan enterprise. What Chomsky (1986: 38) is after, on the one hand, is a theory of mind that 'aims to determine the properties of the initial state $S_0$ [of the language faculty]'. On the other hand, 'the brain sciences seek to discover the mechanisms of the brain that are the physical realization of these states'. Nevertheless, on Chomsky's (1986: 38) view,

> There is a common enterprise: to discover the correct character-ization of the language faculty in its initial and attained states, to discover the truth about the language faculty. This enterprise is conducted at several levels: an abstract characterization in

the theory of mind, and an inquiry into mechanisms in the brain sciences. In principle, discoveries about the brain should influence the theory of mind, and at the same time the abstract study of states of the language faculty should formulate properties to be explained by the theory of the brain and is likely to be indispensable in the search for mechanisms. To the extent that such connections can be established, the study of the mind – in particular, of I-language – will be assimilated to the mainstream of the natural sciences.

From these remarks it is clear that Chomskyan linguistics is not concerned with reality at the same level of abstraction as the brain sciences. Yet, as Chomsky (1986: 38) notes 'the interdependency of the brain sciences and the study of mind is reciprocal'. Chomskyan linguistics may be characterized as 'abstract biology' analogous to the kind of work that has been done by Marr and Nishihara on vision. These scholars, as Chomsky (1982: 10) puts it, are 'interested in developing systems of representation and levels of representation which will on the one hand have a basis in physiology, if they can find it, and on the other hand will account for important perceptual phenomena'.[5]

*A golden rule to go by? Consider, Dear Player,*

Maxim Number Four
*Since as a linguist you loathe a laboratory,*
*intrusively locating mind's mechanisms isn't your territory.*

**5.5** Let us then consider the distinction **linguistics vs the natural sciences**. From the remarks quoted above in section 5.4 it is clear that Chomsky holds out some hope that his form of linguistics 'will be assimilated to the main stream of the natural sciences'. If such a process of substantive assimilation did take place, it would go via the biological sciences. As has been pointed out by Chomsky (1980a: 241), he pursues the study of mind 'much as we investigate the body', i.e., 'on the model of a bodily organ' (p. 229). Adopting this model implies to Chomsky that the inquiry is organized by taking as 'basic questions' those about the function, structure, physical basis, development in the individual, and evolutionary development of the 'language organ' (p. 227).[6]

As regards the assimilation of linguistics to the natural sciences, Chomsky, in fact, has gone one important step further. He has not only argued for an assimilation in terms of substance via the biological sciences. He has also presented a case for the metascientific or methodological assimilation of linguistics to the natural sciences. Thus, as we saw in chapter 4, Chomsky has consistently stressed the point that there are fundamental similarities at a metascientific level between his linguistics and the natural sciences. The former and the latter adopt the same basic aim (pursuing depth of insight), the same ontological position ('sophisticated' realism), the same epistemological stance ('tolerant' falsificationism) and the same methodological means (e.g. idealization).

Recently, as we noted in section 4.3.2, Chomsky has stressed these similarities by contending that generative grammarians, like physicists, have adopted the 'Galilean style' of inquiry. He (1980a: 197) has argued, in fact, that the metascientific differences between his form of linguistics and the natural sciences – e.g. those concerning 'intrusive experimentation' – are not 'differences of principle'. Thus, so far as method is concerned, Chomsky sees generative grammar as a natural science.

Given that Chomskyan linguistics is similar to the natural sciences both in substance and in method, the question arises why it should be considered a distinct discipline. Chomsky's (1986: 37) reply is informative:

> The study of language structure as currently practiced should eventually disappear as a discipline as new types of evidence become available, remaining distinct only insofar as its concern is a particular faculty of the mind, ultimately the brain: its initial state and its various attainable mature states.

*Would you believe, Dear Player, that a battle to the death – with undertones of a holy war – was fought about the fork 'linguistics vs natural science'? As we saw in section 4.2.1 above, Quine, Putnam and other philosophers of the same intellectual phylum have contended that linguistics and psychology are affected by an insuperable form of indeterminacy.*[7] *They have claimed that linguistic and psychological theories are incorrigibly underdetermined by the available evidence: given two or more extensionally equivalent theories in linguistics or psychology, it is impossible to determine which one correctly characterizes the mechanisms underlying the data. They have insisted, moreover, that linguistics and psychology are in this respect distinct from physics, hence that there is a 'linguistics/psychology vs physics' fork.*

*The Master fought off the fellows of this phylum with verve, shooting straight from the shoulder. On the one hand, he (1980a: 16ff; 1986: 13) shot back, Quinian indeterminacy amounts to nothing more than the normal underdetermination of theory by the evidence:*

> *I do not think that he succeeded in showing that some novel form of indeterminacy affects the study of language beyond the normal underdetermination of theory by evidence; his own formulations of the thesis furthermore involve internal inconsistency. (Chomsky 1986: 13)*

*On the other hand, he (1980a: 22) flayed the Philosophers of the Phylum for having confronted linguistics and psychology with questions of indeterminacy that have been dismissed in the case of the natural sciences:*

> *I think it is worth remarking on the fact that these issues have been so much debated in the past twenty years in the domain of psychology and language, while the comparable questions concerning indeterminacy in the natural sciences have received far less attention; and where they have been investigated, in connection with the question of realism, the framework and conclusions have been entirely different. What has happened, in fact, is that psychology has been asked to confront questions that are simply dismissed in the case of the natural sciences, where no one is much concerned with the fact that two samples might in principle be differently constituted, that theories are undetermined by evidence, and so on. This seems a strange state of affairs. Questions of a fundamental nature should be raised where the hope of gaining illumination is highest; in this case in physics, not psychology.*

*And, taking his revenge, The Master (1980a: 23) riddled the Quinian position from end to end with his own brand of resounding rhetoric:*

*It is a fair rule of thumb that questions should not be raised concerning the foundations of psychology if they cannot be answered in some measure at least in the case of physics. This reasonable principle has been drastically violated, with the obvious consequence that nothing much comes of the discussion, even when confusions are eliminated.*

*The Quinian proposal to distinguish linguistics and psychology in principle from the natural sciences comes down to nothing more than the arbitrary acceptance of a Bifurcation Thesis – a point which The Master has taken over from Hockney. And it is this very thesis which The Master (1980a: 16) has made into a missile, guiding it with awesome accuracy to blow up the phylum's fortress:*

*What is really at stake is only what Donald Hockney has called 'the bifurcation thesis', that is, the thesis that theories of meaning, language and much of psychology are faced with a problem of indeterminacy that is qualitatively different in some way from the underdetermination of theory by evidence in the natural sciences (n. 28). For this conclusion, no argument at all has been presented; and as Hockney shows, the bifurcation thesis leads to contradiction within Quine's system.*

*Let us then, in honour of one Hockney, try to remember the 'linguistics/psychology vs the natural sciences' fork as the Bifurcation Bifurcation. Your Fifth and Final Maxim, Dear Player, must take, I fear, the form of an epitaph:*

*Here lie the Philosophers of the Fake-fork Phylum*

★　　★　　★

*How frightful is the self-inflicted fate*
*of learned men who cleverly create*
*strange forks that, prongless, fail to bifurcate.*

Let us, in conclusion, return to the general questions addressed in this section: How is Chomskyan linguistics related to what have been considered to be adjacent but separate fields of study? Where does Chomskyan linguistics fit into science in general? A synoptic answer to these questions, necessarily simplified, is presented in the diagram below:

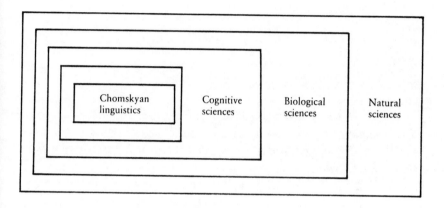

This diagram is complemented by and should be considered in conjunction with diagram (2) of section 1.5, which shows where Chomskyan linguistics fits into the larger field of linguistics.

# Afterthoughts

So here at last we are back, Dear Reader, at the gates of The Garden, having completed a guided tour of considerable conceptual mileage. Perhaps you feel a sense of relief as you reflect that The Garden is not one of remembrance so far as you are concerned. But before you leave for pastures less perilous – but more prosaic, I hasten to warn – let us pause for a moment's further reflection.

Reflection, not on what you have been shown of the limbs of linguistics, the meat of mentalism, the thews of theory, the muscle of method or the sinews of science. Not on what you have seen of players with more courage than cool, more heart than head, more pretence than sober sense. Not on what you now know about The Master's fortitude under fire, power in play or ruthlessness in retaliation.

No, let us think back about the quality of the guidance that you have been given. Having survived trials and tribulations, tense times and tight turns, do you not graciously concede that your Guide has been a credit to his trade? But not everyone would agree.

Take certain Past Players. They would complain (if indeed a Garden Grave is a place from which one can grumble) that they more than matched The Master – but that, in the yarns I spin, I give the credit to him. Or take certain Present Players. They would protest that they have been taking The Garden by storm – but that, in my story of The Game, I make no mention of their glorious name.

And don't forget the Serious Scholars who, against my advice, have grimly 'worked' their way through all that I have had to say. Untiring, unyielding, unsmiling, they keep carping away about forks *that have been fogged, corners that have been cut, incidents that have been inflated and encounters that have been exaggerated in my Grammar of The Game.*

*Always in attendance, of course, is the Lord of the Labyrinth himself. The Master Maze-maker and Minder, how could he ever rest content? My map of his maze is sure to fall short of his standards of surveying. And another certain bone of contention will be that I portray (at least) some ploys and principles of play in a way that is less than laudatory to him.*

*Generously granting me the last word, Dear Reader, you would like to hear my defence? But then, do I really need to say much? It seems to me that two or three questions and observations should do. For example, take all those dozens of conceptual distinctions – devilish in their delicacy and diversity. How do you suppose they would taste, were they to be served straight or sec to Novices and Neophytes? Or, again, what quicker way is there for an Out-of-form Fighter to upgrade his game – to secure survival in a land of lethal lanes, deadly drops and frightening forks? And what better to whet the appetite for action of Visiting Scholars lured from distant domains by the name of The Game?*

*Ultimately, then, I have been addressing myself to those who have a taste and a talent for conceptual combat – whether these attributes are in the bud only or have already begun to bloom. The manual patiently presented here, the verbal maps diligently drawn, and the many memory aids freshly minted will be instrumental, I hope, in producing a new generation of Players equipped to challenge The Generative Gladiator in his Garden with greater competence and credibility. But in essence my aims have been simple and my efforts quite modest. I have tried to assist in populating The Garden with people of 'the right stuff', players who have The Game in their genes. And I have tried to contribute to raising the general level of The Game. In a phrase: more contenders of calibre, more play of the proper proficiency. That's what it has been all about, Dear Reader.*

# Notes

## 1  The Lie of the Land

1   Chomsky (1986: 3) recently reiterated the point that ' "generative" means nothing more than "explicit" '. Note, incidentally, that in Chomsky's linguistics a grammar is not a description of a language in the conventional sense, as will be explained in sections 2.5.10 and 2.5.13 below. At this stage, however, this conventional view of the object described by a grammar won't do much harm.

2   Formalized rules are stated in terms of unambiguous symbols which have been specially chosen for the purpose. Formalization may be carried a step further by axiomatizing the rules constituting a grammar. For the distinction between formalization and axiomatization cf. Botha 1981: 168–9.

3   This is why Derek Bickerton (1981: 104–5) was able to claim that both his 'dynamic' model of language and Chomsky's 'static' model were 'generative'. For a recent version of Bickerton's views cf. Bickerton 1984.

4   This was such a common misconception that Bach (1974: 27), in his widely used textbook, found it necessary to point out with respect to the notion 'generate' that 'No connotations about actual production are intended'.

5   We will see in section 2.5.21 below that Chomsky has lately come to believe that knowledge of language should not be viewed as a rule system in the conventional sense. At this point of the discussion, however, the conventional Chomskyan view of language as a system of rules will do.

6   Hornstein and Lightfoot (1981c: 7) formulate this problem as follows: 'The goal of our research program is to explain how children come to know what they know in the linguistic domain.' Or, as formulated

by Lightfoot (1982: 15): 'The central problem is to characterize how children can master their native languages.'

7 A number of the different ontological interpretations that may be assigned to recent linguistic theories in the domain of syntax are discussed insightfully by Stockwell (1980: 354). Katz (1981: 18) argues that Bresnan (1978) and Fodor and Garrett (1975) also hold a view of the ontological status of linguistic theories that differs from Chomsky's mentalistic conception. Sober (1980: 38–9) holds the view that certain linguistic regularities have the status of 'social regularities'. In section 4.2.1 below, we return to the question of the ontological status of Chomskyan linguistic theories. For a discussion of the possibility of assigning more than one alternative ontological interpretation to a single linguistic theory cf. also Botha 1980: 26–8.

8 A historical note may be informative at this juncture: in assigning the questions (1) (a)–(c) the status of 'basic questions' – thereby making central concerns of the nature [(1) (a)], origin [(1) (b)] and use [(1) (c)] of language – Chomskyan generative grammar, on Chomsky's (1986: 3) view, represents 'a significant shift of focus in the approach to problems of language. Put in the simplest terms, to be elaborated below, the shift of focus was from behavior or the products of behavior to states of the mind/brain that enter into behavior'. Chomskyan linguistics, thus, is the result of a fundamental conceptual shift away from the concerns of traditional and structural grammar which – on Chomsky's (1986: 6) analysis – did not deal with the questions of (1). To a second fundamental conceptual shift, one that has taken place within Chomskyan linguistics, we return in sections 2.4.4, 2.5.21 and 2.6.5 below.

9 Soames (1984) has made a similar move by drawing a distinction between 'C(ognitive) linguistics' which studies language as represented in the minds/brains of the members of a speech community and 'A(bstract) linguistics' which studies language in abstraction from its mental/biological basis. For a critical discussion of this distinction cf. Chomsky 1986: 34–6.

10 The need for transformations has been questioned by, for example, Brame (1978) and Gazdar (1981), linguists who oppose Chomsky on other major points as well. Many, more recent examples illustrating this distinction are to be found in Chomsky's *Lectures on Government and Binding* (1981b), specifically in the notes. Consider, as an illustrative case, note 67 (p. 143) in which Chomsky briefly mentions a number of disagreements between himself on the one hand and on the other hand Chomskyan linguists such as Wilkins (1977, 1979), Koster (1978b, 1978c, 1980) and Kayne (1980). These disagreements

concern the structural aspects of language accounted for with the aid of theoretical notions such as 'subjacency', 'binding', 'bounding', 'government' etc. Other examples that clearly illustrate the distinction between Chomskyan linguistics and Chomsky's linguistics may be found in anthologies such as *Levels of Syntactic Representation* (edited by Koster and May, 1981) and *Theory of Markedness in Generative Grammar* (edited by Belletti, Brandi and Rizzi, 1981).

11 Cf. Newmeyer 1980: ch. 5 for a discussion of the main variants of generative semantics.

12 Cf. Katz 1980 for some discussion of this point.

13 For some discussion of the way in which Chomsky lost followers and the ensuing paradigm fragmentation cf., for example, Botha 1981: 429–30; Newmeyer 1980: 249–50; and Chomsky 1982: 42ff.

14 Cf., for example, Dougherty 1975 and Botha 1977: 74ff for some discussion of this point.


## 2 The Maze of Mentalism

1 Lightfoot (1982: 15), for example, states that 'The problem is one of the deficiency of the stimulus: people come to have a very rich, complex and varied capacity that goes far beyond what they can derive only from their childhood experience . . . .'

2 For some observations by Chomskyans on the psychological problem of language acquisition cf., for example, Chomsky 1981a: 34; Dresher 1981: 114–15; Kean 1981: 196–9; Hornstein and Lightfoot 1981c: 26; and White 1981: 252ff.

3 Cf. section 2.3.1 below for more particulars about Chomsky's distinction between the initial and the steady state of the language faculty.

4 Chomsky (1986: xxviii) considers the study of Orwell's problem to be 'primarily a matter of accumulating evidence and examples to illustrate what should be fairly obvious to a rational observer even on superficial inspection, to establish the conclusion that power and privilege function much as any rational mind would expect, and to exhibit the mechanisms that operate to yield the results that we observe'.

5 As noted by Chomsky (1986: 7) this view of the poverty of the stimulus differs sharply from the standard structuralist belief of thirty years ago that language, as a habit system, is 'much overdetermined by available evidence'.

6 Cf., for example, Lightfoot 1982: 17–18 for such an illustration.

7   Specific claims about the poverty of the stimulus may be challenged on factual grounds. For further observations on this point cf. section 4.4.2 below.

8   'Motherese', alternatively referred to as 'caretaker speech' or 'baby talk', is defined by Richards, Platt and Weber (1985: 34) as 'the simple speech used by mothers, fathers, babysitters, etc. when they talk to young children who are learning to talk. Caretaker speech usually has: (a) shorter utterances than speech to other adults, (b) grammatically simple utterances, (c) few abstract or difficult words, with a lot of repetition, (d) clearer pronunciation, sometimes with exaggerated INTONATION patterns'. For further discussion of the properties of motherese and its alleged role in language acquisition cf., for example, Ferguson and DeBose 1977 and Snow and Ferguson 1977. For critical appraisals of the role of such so-called simplified data in language acquisition cf., for example, Bickerton 1981: 139ff; Gleitman and Wanner 1982: 39ff; Newmeyer 1983: 22; and Romaine 1985: 261.

9   Cf., for example, Baker 1978: 411–13; Hornstein and Lightfoot 1981c: 20; and Lightfoot 1982: 17 for this view.

10  Cf. Lightfoot 1982: 17.

11  Cf. Hornstein and Lightfoot, 1981c: 20.

12  Baker refers here to studies by Braine 1971 and Brown and Hanlon 1970.

13  Or, rather, 'knowledge of grammar', as we will see below in section 2.5.15.

14  The genotype is the inherited set of genes that 'determines the organism's potential for adapting to its environment; it sets the boundaries of an organism's performance by determining what its cells can do' (Lightfoot 1982: 5). An organism's phenotype is 'the set of acquired characteristics, like having axial flowers or being tall, dark, and handsome; it is the mature expression of the genotype within a given environmental setting' (Lightfoot 1982: 6).

15  (3) does not represent an exhaustive list of the terminological pairs that may be used synonymously to denote the initial and steady states of the language faculty. Thus, in note 39 below, we will see that Chomsky (1980a: 4) has also used the expression 'first order capacity' to denote the steady state, and the converse expression 'second order capacity' in referring to the initial state.

16  This distinction was drawn by Piattelli-Palmarini (ed.) (1983: 18), an organizer of the debate between Chomsky and Piaget at the Abbaye de Royaumont near Paris. Piattelli-Palmarini illustrates the distinction *steady state vs stable state* as follows: 'A billiard ball coming to rest

at the bottom of a basin, or crystals being formed under progressive saturation of a solution, constitute canonical examples of stable equilibrium states. In dynamic processes, whenever a constant turnover of matter is geared to a uniform flow of transformable energy, steady states may appear. The canonical example is the flame of a candle in an environment devoid of turbulence.'

17  What is called 'language-specificity' here has also been referred to as 'domain-specificity', for example in Caplan 1981: 60.

18  Putnam takes the fact that a chimpanzee such as Washoe can 'learn language' successfully to provide evidence for his own theory of language acquisition and against Chomsky's. We return to this point in section 2.5.17 below.

19  Subjacency is a general condition 'which states that a transformation cannot move a phrase "too far" in a well-defined sense' Chomsky 1986: 72). In an informal, relatively early formulation, Subjacency stated that a phrasal constituent cannot be moved out of two bounding categories (cf., for example, Chomsky 1978a: 16 and Radford 1981: 227 for such a formulation). The ill-formedness of the *wh*-question in (a) below may be explained by invoking, amongst other things, Subjacency: to derive (a) the constituent *in whom* has to be moved out of two bounding categories – the circled NP and S – in (b) (cf. Chomsky 1978a: 16).

(a)  *in whom did your interest surprise me
(b)  *[$_{\bar{S}}$ COMP [ (S) [ (NP) your interest [$_{WH}$in whom] ] surprised me] ]

As for binding theory, it contains the principles that govern the relations between various kinds of (pro)nominal elements and their possible antecedents. Cf. Chomsky 1986: 77, 164ff.

20  We will consider Piaget's theory of language acquisition in section 2.4.6 below.

21  The function that idealizations such as that of uniformity in the species have in Chomskyan linguistics will be considered from a metascientific point of view in section 4.1.4 below.

22  Chomsky (1986: 204, n. 3) refers to Borer and Wexler 1984 for an illustration of how this assumption may be used in explaining phenomena of child language.

23  For the distinction 'genetic vs epigenetic' cf., for example, Catlin 1978: 276–7; Cromer 1980: 18; and Lightfoot 1982: 12.

24  On Catlin's view, Lenneberg's (1967) approach is of the epigenetic sort.

25  This characterization presupposes a distinction between, on the one hand, characterizing the language faculty at a concrete,

neurophysiological level and, on the other hand, characterizing this faculty at an abstract, mental level. We will go into this and related distinctions in some detail in sections 3.7.2 and 4.2.4 below.

26  NP stands for Noun Phrase (e.g., *the boy*, *the bright boy*, *the boy who is bright* etc.), S for Sentence (e.g., *The boy is bright* etc.), and S̄ for a structure consisting of a sentence (S) introduced by a complementizer (COMP) (e.g., (*He claims*) *that the boy is bright* etc.).

27  English, Italian and French, thus, differ in their use of Subjacency in only a relatively minor respect. This relatively small difference, however, lies at the basis of what superficially appear to be substantial differences in phrase structure. The latter differences are reflected by the fact that, whereas certain structures would be ungrammatical in English, parallel structures would be grammatical in French and Italian. For an illustration of this point cf. Chomsky 1981a: 55-6.

28  Throughout the discussion it has to be kept in mind that Chomsky is concerned with the process by which a child acquires its native language and not processes specific to the acquisition of a second or third language.

29  Chomsky (1980b: 47-8) proceeds: 'McCawley takes the criterial property of "learning" to be individuation; since our mind can acquire knowledge of several languages, acquisition of language is "learning" (so that if it turned out that "coordinate bilingualism" is impossible, rather only "compound bilingualism", in which knowledge of one language is built on knowledge of another, then first-language acquisition would not be "learning"). Clearly, this does not respond to the point I discussed.'

30  Thus, Chomsky (1980b: 14) argues that if one wished to take the abduction metaphor 'partially seriously, then under this concept of learning as "abduction" or "self-design" [a notion to which we will turn below], the question whether language is learned or grows will depend on whether the mind equipped with universal grammar presents a set of grammars as hypotheses to be selected on the basis of data and an evaluation metric, or whether the steady-state grammar arises in another way – for example, by virtue of a hierarchy of accessibility (stated, perhaps, in terms of the very same evaluation metric) and a process of selection of the most accessible grammar compatible with given data. The distinction between such alternatives lies so far beyond conceivable research that the question whether knowledge is the result of learning or growth is hardly worth considering, if learning is characterized in these terms.'

31  Chomsky (1983: 73) has also rejected Cellérier's (1983: 70) portrayal of language learning as analogous to 'hill climbing' in artificial

intelligence, in which it represents an 'adaptive or self-optimizing servo-mechanism'. Cellérier takes over Minsky's (1963: 410) characterization of 'hill climbing' as a way of getting to the top of a hill in a dense fog: 'the obvious approach is to explore locally about a point, finding the direction of steepest ascent. One moves a certain distance in that direction and repeats the process until improvement ceases'. Chomsky (1983: 73), however, contends that 'hill climbing is one technique that is very special and possibly correct (though I am rather skeptical) for gaining cognitive structures sometimes; but whether it is *the* method here, I'm rather skeptical. In fact it seems to me possibly more likely in this case to be a *matter of successive maturation of specialized hardware* (to use one of Cellérier's expressions)'.

32   Jerne's prime example of such replacement involves theories dealing with the development of antibodies to the immune system (cf. Chomsky 1980a: 137). At first it was assumed to be a learning process in which the antigen played an instructive role. In view of the huge number of antigens, no other account seemed conceivable. This instructive theory, however, was abandoned, and antibody formation has been portrayed as a selective process in which the antigen plays a selective and amplifying role. It has been argued that an animal 'cannot be stimulated to make specific antibodies, unless it has already made antibodies of this specificity before the antigen arrives'.

33   To the nature of the periphery alluded to in this quotation we return in section 2.5.19 below.

34   The 'peripheral processing mechanisms' alluded to in this quotation are located in 'the receptor system' and 'lower cortical centers' on Chomsky's (1965: 205, n. 27) view.

35   The first, that of the species-specificity of these structures, was considered in section 2.3.2. above.

36   Piaget (1983: 30) characterizes 'autoregulation' as 'a mechanism which is as general as heredity and which even, in a sense, controls it'.

37   For a characterization of these linguistic entities and their relevance to the appraisal of theories of language acquisition cf., for example, Chomsky 1983: 39ff.

38   In section 4.3.1 we will take a closer metascientific look at the 'Piagetian dogma'.

39   Note that in his discussion of knowledge of language Chomsky has drawn a number of secondary distinctions. First, with reference to the nature of capacities, Chomsky (1980a: 4–5; 1980b: 1) draws a distinction between first-order and second-order capacities: a person's capacity to use his language represents a first-order capacity; a human's

capacity to construct the mental structures that underlie first-order capacities represents a second-order capacity. Chomsky (1980a: 5) notes in addition that the term 'capacity' is also 'used more loosely, as when we speak of "capacities" in the sense of "mental faculties"'.

Second, Chomsky (1980a: 4) also distinguishes between 'having the capacity to do so-and-so' and 'knowing how to do so-and-so'. In 'knowing how', there is for Chomsky 'a crucial intellectual component' which is absent from 'having a capacity'.

Third, Chomsky (1980a: 4) draws a distinction between 'what one is able to do at will and what falls within one's capacity, though we cannot do it at will'. Chomsky's example is that of a baseball player who 'had the capacity to hit a home run, but not at will, whereas he had the capacity to lift a bat at will'.

40 In justification of this claim Chomsky (1980a: 74–5) presents typical examples of a set of facts – facts about knowledge of language – that call for explanation by linguistic theories: 'Consider again a specific set of facts, say, those already used for illustration: the sentence "the candidates wanted each other to win" has roughly the meaning that each wanted the other to win, whereas "the candidates wanted me to vote for each other" is not a well-formed sentence meaning that each wanted me to vote for the other. These are things that we know, in anyone's sense of "know". These instances of our knowledge are on a par with some fact about the light emitted by the sun. The facts don't have to come out this way on any logical grounds; these are empirical facts, if anything is. It is difficult to see any reason, then, for denying that it makes sense to seek an explanation as to why the facts come out this way rather than some other way.'

41 The rules mentioned in this quotation include, for example, phrase structure rules such as (A):

(A)  S  $\rightarrow$  NP  VP
     VP  $\rightarrow$  V  NP
     NP  $\rightarrow$  DET  N'
     N'  $\rightarrow$  N  S

Constrained by principles (cf. the quote) such as (B) (a rough, informal approximation of a principle of $\overline{X}$-theory) these rules generate (syntactic) representations such as (C).

(B)  A Noun Phrase consists of a Specifier – e.g., a Determiner – and a Noun or Noun Phrase.

(C)  $[_S[_{NP}[_{N'}\text{John}]] \; [_{VP}[_V\text{hit}] \; [_{NP}[_{DET}\text{the}] \; [_{N'}\text{boy}]]]]$

215

For a recent introductory account of such rules, principles and representations cf. Chomsky 1986: ch. 3.

42  Unconscious knowledge should be distinguished from 'conscious but unverbalized knowledge'. Chomsky (1986: 271) considers 'our knowledge of properties of perceptual space and the behavior of objects in it' to represent an example of the latter kind of knowledge. He does not agree, however, with Dummett that a speaker's knowledge of meaning represents such 'conscious but unverbalized knowledge'.

43  Over the years Chomsky and Searle have been involved in a series of disagreements over this issue. We return to this point in section 4.2.3 below.

44  It is not clear to me how Chomsky would draw a distinction, *in general terms*, between a skill and an ability.

45  In similar vein Chomsky (1986: 265–6) states 'Knowledge of language involves (perhaps entails) standard examples of propositional knowledge: knowledge that in the word *pin*, /p/ is aspirated, whereas in *spin* it is not; that the pronoun may be referentially dependent on *the men* in (9i), but not in the identical phrase in (9ii), and so forth:

(i)   I wonder who [the men expected to see them]   (9)
(ii)  [the men expected to see them]

If these are not instances of knowledge, it is hard to see what is.'

46  The opacity principle, informally, governs the choice of antecedents: variable-like elements can't be free in opaque domains (cf. Chomsky 1980a: 91).

47  These remarks Chomsky (1980a: 94) believes to 'carry over . . . to other kinds of knowledge and belief, for example, our knowledge of the properties and behavior of objects'. This view was challenged in an interesting way by Rollin (1980: 31–2) and was defended in some detail by Chomsky (1980b: 50–1).

48  We return to this point in section 2.5.8 below.

49  As will be shown below, this view of Chomsky's has been challenged by Katz (1981: 79–80).

50  The remaining part of this passage of Katz's (1981: 79–80) reads as follows: 'One can appreciate that, in connection with these notions as with many others, adjustments of the ordinary notion may be required in their scientific, formal explication. But nothing warrants the astounding claim that "English", "French" etc. and "natural language" are not concepts of *linguistic* science.'

51  The ideal speaker–listener has a third ideal side: when using his language, he is not affected by grammatically irrelevant conditions. Chomsky's (1965: 3) full characterization of the notion 'the ideal

speaker–listener', thus, reads as follows: 'Linguistic theory is concerned primarily with an ideal speaker–listener, in a completely homogeneous speech-community, who knows its language perfectly and is unaffected by such grammatically irrelevant conditions as memory limitations, distractions, shifts of attention and interest, and errors (random or characteristic) in applying his knowledge of the language in actual performance.' The third side of Chomsky's idealization will be considered in section 2.6.1 below.

52   Cf. Newmeyer 1983: 75 for this characterization, and Botha 1981: 32–3 for further discussion of the point in question.

53   Cf. also Newmeyer 1983: 74–5 for evidence indicating that the idealization of the ideal speaker–listener is as old as the Western grammatical tradition, a tradition including Saussurean structuralism, Praguian functionalism and Bloomfieldian as well as post-Bloomfieldian taxonomic linguistics.

54   With reference to the passage quoted in note 51 above, Newmeyer (1983: 73) observes: 'If a sampling of the critical literature is any indication, no paragraph in any generativist work has engendered as many misunderstandings . . .'

55   Cf. Newmeyer 1983: 74 for some discussion of the essentially empty nature of these charges.

56   Chomsky (1980a: 26) has also observed that 'Once the issues are clarified, it is hard to see how anyone could reject the idealization, and, to my knowledge no one in fact does, including its most vocal opponents, as we see when we look in detail at their actual work on such topics as dialect variation. This is unfortunately typical of the kind of debate that beclouds the issue of idealization all too often.' In section 4.1.4 below we will return to Chomsky's metascientific motivation for using idealizations such as the one under consideration.

57   On Chomsky's interpretation, Saussure took a language to be a system of sounds and an associated system of concepts; Bloomfield viewed a language as the totality of utterances that can be made in a speech community; and, more recently, David Lewis defined language as a pairing of sentences and meanings over an infinite range.

58   We will return to the metascientific status of the notion 'truth' in Chomskyan linguistics in section 4.2.1 below.

59   A language is recursively enumerable if 'it can be defined by a definite formal system of some sort' (Bach 1974: 194). Turing machines are considered to be the most general formal systems known.

60   Chomsky (1986: 49), n. 17) presents details such as the following to account for the 'E-language nature' of his characterization of language quoted above: 'As for the publishing history, the earliest

publications on generative grammar were presented in a framework suggested by certain topics in automata theory (e.g., my *Syntactic Structures*, 1957 – actually course notes for an undergraduate course at MIT and hence presented from a point of view related to interests of these students). Specifically linguistic work, such as Chomsky (1975a), was not publishable at the time. In the latter, considerations of weak generative capacity (i.e., characterizability of E-languages), finite automata and the like were completely absent, and emhasis was on I-language, although the term was not used.' Cf. also Chomsky 1982: 62–3 for remarks in the same vein.

61  Cf. Newmeyer 1983: 37–8 for some discussion of attempts to use 'communicative competence' as a basic notion in linguistic theorizing.

62  Chomsky (1986: 48, n. 10) has indicated his awareness of the use by other linguists of the notion 'communicative competence', but, has, to my knowledge, not commented directly on its merits/limitations.

63  The thematic structure of a sentence is characterized in terms of notions such as 'Agent', 'Instrument', 'Goal', 'Location' etc. which represent 'semantic roles' of NPs. As regards 'aitiational factors', Chomsky (1980a: 55) adopts Moravcsik's idea that concepts have an 'aitiational structure' that can be characterized in terms of such 'generative factors' as 'origin', 'function', 'material constitution', and so on.

64  Cf. Chomsky 1981a: 38–9.

65  We return to the empirical nature of markedness claims in section 4.4.3 below. Cf. also Lightfoot 1979: 76ff for some discussion of this point.

66  Cf. Chomsky's paper 'Markedness and core grammar' that circulated for a long time in mimeographed form ( = Chomsky 1979a) and that was only published formally in 1981 in A. Belletti, L. Brandi and L. Rizzi (eds), *Theory of Markedness in Generative Grammar* ( = Proceedings of the 1979 GLOW Conference). Pisa: Scuola Normale Superiore.

67  For an analysis of the rhetorical nature of this claim and others related to it cf. Botha 1982a: 29ff.

68  For this point about Galileo cf. Feyerabend 1979: 30 and the references in note 37 of Botha 1982a: 46. The latter study presents a fuller discussion of Chomsky's 'Galilean style' of inquiry.

69  The first conceptual shift, we saw in section 2.5.13 above, was the shift in focus from the study of E-language to the study of I-language.

70  For a schematic representation of Chomsky's 'pre-shift' views of production, interpretation, processing and intuitive judgement as three basic aspects of linguistic behaviour/performance cf. Botha 1981: 30ff).

71 Cf. Newmeyer 1983: 35.

72 For a discussion of concrete cases of these general criticisms cf. Newmeyer 1983: 35ff.

73 Kripke (1982) only refers to Chomsky in three footnotes (pp. 30, 72, 97).

74 Chomsky (1986: 240) attributes the term 'constructive skepticism' to Richard Popkin. This form of scepticism was 'developed by Mersenne and Gassendi in response to the skeptical crisis of the seventeenth century, their "new outlook, . . . doubting our abilities to find grounds for our knowledge" and recognizing that "the secrets of nature, of things-in-themselves, are forever hidden from us", while "accepting and increasing the knowledge itself" '.

75 In section 4.2.3 we will consider a further, metascientific, distinction that is relevant to the idea that language use is rule-following.

76 For further discussion of the status of the notion of 'body' cf. Chomsky 1982: 34ff.

77 To the distinction between 'subcomponents of the rule system' and 'subsystems of principles' we return in section 3.2.4 below where a brief, nontechnical characterization of the various subcomponents and subsystems will be presented as well.

78 Consider again the following remark by Chomsky quoted above: 'On the contrary, it is difficult to imagine by what inductive, associative, or other "learning process" this [i.e., number] capacity might have derived from experience (though, as I noted, it may be triggered by experience.' This remark may be construed as an argument from ignorance – a construal which, if correct, would cause Chomsky some embarrassment. A few lines higher up in the same passage Chomsky takes others to task for using this kind of argument: 'There is, of course, a traditional view that "higher-level" processes are uniform even if sensory and perceptual systems are modular; perhaps so, but it seems to me a dubious argument from ignorance.'

79 For the notion of 'poverty of the stimulus' cf. section 2.2.1 above.

80 For the distinction between rationalists, empiricists and constructivists cf. sections 2.4.5 and 2.4.6 above.

81 Cf. Chomsky 1975b: 176ff and Newmeyer 1983: 2–4.

82 For some discussion of the nature of such 'extragrammatical' (systems of) principles cf. Newmeyer 1983: 96ff.

83 Newmeyer (1983: 2–4), incidentally, holds the view that Chomsky's thesis of the autonomy of formal grammar and his conception of modularity represent the two characteristics that 'distinguish "transformational generative grammar" from other current theories of language'.

84 'Guys' has no sexist connotation – cf., for example, Barbara Hall Partee's (1975) attack of Chomsky's autonomy thesis. The 'Good Guys' were those defending interpretive semanticist positions, the 'Bad Guys' those championing generative semanticist beliefs.

85 For some discussion of these issues and reasons cf., for example, Botha 1973: chs 5 and 6; Newmeyer 1980: ch. 5.

86 Some of these duels are described in the works referred to in note 85 above.

87 For some discussion of this 'so-called' revolution cf., for example, Katz and Bever 1977; Botha 1981: 424ff; Newmeyer 1980: ch. 2. Not everyone agrees that generative grammar was born in a revolutionary manner – hence the qualification 'so-called'.

88 For typical examples of man-to-man confrontations that took place in the 'Chomskyan Revolution' cf., for example, Hill 1962 (ed.); Woodworth and DiPietro 1962 (eds).

89 The sociological structure of linguistic (in-)fighting is complex: some linguists who had been flag-bearers of Chomsky's in the 'Revolution' fiercely fought him in the 'Wars'; others who battled on Chomsky's side in the 'Wars' have lately been challenging him in 'The Game'.

90 Cf. Newmeyer 1983: 119.

91 Cf. Newmeyer 1983: 119. *Syntactic Structures* (1957) represents Chomsky's first major publication.

92 Recently, Chomsky (1980a: 230) once again asked the question 'What does it mean to say that language has an "essential purpose"?' And he went on to observe: 'Suppose that in the quiet of my study I think about a problem, using language, and even write down what I think. Suppose that someone speaks honestly, merely out of a sense of integrity, fully aware that his audience will refuse to comprehend or even consider what he is saying. Consider informal conversation conducted for the sole purpose of maintaining casual friendly relations, with no particular concern as to its content. Are these examples of "communication"? If so, what do we mean by "communication" in the absence of an audience, or with an audience assumed to be completely unresponsive, or with no intention to convey information or modify belief or attitude?' Given these questions and observations, Chomsky (1980a: 230) came to the conclusion that 'either we must deprive the notion "communication" of all significance, or else we must reject the view that the purpose of language is communication.' And he proceeded to argue that 'While it is quite commonly argued that the purpose of language is communication and that it is pointless to study language apart from its communicative function, there is no formulation of this belief, to my knowledge, from which any

220

substantive proposals follow. The same may be said of the idea that the essential purpose of language is to achieve certain instrumental ends, to satisfy needs, and so on. Surely language can be used for such purposes – or for others. It is difficult to say what 'the purpose' of language is, except, perhaps, the expression of thought, a rather empty formulation. The functions of language are various. It is unclear what might be meant by the statement that some of them are "central" or "essential".'

93   In terms of an informal characterization of Chomsky's (1983: 39) a rule is structure-independent if it requires (in its structural description) that a linguistic form (e.g., a declarative) be analysed into successive words *only*. A rule is structure-dependent if it requires that such a form be analysed into successive words *and also* abstract phrases such as 'noun phrase'.

94   For a representative sample of linguists who have this kind of commitment to some or other notion of 'communication' cf. Newmeyer 1983: 100ff. The 'Comrades of Communication' are those linguists, philosophers etc. who have claimed on *a priori grounds* that the 'essential purpose' of language is 'communication' and that the 'structure' of language reflects this 'purpose'. Linguists who have argued *on empirical grounds* for a limited measure of iconicity in restricted domains between form and meaning, clearly, are not related in any essential way to these 'Comrades'. For perceptive empirical observations about such iconicity cf., for example, Bolinger 1980: 19–21, 28.

### 3   The Terrain of Theory

1   Newmeyer (1983: 75) proceeds to point out that 'the equation of "linguistic theory" (or an equivalent term) with "theory of grammar" was not Chomsky's innovation. Saussure explicitly distinguished the "science of language" (theorizing about grammar) from linguistics as a whole.'

2   The distinction under consideration goes back at least to *The Sound Pattern of English* (1968: 4) in which Chomsky and Halle drew a distinction between 'essential' and 'accidental' universals. They illustrated this distinction by sketching an imaginary situation in which only the inhabitants of Tasmania survive a future war. Every principle of the Tasmanian grammar would then apply to all human languages, since there would be only one. Every principle of Tasmanian would have become an accidental universal.

3   Comrie (1981: 26) characterizes Chomsky's approach to linguistic universals as one that 'argues that the best way of studying language

universals is by detailed, abstract study of an individual language, the main explanation for language universals being that they are innate properties of the human'. In section 4.4.4 below we will consider from a metascientific point of view the distinction 'evidence from a single language vs evidence from a diversity of languages'.

4　Newmeyer refers in this quotation to the following study: Joseph Greenberg, Charles Ferguson, and Edith Moravcsik (eds), *Universals of Human Language*. Stanford: Stanford University Press, 1978. Cf. also Lightfoot (1982: 64) for some discussion of the problems involved in attempts to interpret the 'typologist's percentages' within the framework of Chomsky's theory of grammar.

5　For a relatively nontechnical and more informative characterization of the various subcomponents of rule systems cf. Chomsky 1986: 56ff.

6　A not overly technical account of the various subsystems of principles is given in Chomsky 1986: 56ff.

7　We will consider the type to which a description or characterization of this sort belongs in section 4.2.4 below.

8　Referring to the distinction 'E-language vs I-language', Chomsky (1986: 29) recently presented the gist of this point as follows: 'The term "grammar" was then used with systematic ambiguity, to refer to what we have here called "I-language" and also to the linguist's theory of the I-language; the same was true of the term UG, introduced later with the same systematic ambiguity, referring to $S_0$ [i.e., the initial state of the language faculty] and the theory of $S_0$.'

9　Cf. Chomsky 1965: 60–2 for an early explication of this distinction.

10　Chomsky's (1980b: 4) account runs as follows: 'Consider, for example, the process of forming questions. We select some noun phrase in a sentence, replace it by an appropriate question word, place the latter at the beginning of the sentence, and with other mechanical operations, form a question. Thus, on the model of the sentence, "John saw a man", we can form "Whom did John see?" Or, to take a more complex case, on the model of the sentence, "The teacher thought that his assistant had told the class to study the lesson", we can question "the class" and ask: "Which class did the teacher think that his assistant had told to study the lesson?".'

## 4　The Marshes of Method

1　For a critical explication of Chomsky's notions 'unifying' and 'deductive depth', cf. Botha 1982a: 6ff and Sinclair 1985: sections 4.2, 7.2.2.2.

2   In contrast to (i) below, (ii) violates the Complex Noun Phrase
    Constraint: in (ii), an element realized as *who* in sentence-initial
    position has been removed from the italicized appositional clause
    (complex NP):

    (i)   who do you think that Ed claimed that Joan married?
    (ii)  *who do you think that Ed made *the claim that Joan married?*

3   In contrast to (i) below, (ii) violates the WH-Island Constraint: in (ii),
    an element realized as *what* in sentence-initial position has been
    removed from the italicized clause introduced by *who*:

    (i)   what did he notice (that) the CIA discovered (that) Joan had
          read?
    (ii)  *what did he notice (that) the CIA discovered *who had read?*

4   In contrast to (i) below, (ii) violates the Sentential Subject Condition:
    in (ii), an element realized as *what* in sentence-initial position has
    been removed from the italicized sentential subject, which also occurs
    in (iii):

    (i)   what was it expected that Joan would read?
    (ii)  *what was *that Joan would read* expected?
    (iii) *that Joan would read this* was expected

5   In contrast to (i) below, (ii) violates the Phrasal Subject Constraint:
    in (ii), an element realized as *who* in sentence-initial position has been
    removed from the italicized complex nominal subject:

    (i)   who did you find a picture of?
    (ii)  *who did *a picture of* frighten Joan?

6   In contrast to (ii) below, (iii) violates the Upward Boundedness
    Constraint: in (iii), an element, the sentential subject *that the moon
    is a piece of green cheese*, has been moved rightwards out of the clause
    containing it:

    (i)   that [that the moon is a piece of green cheese] is obvious is
          not clear
    (ii)  that it is obvious [that the moon is a piece of green cheese]
          is not clear
    (iii) *that it is obvious is not clear [that the moon is a piece of
          green cheese]

7   Chomsky's (1978a: 16) informal characterization of the notion 'binding
    category' reads as follows: 'we identify a class of what is called binding
    categories, including NP and S which are alike in many respects, that

is, each of them involves the basic grammatical relations of subject etc., each serves as the domain of transformational rules and so on.'

8   These idealizations were considered individually in chapter 2 above.

9   For a critical analysis of Chomsky's astrophysical analogy cf. Botha 1980: 12ff.

10  The characterization given above of the 'various stances' on theoretical discourse is quite crude. For a more careful discussion cf. Botha 1968: 87ff.

11  The thesis of the indeterminacy of translation applies to translation between languages, claims expressed by linguistic theories – e.g., claims about the boundaries between phrases and the categories to which phrases belong – and so on. The thesis, as characterized by Chomsky (1980a: 15) says that 'there is no fact of the matter in such cases as these [i.e., cases involving the postulation of phrase boundaries and categories], and therefore no sense to the construction of a theory of language and mind that tries to establish that the rules of grammar assign phrases in one or another way in mental representations (n. 22).'

12  Occam's Razor, on Harré's (1961: 16) characterization, embodies the criterion 'Don't invent any more entities than you really need for an explanation'. Einstein's Chopper gives substance to a related criterion: 'The simpler a theory the more acceptable it is, provided that it accounts for all the facts; that is, don't invent more processes than you really need in an explanation'. Continuing in this vein, Harman's Hatchet may be characterized as expressing the criterion: 'Mental entities may be postulated only if there is evidence different in sort from the evidence that bears on the ability of a theory to bring order to the domain of linguistic phenomena'. Harman's Hatchet is an instrument for cutting away those aspects of a theory that represent 'artifacts of notation'.

13  If one wishes to operate with a notion of 'psychological reality', a (further) distinction has to be drawn on Chomsky's (1980b: 56) view: viz. between the psychological reality of a theory and its hypotheses on the one hand, and the psychological reality of the entities attributed by the theory to the mind/brain on the other hand.

14  'Move alpha' is a general movement transformation that plays a role in deriving a variety of constructions including *wh*-questions, passives, and so on. Cf. Chomsky 1986: 73ff for more details on this rule.

15  It was in reply to criticisms by Piaget that Chomsky (1983: 125) argued that a distinction should be drawn between what was biologically unexplained (for accidental reasons) and what was biologically inexplicable.

16 The basic idea was that a type of (theoretically postulated) entity was not uniquely identifiable if an arbitrary specimen could not be identified by a scientist as an instance of the type. Unique identifiability presupposes neither direct observability nor logical proof of the existence of the entity. For some discussion of these points cf. Botha 1980: 22–3.

17 For a reply to Slezak 1981, cf. Botha 1982b.

18 The distinction between descriptive and explanatory adequacy goes back at least to the early sixties when it formed part of the tripartite distinction that included observational adequacy too. At that juncture, Chomsky explicated the distinction as follows: A grammar is observationally adequate if it 'presents the observed primary data correctly' (Chomsky 1964: 28). A grammar is descriptively adequate to the extent that it is psychologically real, i.e. 'to the extent that it correctly describes the intrinsic competence of the idealized native speaker' (Chomsky 1965: 24). A general linguistic theory is explanatorily adequate if it 'provides a general basis for selecting a grammar that achieves . . . success over other grammars consistent with the relevant observed data', i.e. the descriptively adequate grammar for that language (Chomsky 1964: 28).

19 For further explication of this point cf. Botha 1981: 235.

20 For a discussion of this aspect of the Linguistic Wars cf. Botha 1973: 286ff; 1981: 318; Newmeyer 1980: ch. 5.

21 Cf. Lightfoot 1982: 93ff for remarks on the status of falsificationism in Chomskyan linguistics.

22 For a metascientific analysis of this style of inquiry cf. Botha 1982a and for an illustration of its use in morphological and semantic analysis cf. Botha 1984.

23 Cf. Botha and Sinclair (forthcoming) for a critical discussion of Brame's analysis of what Chomsky's epistemological tolerance entails.

24 Cf. Botha 1973: 283–4 for some discussion of the way in which the distinction under consideration was used by interpretive semanticists against generative semanticists.

25 For Quine's thesis of the indeterminacy of translation cf. n. 11 above.

26 For Chomsky's astrophysical analogy cf. section 4.2.1 above and Botha 1980: 12ff.

27 Lightfoot (1982: 15) has characterized the argument from poverty of the stimulus, as the 'basic line of reasoning' adopted by Chomskyans, in the following terms: 'Since our perspective is a biological one, we shall tease out hereditary and environmental contributions to people's use of language. Properties of the phenotype will be identified which cannot arise through the shaping effect of the environment but which

are due to genetic inheritance. As is usual amongst biologists, arguments from the deficiency of the stimulus will be relevant as a means to pin down the genetic contribution to somebody's eventual language capacity.'

28  For the distinction 'internal (linguistic) evidence vs external (linguistic) evidence' cf., for example, Botha 1980: 36–7; 1981: 302, 323.

29  Cf., for example, Botha 1980: 77ff; 1981: 323; Lightfoot 1979: 76–7; Stich 1980: 40.

30  For some discussion of controversial aspects of the various notions of 'simplicity' that have played a role in generative grammar cf., for example, Botha 1973: 291–2; Sober 1975; White 1982: 91ff; and Newmeyer 1983: 41–2.


### 5  Locus in the Landscape of Learning

1  Chomsky (1982: 5) considers 'The chance of extracting answers to those [i.e., philosophical] questions from linguistics . . . very slight. I cannot imagine why linguistics would offer any particular insight into the specific topics that happen to interest people like Zeno Vendler.'

2  Chomsky (1982: 56) is of the opinion that this kind of philological work by ordinary language philosophers and 'other work that comes out of it on speech acts and performatives' could be thought of as 'a type of linguistics'.

3  For some discussion cf., for example, Chomsky 1982: 17ff.

4  For some discussion of this point cf. Leiber 1975: 140ff; Lyons 1970: 83ff; 1981: 230–1.

5  For more details on the work of Marr and his group cf. Chomsky 1982: 9–11.

6  In addition to 'organ' Chomsky has also adopted the biological notions of 'growth' and 'maturation' in his theory of language acquisition. For this point cf. section 2.4.1 above.

7  Cf. note 11 of chapter 4 for the Quinian notion of 'indeterminacy'.

# Bibliography

Alatis, J. (ed.) 1970: *Georgetown University Round Table on Languages and Linguistics 1969*. Washington, DC: Georgetown University Press.

Austerlitz, R. (ed.) 1975: *The Scope of American Linguistics*. Lisse: Peter de Ridder Press.

Bach, E. 1974: *Syntactic Theory*. New York: Holt, Rinehart and Winston.

Baker, C. L. 1978: *Introduction to Generative-Transformational Syntax*. Englewood Cliffs, NJ: Prentice Hall.

Baron, N. 1981: *Speech, Writing, and Sign*. Bloomington: Indiana University Press.

Belletti, A., Brandi, L. and Rizzi, L. (eds) 1981: *Theory of Markedness in Generative Grammar*. Proceedings of the 1979 GLOW Conference. Pisa: Scuola Normale Superiore.

Bever, T. A. 1974: The ascent of the specious or there's a lot we don't know about mirrors. In Cohen (ed.) 1974: 173–200.

—— 1982: The nonspecific bases of language. In Wanner and Gleitman (eds) 1982.

Bever, T. G., Katz, J. J. and Langendoen, D. T. (eds) *An Integrated Theory of Linguistic Ability*. Hassocks, Sussex: The Harvester Press.

Bickerton, D. 1981: *Roots of Language*. Ann Arbor, Mich.: Karoma Publishers.

—— 1984: The language bioprogram hypothesis. *The Behavioral and Brain Sciences*, 7: 173–88.

Bolinger, D. L. 1980: *Language – the Loaded Weapon*. London and New York: Longman.

Borer, H. and Wexler, K. 1984: *The Maturation of Syntax*. Unpublished manuscript, UC-Irvine.

Botha, R. P. 1968: *The Function of the Lexicon in Transformational Generative Grammar*. (Janua Linguarum, Series Maior 38.) The Hague: Mouton.

Botha, R. P. 1973: *The Justification of Linguistic Hypotheses: A study of non-demonstrative inference in transformational grammar.* (Janua Linguarum, Series Maior 84.) The Hague: Mouton.

—— 1977: *On the Logic of Linguistic Research* (Utrecht Working Papers in Linguistics 2.) Utrecht: Instituut voor Algemene Taalwetenschap.

—— 1980: Methodological bases of a progressive mentalism. *Synthese*, 44; 1–112.

—— 1981: *The Conduct of Linguistic Inquiry. A systematic introduction to the methodology of generative grammar.* (Janua Linguarum, Series Practica 157.) The Hague: Mouton.

—— 1982a: On the 'Galilean style' of linguistic inquiry. *Lingua*, 58; 1–50.

—— 1982b: On Chomskyan mentalism: a reply to Peter Slezak. *Synthese*, 53; 123–41.

—— 1984: *A Galilean Analysis of Afrikaans Reduplication.* (Stellenbosch Papers in Linguistics 13.) Stellenbosch: Department of General Linguistics. (Also published as *Form and Meaning in Word Formation. A Study of Afrikaans Reduplication.* Cambridge: Cambridge University Press, 1988.)

—— 1985: *The Language Lottery:* Promises, promises . . . *Studies in Language*, 9; 109–21.

Botha, R. P. and Sinclair, M. (forthcoming): *Brame on Chomsky's Epistemological Tolerance.* (Stellenbosch Papers in Linguistics.)

Braine, M. D. 1971: On two types of models of the internalization of grammars. In Slobin (ed.) 1971: 153–86.

Brame, M. 1978: *Base Generated Syntax.* Seattle: Noit Amrofer Press.

—— 1985: Universal word induction vs. Move α. *Linguistic Analysis*, 14; 313–52.

Bresnan, J. 1978: Toward a realistic model of transformational grammar. In Halle, Bresnan and Miller (eds) 1978: 1–59.

Brown, R. and Hanlon, C. 1970: Derivational complexity and order of acquisition in child speech. In Hayes (ed.) 1970.

Caplan, D. 1981: Prospects for neurolinguistic theory. *Cognition*, 10; 59–64.

Catlin, J. 1978: Discussion of the Chapters by Stolzenberg and Chomsky. In Miller and Lenneberg (eds) 1978: 271–80.

Cauman, L. S., Levi, I., Parsons, C. and Schwartz, R. (eds) *How Many Questions?* Indianapolis: Hackett.

Cellérier, G. 1983: Cognitive strategies in problem solving. In Piattelli-Palmarini (ed.) 1983: 67–70.

Chomsky, N. 1957: *Syntactic Structures.* (Janua Linguarum IV.) The Hague: Mouton.

—— 1962: Contribution to the discussion. In Hill (ed.) 1962: 124–58.

—— 1964: *Current Issues in Linguistic Theory. (Janua Linguarum, Series Minor 38). The Hague: Mouton.*

—— 1965: *Aspects of the Theory of Syntax.* Cambridge, Mass.: MIT Press.

—— 1972: *Language and Mind*, enlarged edn. New York: Harcourt Brace Javanovich.

—— 1975a: *Reflections on Language.* New York: Pantheon Books.

—— 1975b: Questions of form and interpretation. In Austerlitz (ed.) 1975: 159–96.

—— 1977: On *Wh*-movement. In Culicover, Wasow and Akmajian (eds) 1977: 71–132.

—— 1978a: A theory of core grammar. *Glot*: 1, 7–26.

—— 1978b: Interview with Sol Saporta. *Working Papers in Linguistics*, Supplement Number 4. Department of Linguistics, University of Washington.

—— 1979a: Markedness and core grammar. Mimeo. (Published later in A. Belletti, L. Brandi and L. Rizzi (eds), *Theory of Markedness in Generative Grammar.* Pisa: Scuola Normale Superiore, 1981.)

—— 1979b: *Language and Responsibility.* Translated from the French by John Viertel. Hassocks, Sussex: The Harvester Press.

—— 1980a: *Rules and Representations.* New York: Columbia University Press.

—— 1980b: Rules and Representations. *The Behavioral and Brain Sciences*, 3, 1–15, 42–61.

—— 1981a: Principles and parameters in syntactic theory. In Hornstein and Lightfoot (eds) 1981a: 32–75.

—— 1981b: *Lectures on Government and Binding.* Dordrecht: Foris Publications.

—— 1982: *The Generative Enterprise. A discussion with R. Huybregts and H. van Riemsdijk.* Dordrecht: Foris Publications.

—— 1983: On cognitive structures and their development: A reply to Piaget. As well as other contributions to the Abbaye de Royaumont debate (October 1975). In Piattelli-Palmarini (ed.) 1983.

—— 1986: *Knowledge of Language: Its nature, origin and use.* New York: Praeger.

—— 1987: Reply to George 1987. *Mind and Language*, 2, 178–97.

Chomsky, N. and Halle, M. 1968: *The Sound Pattern of English.* New York: Harper and Row.

Cohen, D. (ed.) 1974: *Explaining Linguistic Phenomena.* Washington, DC: Hemisphere.

Comrie, B. 1981: *Language Universals and Linguistic Typology. Syntax and morphology.* Oxford: Basil Blackwell.

Cromer, R. F. 1980: Empirical evidence in support of non-empiricist theories of mind. *The Behavioral and Brain Sciences*, 3, 16–18.

Culicover, P., Wasow, T. and Akmajian, A. (eds) 1977: *Formal Syntax*. New York: Academic Press.

Davis, S. 1976: *Philosophy and Language*. Indianapolis: Bobbs-Merrill.

Dennett, D. C. 1978: *Brainstorms. Philosophical essays on mind and psychology*. Hassocks, Sussex: Harvester Press.

Donnellan, K. 1977: Review of Gunderson (ed.) 1975. *Language*, 53, 720.

Dougherty, R. C. 1975: The logic of linguistic research. Mimeo.

Dresher, B. E. 1981: Abstractness and explanation in phonology. In Hornstein and Lightfoot (eds) 1981a: 76–115.

Dummett, M. 1975: What is a theory of meaning?: Part 1. In Guttenplan (ed.) 1975: 97–138.

—— 1981: Objections to Chomsky. *London Review of Books*, 3–16 September, 1981.

Edgley, R. 1970: Innate ideas. In Vesey (ed.) 1970.

Feigenbaum, E. A. and Feldman, J. (eds). 1963: *Computers and Thought*. New York: McGraw-Hill.

Ferguson, C. A. and DeBose, C. E. 1977: Simplified registers, broken language, and pidginization. In Valdman (ed.) 1977: 99–125.

Feyerabend, P. K. 1979: *Against Method. Outline of an anarchist theory of knowledge*, verso edn, 2nd printing. London: New Left Books.

Fodor, J. A. and Garrett, M. F. The psychological unreality of semantic representations. *Linguistic Inquiry*, 6, 515–32.

Freidin, R. 1978: Cyclicity and the theory of grammar. *Linguistic Inquiry*, 9, 519–49.

Gardner, H. 1985: *The Mind's New Science. A history of the cognitive revolution*. New York: Basic Books.

Gazdar, G. 1981: Unbounded dependencies and coordinate structure. *Linguistic Inquiry*, 12, 155–84.

George, A. 1987: Review discussion of Chomsky 1986. *Mind and Language*, 3, 155–64.

Gleitman, L. and Wanner, E. 1982: Language acquisition: State of the art. In Wanner and Gleitman (eds) 1982.

Gunderson, K. (ed.) 1975: *Language, Mind, and Knowledge*. Minneapolis: University of Minnesota Press.

Guttenplan, S. (ed.) 1975: *Mind and Language*. London: Oxford University Press.

Hahn, E. 1978: *Look Who's Talking!* New York: Crowell.

Halle, M., Bresnan, J., Miller, G. (eds) *Linguistic Theory and Psychological Reality*. Cambridge, Mass.: MIT Press.

230

Harman, G. 1980: Two quibbles about analyticity and psychological reality. *The Behavioral and Brain Sciences*, 3, 21–2.

Harman, G. and Davidson, D. (eds) 1972: *Semantics of Natural Language*. Dordrecht: D. Reidel.

Harré, R. 1961: *Theories and Things. A brief study in prescriptive metaphysics*. London and New York: Sheed and Ward.

Hayes, J. R. 1970: *Cognition and the Development of Language*. New York: John Wiley and Sons.

Higginbotham, J. 1983: Is grammar psychological? In Cauman, Levi, Parsons and Schwartz (eds) 1983.

Hill, A. A. (ed.) 1962: *Proceedings of the Second Texas Conference on Problems of Linguistic Analysis in English*. Austin: Texas University Press.

Hintikka, J. 1977: Quantifiers in natural language: some logical problems 2. *Linguistics and Philosophy*, 1, 153–72.

Hiż, H. 1967: Methodological aspects of the theory of syntax. *The Journal of Philosophy*, LXIV, 67–74.

Hornstein, N. and Lightfoot, D. (eds) 1981a: *Explanation in Linguistics. The logical problem of language acquisition*. London and New York: Longman.

Hornstein, N. and Lightfoot, D. 1981b: Preface. In Hornstein and Lightfoot (eds) 1981a: 7–8.

—— 1981c: Introduction. In Hornstein and Lightfoot (eds) 1981a: 9–31.

Hunter, J. F. M. 1973: *Essays after Wittgenstein*. Toronto: University of Toronto Press.

Huxley, R. A. and Ingram, E. (eds) 1971: *Language Acquisition: models and methods*. New York: Academic Press.

Hymes, D. 1971: Competence and performance in linguistic theory. In Huxley and Ingram (eds) 1971: 3–24.

Inhelder, B., Sinclair, H. and Bovet, M. (eds) 1974: *Learning and the Development of Cognition*. Cambridge, Mass.: Harvard University Press.

Kac, M. G. 1980: Corepresentational grammar. In Moravscik and Wirth (eds) 1980: 97–116.

Katz, J. J. 1980: Chomsky on meaning. *Language*, 56, 1–41.

—— 1981: *Language and Other Abstract Objects*. Oxford: Basil Blackwell.

Katz, J. J. and Bever, T. G. 1977: The fall and rise of empiricism. In Bever, Katz and Langendoen (eds) 1977: 11–64.

Kayne, R. 1980: ECP extensions. Mimeo.

Kean, M. L. 1981: Explanation in neurolinguistics. In Hornstein and Lightfoot (eds) 1981a: 174–208.

Keyser, S. J. (ed.) 1978: *Recent Transformational Studies in European Languages*. (Linguistic Inquiry Monograph No. 3.) Cambridge, Mass.: MIT Press.

Kintsch, W. et al. 1974: *The Representation of Meaning in Memory*. New York: John Wiley and Sons.

Koster, J. 1978a: Why subject sentences don't exist. In Keyser (ed.) 1978: 53–64.

—— 1978b: *Locality Principles in Syntax*. Dordrecht: Foris Publications.

—— 1978c: Conditions, empty nodes, and markedness. *Linguistic Inquiry*, 9, 551–93.

—— 1980: Configurational grammar. Mimeo, Max-Planck-Institute, Nijmegen.

Koster, J. and May, R. (eds) 1981: *Levels of Syntactic Representation*. Dordrecht: Foris Publications.

Kripke, S. 1982: *Wittgenstein on Rules and Private Language*. Cambridge, Mass.: Harvard University Press.

Labov, W. 1970: The logic of nonstandard English. In Alatis (ed.) 1970: 1–44.

Lakoff, G. 1974: Discussing language with Herman Parret. In Parret 1974: 150–78.

—— 1980: What ever happened to deep structure? *The Behavioral and Brain Sciences*, 3, 22–3.

Lear, J. 1978: Going native. *Daedalus*, Fall 1978.

Leiber, J. 1975: *Noam Chomsky. A Philosophical Overview*. New York: St Martin's Press.

Lenneberg, E. H. 1967: *Biological Foundations of Language*. New York: John Wiley and Sons.

Lewis, D. 1975: Languages and language. In Gunderson (ed.) 1975.

Li, C. (ed.) 1976: *Subject and Topic*. New York: Academic Press.

Lightfoot, D. W. 1979: *Principles of Diachronic Syntax*. Cambridge: Cambridge University Press.

—— 1982: *The Language Lottery: towards a biology of grammars*. Cambridge, Mass.: MIT Press.

Luria, A. R. 1975: Scientific perspectives and philosophical deadends in modern linguistics. *Cognition*, 3, 377–85.

Lyons, J. 1970: *Chomsky*. Fontana/Collins.

—— 1981: *Language and Linguistics. An introduction*. Cambridge: Cambridge University Press.

McCawley, J. D, 1980: ¡Tabula si, rasa no! *The Brain and Behavioral Sciences*, 3, 26–7.

McGinn, C. 1981: Review of [Chomsky 1980a]. *The Journal of Philosophy*, 78, 288–98.

Miller, G. A. and Lenneberg, E. (eds) 1978: *Psychology and Biology of Language and Thought*. New York: Academic Press.

Milner, J.-Cl. 1978: Reply to the GLOW Manifesto concerning the object of inquiry. *GLOW Newsletter* No. 1.

Minsky, M. 1963: Steps towards artificial intelligence. In Feigenbaum and Feldman (eds) 1963: 406–50.

Moravscik, E. A. and Wirth, J. R. (eds) 1980: *Syntax and Semantics vol. 13: Current Approaches to Syntax*. New York: Academic Press.

Moravscik, J. M. 1980: Chomsky's radical break with modern traditions. *The Behavioral and Brain Sciences*, 3, 28–9.

Newmeyer, F. 1980: *Linguistic Theory in America*. New York. Academic Press.

—— 1983: *Grammatical Theory. Its limits and its possibilities*. Chicago and London: University of Chicago Press.

—— 1986: Has there been a 'Chomskyan revolution' in linguistics? *Language*, 62, 1–18.

Parret, H. 1974: *Discussing Language*. (Janua Linguarum, Series Maior 93.) The Hague: Mouton.

Partee, Barbara Hall 1975: Comments on C. J. Fillmore's and N. Chomsky's papers. In Austerlitz (ed.) 1975: 197–209.

Pateman, T. 1987: *Language in Mind and Language in Society. Studies in Linguistic Reproduction*. Oxford: Clarendon Press.

Piaget, J. 1983: The psychogenesis of knowledge. In Piattelli-Palmarini (ed.) 1983: 23–34.

Piattelli-Palmarini, M. (ed.) 1983: *Language and Learning. The debate between Jean Piaget and Noam Chomsky*. London: Routledge and Kegan Paul.

Putnam, H. 1981: *Reason, Truth and History*. Cambridge: Cambridge University Press.

—— 1983a: What is innate and why: comments on the debate. In Piattelli-Palmarini (ed.) 1983: 287–309.

—— 1983b: Comments on Chomsky's and Fodor's replies. In Piattelli-Palmarini (ed.) 1983: 335–40.

Quine, W. V. O. 1972: Methodological reflections on current linguistic theory. In Davidson and Harman (eds) 1972: 442–54.

Rachlin, H. 1980: Cross purposes. *The Behavioral and Brain Sciences*, 3, 30–1.

Radford, A. 1981: *Transformational Syntax*. Cambridge: Cambridge University Press.

Richards, J., Platt, J. and Weber, H. 1985: *Longman Dictionary of Applied Linguistics*. Harlow: Longman.

233

Rollin, B. E. 1980: Innate and *a priori*. *The Behavioral and Brain Sciences*, 3, 31–2.

Romaine, S. 1985: Why the problem of language acquisition should not be explained logically. *Studies in Language*, 9, 255–70.

Rosenthal, D. M. 1980: The modularity and maturation of cognitive capacities. *The Behavioral and Brain Sciences*, 3, 32–4.

Sanders, G. 1980: Equational rules and rule functions in syntax. In Moravscik and Wirth (eds) 1980: 231–66.

Schank, R. C. 1980: An artificial intelligence perspective on Chomsky's view of language. *The Behavioral and Brain Sciences*, 3, 35–7.

Searle, J. R. 1972: Chomsky's revolution in linguistics. *New York Review of Books*, June 29.

—— 1976: Discussion in *Times Literary Supplement*, 10 September 1976.

—— 1980: Rules and causation. *The Behavioral and Brain Sciences*, 3, 37–9.

Simon, H. 1970: *Sciences of the Artificial*. Cambridge, Mass.: MIT Press.

Sinclair, M. 1985: *The Rationality of Chomsky's Linguistics*. (Stellenbosch Papers in Linguistics 14.) Stellenbosch: Department of General Linguistics.

Slezak, P. 1981: Language and psychological reality: a discussion of Rudolf Botha's study. *Synthese*, 49, 427–40.

Slobin, D. I. (ed.) 1971: *The Ontogenesis of Grammar: a theoretical symposium*. New York: Academic Press.

Snow, C. E. and Ferguson, C.A. (eds) 1977: *Talking to Children: language input and acquisition*. Cambridge: Cambridge University Press.

Soames, S. 1984: Linguistics and psychology. *Linguistics and Philosophy*, 7, 155–79.

Sober, E. 1975: *Simplicity*. Oxford: Clarendon Press.

—— 1980: Representation and psychological reality. *The Behavioral and Brain Sciences*, 3, 38–9.

Steinberg, D. D. 1975: Chomsky: from formalism to mentalism and psychological invalidity. *Glossa*, 9, 218–52.

Stich, S. P. 1978: Empiricism, innateness, and linguistic universals. *Philosophical Studies*, 33, 273–85.

—— 1980: What every speaker cognizes. *The Behavioral and Brain Sciences*, 3, 39–40.

Stockwell, R. P. 1980: Summation and assessment of theories. In Moravscik and Wirth (eds) 1980: 353–81.

Strawson, P. F. 1970: *Meaning and Truth*. London: Oxford University Press.

Valdman, A. (ed.) 1977: *Pidgins and Creoles*. London and Boston: Routledge and Kegan Paul.

Vesey, G. N. A. (ed.) 1970: *Knowledge and Necessity*. London: Macmillan.

Wanner, E. and Gleitman, L. (eds) 1982: *Language Acquisition: state of the art*. Cambridge: Cambridge University Press.

White, L. 1982: *Grammatical Theory and Language Acquisition*. Dordrecht: Foris Publications.

—— 1981: The responsibility of grammatical theory to acquisitional data. In Hornstein and Lightfoot (eds) 1981: 241–71.

Wilkins, W. 1977: The variable interpretation convention. PhD Dissertation, UCLA.

—— 1979: Adjacency and variables in syntactic transformations. Mimeo, UCLA.

Wittgenstein, L. 1953: *Philosophical Investigations*. Oxford: Basil Blackwell.

Woodworth, E. D. and DiPietro, R. J. (eds) 1962: *Monograph Series on Languages and Linguistics* 25. Washington: Georgetown University Press.

# Index